Friday

MW01043232

For Thérèse MacNeil

Thank you for help, Kindness & Support you have shown me

best wishes for continued future Success

W. Michael S. Court

FIFTY YEARS IN THE PRACTICE OF LAW

Pilot Officer F.M. Covert, ca. 1943

Frank Manning Covert

Fifty Years in the Practice of Law

EDITED BY
BARRY CAHILL

McGill-Queen's University Press
Montreal & Kingston · London · Ithaca

© McGill-Queen's University Press 2005
ISBN 0-7735-2809-1

Legal deposit first quarter 2005
Bibliothèque nationale du Québec

Printed in Canada on acid-free paper that is 100% ancient forest free
(100% post-consumer recycled), processed chlorine free

McGill-Queen's University Press acknowledges the support of the Canada
Council for the Arts for our publishing program. We also acknowledge
the financial support of the Government of Canada through the Book
Publishing Industry Development Program (BPIDP) for our publishing
activities.

Library and Archives Canada Cataloguing in Publication

Covert, Frank Manning, 1908–1987
    Fifty years in the practice of law/Frank Manning Covert:
    edited by Barry Cahill.
    Includes bibliographical references and index.
    ISBN 0-7735-2809-1
    1. Covert, Frank Manning, 1908–1987. 2. Lawyers – Nova Scotia –
Biography. 3. Corporate lawyers – Canada – Biography. 4. Businessmen –
Canada – Biography. 5. Directors of corporations – Canada – Biography.
I. Cahill, Barry. II. Title.
    KE416.C68A3 2004   340'.092   C2004-903652-1   KF345.Z9C68 2004

Typeset in Sabon 10.5/13
by Caractéra inc., Quebec City

Contents

Editor's Foreword

Autobiographical literature on Canadian lawyers is in its infancy. There are the memoirs of a former attorney general of Ontario, a prominent Toronto criminal defence counsel, a corporate executive, a federal Progressive Conservative politician, and an early Jewish lawyer in Halifax; that is all.[1] Biographical literature, on the other hand, is flourishing.[2] The author of these memoirs was, from 1955 to 1975, one of Canada's leading corporation lawyers. Frank Covert's continuing celebrity was such that David Ricardo Williams, deeming Covert to be "the logical choice for the Atlantic region," included him in his collective biography of élite lawyers, each of whom "attained, in his own particular way, the pinnacle of the legal profession not only in his own province and region but also in the entire country."[3] Covert's memoirs, not written for publication, are an important historical document shedding considerable light on how corporation lawyers came both to epitomize the legal élite and to dominate the business élite in post-war Canada.[4]

Frank Covert was both businessman and businessman's lawyer. Indeed he was so highly respected as a corporate lawyer that he exercised more power and influence in the business world than most businessmen. In his time one of Canada's top 100 bank directors and a senior director of the Royal Bank, Covert was a leading figure in the business establishment. A linchpin of the Canadian corporate elite, in Atlantic Canada he defined it. In the field of industrial relations, which he introduced and made his own, Covert was a pioneer – years ahead of his time. He "sold" the idea of trade unions to sceptical Maritime tycoons like R.A. Jodrey and for thirty years personally negotiated collective agreements on behalf of management, even occasionally accepting unions as clients. Covert's clients included the most prominent regional corporate capitalists of his time – Jodrey, Ralph Bell, George Chase, Fred C. Manning and Frank Sobey. Like Jodrey, whose conglomerate remains private and family-owned, Covert was a proud and loyal Maritimer who was at home on Bay Street but believed that business could be done and was worth doing in the Maritimes.[5] So valued was Covert's counsel that he served not only as a director of many important national companies, such as Sun Life, but also as president or vice-president of regional concerns.[6] If Frank Covert was Nova Scotia's Mr Lawyer,[7] then it was because he was also Atlantic Canada's Mr Businessman and Mr Financier. He recognized that corporation law – especially securities regulation and income tax – was of supreme importance to business development and he exploited that knowledge to the benefit of every company with which he was associated as legal adviser or director or – frequently – both. He was more corporate captain than "corporate navigator" – a lawyer whom big business-men trusted so completely that they not only depended on his legal and financial advice; they also invited him to organize, reorganize, or run their companies – and talk to organized labour on their behalf. Though for him business was not in any degree beyond the law, Frank Covert truly was "more than a lawyer."[8] He was himself, in Peter Newman's memorable phrase, one of Canada's greatest businessmen in whom the flame of power burned brightly.

Frank Manning Covert was born in Canning, NS on 13 January 1908,[9] the second son and third of four children of Archibald Menzies Covert MD and Minnie Alma Clarke.[10] Dr Covert had followed his parents from New Brunswick to Nova Scotia, settling first in Lakeville (Kings County), before removing to Canning after his marriage in 1904 to a farmer's daughter. Originally the site of an Acadian village, Canning had been given a new lease on life by the arrival of American Loyalists in 1783. By 1908 it was a thriving riverport village. Archibald Covert, like many small-town doctors of his time and ours, had political ambitions. Though the Covert family were stalwart Conservatives,[11] Dr Covert defected to the Lib-erals – the party of his wife's family[12] – and served for twelve years as a municipal councillor in Kings County. He went on to become a Liberal member of the Nova Scotia House of Assembly and then of the Legislative Council (until 1928 the provincial senate), before dying prematurely of cirrhosis in 1922, aged fifty-two. Dr Covert's legacy to Frank was threefold: the Liberal Party of F.W. Borden, Wilfrid Laurier, and William Lyon Mackenzie King – Frank's devotion to which never faltered; the learned professions, though Frank would follow a different one from his father; and diary-keeping, which turned Frank into a lifelong documenter of himself. Frank was fourteen when Dr Covert died; the teenager, who was the apple of his father's eye, never got over the loss. Throughout his life he was always the son, never the father, and this attitude inevitably coloured and complicated his relationship with his own children.

Had his father lived longer, Frank Covert would have followed a profession other than law. His choice, approved by his father but vetoed after his father's death by his formidable mother, was engineering. Though Dr Covert's family was Church of England,[13] his mother's was Baptist, so, by way of compromise, Covert went to Presbyterian Dalhousie rather than the University of King's College or Acadia University. Arriving in Halifax in 1924, Covert lived at Mount Amelia in Dartmouth with his Covert first cousins. Among them was eleven-year-old Mary Louise Stuart (Mollie), with whom he would later fall in love and marry in 1934. Walter Harold Covert, Dr Covert's older brother, was an élite corporate lawyer and a power in the Conservative Party. Young Frank was impressed with city life, but not with Dalhousie. He intensely disliked and therefore did not distinguish himself in the arts course. His brilliant performance in the Law School, however, showed how wise was his mother's choice of career for him. Not only did he win the coveted Smith Shield for advocacy in the moot court; he carried off the university medal in law on graduating two years later.

In 1927 Covert had met the person who would dominate his life for the next three decades. James McGregor Stewart was the fastest-rising star on the Halifax legal firmament.[14] A mere thirty-eight years old, he would become head of his law firm – now Stewart McKelvey Stirling Scales – before the year was out and eventually the foremost Canadian corporation lawyer of his day. Small wonder that W.H. Covert, standing in loco parentis, chose Stewart, a close business and political associate, as the right person to whom to article his "green country boy," as Covert described himself. It was the beginning of an intense father-son relationship which endured until Stewart's death in 1955. When Covert was called to the bar in February 1930, he was prepared to return home to practise in Canning, which then had no resident barrister. Instead Stewart offered him a place in his own firm, which Covert gratefully accepted. He never looked back.

Stewart's offer to Covert was not made from mere generosity. The cornerstone of Stewart's human resources development policy was to recruit annually the winner of the university medal in law, the crème de la crème of the rising generation of the legal profession. Stewart took the view that trial work was good exercise for someone becoming a corporate lawyer. It was corporation law that mattered, for it separated the men from the boys, the wheat from the chaff. As Stewart's protégé, Covert was drawn into the business world early on. By 1936, when he became a full partner in the law firm, Covert was well out of the courtroom and into the boardroom, where he would make his name as a solicitor and counsel and, in due course, as a director and executive.

When the Second World War broke out, in the autumn of 1939, Covert was over thirty and both a husband and a father. He went to Ottawa in 1940 to work in the Department of Munitions and Supply (M&S), rising to be assistant general counsel in the legal branch. But a desk job was not enough; he wanted nothing less than active service overseas. Stung to the quick by the parliamentary Opposition's allegation that lawyers in the bureaucracy were shirkers and deeply affected by the accidental deaths of both his infant daughter and his brother-in-law (an Army officer), Covert enlisted in the RCAF. He used his influence with C.D. Howe, the all-powerful "minister of everything," to be sent overseas, where he flew numerous bombing missions as a navigator. He received the Distinguished Flying Cross (DFC) and was on active service when created a king's counsel in 1944.

At war's end Covert resumed the practice of law in the firm from which he had been absent for five years. In 1946 his name was added to the shingle, where it would remain for forty-three years. He resisted repeated offers to move to Toronto to join Borden & Elliot (now Borden Ladner Gervais LLP). Assiduously studying developments in business law during his absence, he quickly identified industrial relations as a growth area and was the first corporate lawyer in Nova Scotia to appreciate how the Trade Union Act could benefit the vested interests. He became a skilled and successful collective bargainer on behalf of management, so his services were much in demand. The brains behind the breaking of the strike against

National Sea Products (now High Liner Foods Inc.) in 1947, Covert was immediately rewarded with a directorship in the company.

By 1957, two years after J. McG. Stewart's death, Covert was numbered by Peter Newman among "Canada's biggest big businessmen." He was astute enough not to accept the presidency of the Dominion Steel and Coal Corporation (predecessor of the now both defunct Sysco and Devco), which he knew was on the verge of collapse. He was also wise to decline the presidency of Industrial Estates Limited (now Nova Scotia Business Inc.) depriving his friend Conservative Premier Robert Stanfield of political kudos. In 1949 he replaced the former minister of finance and justice, J.L. Ilsley, as counsel to the federal Royal Commission on Transportation. Ilsley's House of Commons seat was his for the taking, and only the personal intervention of Prime Minister Louis St-Laurent was sufficient to relieve the pressure on Covert to run in the constituency where he had grown up. Covert could even have replaced the late Angus L. Macdonald as premier in 1954, if he had been interested in the job. Despite their different political affiliations, Covert had learned from Stewart that the corporate lawyer performs more useful party service by financing political parties and party leaders than by running for political office. Covert's faith in the Liberal Party was never really tested, not even in 1972, when the Liberal government nationalized Nova Scotia Light and Power Company Limited (now Emera Energy), an important client of the firm, as well as an important directorship of Covert's. Though he forgave Premier Gerald Regan, Covert did not live to see Nova Scotia Power reprivatized in 1992 and a member of his law firm, Gerald Godsoe QC, appointed its inaugural president.

Among the board memberships that devolved on Covert immediately after J. McG. Stewart's death in 1955 was that of Dalhousie University. Stewart had been chair of the university from 1937 to 1943. Covert served for 21 years, resigning only in 1976 to forestall a possible conflict of interest with Nova Scotia Technical College, of which he had accepted appointment as chair of the board. At Dalhousie Covert was instrumental in creating the office of chancellor, and in having his friend and mentor, C.D. Howe, appointed to the post. The university's faculty pension scheme was Covert's brainchild. Among other Halifax institutions that Covert served were Saint Mary's University, whose transition from a religious to a

secular institution he supervised; the Sisters of Charity, whom he
served as counsel and as member of the financial advisory board;
and the Halifax Infirmary, where, as chair of the board, he assisted
the conversion to public ownership and where, years later, he chose
to die. Covert was the lawyer of choice for official Roman Cathol-
icism in Halifax. He also served as president of the board of management of the Children's Hospital (now IWK Health Centre).

Like his mentor Stewart before him, Covert rose from articled
clerk to head of the firm. He served in that capacity from 1963 to
1978, his 70th year. Frank Covert went on working for as long as
possible, and went down fighting against a disease that gave no
quarter – leukaemia. "How the mighty have fallen," he remarked
towards the end, which came on 1 November 1987. Ironically, René
Lévesque, the former Parti québécois premier of Quebec, died the
same day. Covert, a Trudeaumaniac *avant la lettre*, was committed
to keeping Quebec within Canada – but not at any price. Just as
he had supported the Patriation initiative of 1980–2, so Covert
opposed the Meech Lake Accord. Indeed, his last letter to the editor
of a Halifax newspaper, written less than a month before his death,
dealt with exactly that subject.[15] Small wonder that he described
himself, without exaggeration, as a "passionate Canadian."

Frank Covert's memory has not been well served by the two principal published accounts of his life. David Williams's biographical
essay misrepresents him as being a trial lawyer.[16] Journalist Harry
Bruce's authorized life,[17] a popular biography that draws liberally
on Covert's memoirs, is entertaining but superficial. By far the best
account of Covert's brilliant career is his own. So many people told
him he should write about his fifty years in the practice of law, that
in January 1980 he began to do so – just to see what it was like.
He started reading his old diaries and making notes, but the flood
of memories was so great that he found he could not let go. He
read the highlights of previous years and began compiling a five-
decade chronicle of them, 1929 to 1979. It was while collecting this
information that he really formed the idea of composing an autobiography and set to work on 3 February 1980.[18] Written in long-
hand and neither reread nor revised, Covert's stream-of-
consciousness memoirs are a chronicle of seventy years. Typed by
Covert's faithful secretary, Beulah Mosher, the manuscript runs to
over 500 typewritten pages. Its title, "From the Diaries of Frank
M. Covert: Fifty Years in the Practice of Law," is revealing; Covert

saw his life as his career. Though the manuscript is loosely based on his diaries and includes an abridgment of them, Covert was blessed with a near-photographic memory and his memoirs therefore contain material not found in the original diaries. Covert approached his memoir as he would have done a thick client file – with discipline, candour, and assiduity. Writing them was hard work as he found them stressful psychologically. They are a measure of just how long and how hard he had worked at providing raw material for them. Far from forgetting yesterday, he made remembering it the work of today.

Frank Covert's mother inculcated in him a competitiveness and passion for self-improvement that made him a driven man, an obsessive-compulsive hyperachiever both at work and at play. In his garden – vegetable, of course, not flower – he competed against the seasons, the elements, the rodents, and the last best harvest. Both quality *and* quantity mattered equally to him. Whether at bridge or at golf, he competed less against his opponents than against himself. This attitude of mind accounts for his vicarious interest in competitive sport – baseball, hockey, and horseracing – which he followed with all the enthusiastic attentiveness of the participant he never was. High society and high culture meant nothing to him and he had no intellectual or spiritual life. Still, he knew how to enjoy himself. The only way he could relax was by working. He profoundly loved his family and was loved by them. Yet he ignored them at the same time and remained psychically disengaged from them. Unlike two of their Covert cousins,[19] none of his four surviving children – two sons and two daughters – followed him into the legal profession. The standard that Covert set for himself was attainable by him but not by others. Ultimately it was his clients, not his family, who mattered more. He achieved as much as he did not because he was brilliant, though he *was* brilliant, but because he worked nearly all the time. In fact he was serenely proud of his workaholism. A non-drinker, non-smoker, and fanatical exerciser, he was instinctively hostile to anything that might interfere with his work. He was enamoured of anyone who was, or who could be converted into a client – something his family could not be. For Frank Covert the solicitor-client relationship was the most intimate, most gratifying, and most reciprocating of all human relationships.

Acknowledgments

Frank Covert's memoirs were not written for publication and could not have been published without the approval and assistance of my good friend W. Michael S. Covert and Mary L. S. Covert, respectively Frank Covert's eldest child and his widow. Michael provided me with unrestricted access to his father's diaries and other papers and on every occasion went out of his way to be helpful and encouraging. His efforts have ensured that his father's uniquely valuable archive will be preserved. Mrs Covert candidly shared recollections of her late husband and his family and, in particular, made a generous grant in aid of publication.

J. William E. Mingo QC, formerly chair of the executive committee of Stewart, MacKeen & Covert (now Stewart McKelvey Stirling Scales) provided me with complimentary copies of both Covert's memoirs and his unpublished history of the law firm. Wing Commander Wilbur C. (Wib) Pierce DFC, Covert's wartime comrade-in-arms and lifelong friend, not only read the RCAF chapter and pointed out various editorial errors, but also shared his many vivid recollections and personal papers relating to Number 6 Group, Bomber Command. Dr Gregory P. Marchildon, Canada Research Chair at the University of Regina, reviewed the entire manuscript from the point of view of his own profound knowledge of corporate lawyers and law firms.

In Ottawa I had the benefit of expert research assistance from Susan Villeneuve, Jody Perrun, and Jeff Noakes. Francine Hannam computerized the entire typescript, while Troy Wagner responded graciously to innumerable requests for inter-library loans. My colleagues John MacLeod and Paul Maxner provided valuable information about Jerome Spevack and Twin Cities Cooperative Dairy, respectively. Karen White, Archivist of the Roman Catholic Archdiocese of Halifax, Joanna Andow, formerly Archivist of the Sisters of Charity (Mount Saint Vincent Motherhouse), and Carolyn Scanlan, then Archivist of Mount Saint Vincent University, were all extremely courteous and helpful on Roman Catholic matters.

The Osgoode Society for Canadian Legal History provided a substantial grant-in-aid, without which the research supporting a scholarly edition of Covert's memoirs could not have been undertaken.

Barry Cahill
13 April 2004

Author's Preface

I wrote this book from fifty-two years of diaries, which I have faithfully kept. In the beginning I wrote it for my own family and I dedicate it to my wife Mollie and our four children, all of whom I neglected in pursuit of the law. Then, in the course of preparation, and because seventy per cent of my life has been with the firm of Stewart MacKeen & Covert,[1] I decided I owed it to the firm to dedicate the book to them. Accordingly I also dedicate it to the firm, of which I am so proud. I am not proud of the book. I started reasonably well, but after putting in over 400 hours' work, I tired of it and began a history of the firm.[2] By the time I completed that, I did not have the ambition to do much more than summarize the recent years of my life. Sometime I might try to improve it, but I felt I just had to finish it now.

All I can say is that I have loved life, I have loved the practice of law. I have had an affection for the firm beyond anything that anyone can imagine who has not been a part of it. It has given to me, a green country boy, opportunities to meet people, to do things, and to be part of a scene that I could never have hoped for or dreamed of, let alone experienced. I have had wonderful luck in my partners, in my associates, and in the firm staff. All of them have been so kind and thoughtful that I felt I owed it to them to produce this book as part of their history.

Frank M. Covert
13 December 1980

FIFTY YEARS IN THE PRACTICE OF LAW

"Forget yesterday
Work today
Plan tomorrow"
– *Frank Covert's motto*

CHAPTER ONE

Apple Tree Landing

I was born in Canning,[1] a village in Kings County, Nova Scotia, in 1908, the son of a country doctor and a farmer's daughter and one of a family of four – two girls and two boys.[2] The Canning I knew was a beautiful little village with a tidal river running through it, nestled at the foot of North Mountain, approximately six or seven miles from Kentville (the shire town of Kings County) and about equidistant from the college town of Wolfville.[3] To the north, one went up the side of North Mountain (which is only about 300 to 500 feet high) to the Lookoff, where there was a house with a small tower on it, which one could ascend and look at the surrounding country. It is indeed a magnificent view – rolling countryside, apple orchards, Cape Blomidon, Paddys Island, Minas Basin, Upper and Lower Canard, Pereaux, Kingsport, Habitant, Starrs Point, and so on. The view is breathtaking, especially at apple blossom time. One can go and see Scots Bay, Baxters Harbour or Halls Harbour, or drive down the road to the foot of Cape Blomidon. One could take the road to Kentville and go to Upper and Lower Canard or Starrs Point, or take the road to Sheffield Mills and Centreville. All of these roads I travelled by wagon, sled, and car with my father to tend his patients.

The river at low tide was a stream not more than fifteen feet wide; at high tide, however, the salt water came up from the Bay of Fundy through Minas Basin and flowed into the river basin and was held back by dykes built by the Acadians. The river at high tide would be at least 100 feet wide between the dykes, and between the dykes and the wharves and cribwork that lined the side of the river next to the town. When the tide was in, the river basin was very pretty;

when the tide was out, it was chocolate-coloured marsh mud. These
dykes, which protected vast meadowlands, were eight to ten feet
high and made of earth and marsh mud, interlaced with tree
branches, mainly willow, I believe. Thus at high tide a broad river
formed, which enabled three-masted schooners to be launched from
the shipyard, and the ferries, *Brunswick* and later the *Kipawo*, to
sail in at high tide, unload, settle down into the marsh mud, and
then sail away when the tide rose again.

Nothing obstructed the river from its mouth on Minas Basin to
where it reached the road leading into Canning. In place there was
what the townspeople called an aboiteau (from the French *abbatis*,
a breastwork of felled trees or bent saplings). It consisted of a sluice
with gates, which were closed by the force of the incoming tide and
which prevented the tide going beyond the gates, thus preserving
the meadowlands. When the tide went out, the gates were forced
open by the pressure of the water, which had backed up in the little
river on the other side of the gates. It was a sight to see the tide
rising over thirty feet, then the little river of fresh water growing,
the tide going out of the big river, the three gates opening, and the
water rushing out with great force, and the water level of the little
river going down.

The little river wound its way through lush meadows. About one
and a half miles upstream lay a swimming-hole we boys called the
Red Bank; at high tide the water fell into a place we called the deep,
which was over everyone's head. So at high tide we would go to
the Red Bank, where everyone swam in the bare pelt. It was a good
place to learn to swim because there was the low, which was shal-
low, and the deep, where one ventured when one learned to swim.
At high tide a few of the boys swam in the Big River (we called it
the Canning River – its proper name was the Habitant River).
Though clear at high tide, the Big River was where all the sewage
was deposited, so it was regarded as unsafe by the doctors in town.

At one time Canning had been called Apple Tree Landing, but
that was hardly a name to suit the ideas of the village fathers when
it became a thriving little town. So about 1830 the name was
changed to *Canning*, after the late British prime minister. In later
years Canning was served by the Dominion Atlantic Railway (a
subsidiary of Canadian Pacific), which ran from Kingsport to
Kentville and stopped at Canning, Hillaton, Sheffield Mills, and
Centreville – a route totalling not more than ten miles. Canning

was also served by a steamboat that ran out of Saint John, New Brunswick, and stopped at Kingsport, Canning, and Wolfville. It had a branch of the Bank of Nova Scotia and many shops – two butcher shops, two hardware stores, two drygoods stores, a drug-store,[4] four grocery stores, a barber-shop, a shoemaker, a post office, and a small hotel. No description of the town could fail to mention that right in the centre of it, at the junction of Main Street and the road leading up to the North Mountain, is a huge monument called The Harold Borden Monument.[5] It is in honour of the only son of Sir Frederick William Borden, minister of militia and defence in the Laurier government. Atop the monument is the bust of Harold, who was killed in the South African War. On one side is a lion's head which spouted drinking water for humans, while on the other was a place for horses to drink and three bronze plaques – one describing the son and the events leading to his death, the other two depicting the scene, complete with snipers in the mountains.

Canning had one factory, which made the Blenkhorn axe,[6] famous internationally for its quality. Many an hour I spent in the axe factory watching the trip-hammers pound the glowing steel into shape; then watching the workers temper the blades, polish and paint them, and finally hang them on nails on a barrel to dry – fresh, shiny black, green, blue, and brown, with just the sharp edge of the shining bright steel left unpainted.

There was a vinegar factory making cider vinegar and, at one time (before it burned down), an apple evaporator.[7] One watched the farmers bring the culled [picked] apples here for pressing and one could drink one's fill – indeed we did, until our stomachs were distended – of the fresh apple juice as it came out of the spout and into the big hogsheads. Canning had at least three apple warehouses serviced by the railway. There the farmers brought their apples to be sorted, graded and packed in barrels holding two and a half to three bushels. It was fascinating to see the apples going along the endless belt and falling off into chutes according to size – the men inspecting them for spots and other defects – and finally being packed in barrels. The first layer was on a piece of cardboard with every apple fitted to fill the bottom, then basket after basket until the barrel was filled and the top layer was again fitted apple by apple. Then the apples were shaken down and over them was placed a heavy paper container filled with excelsior;[8] the barrel head was placed on top, pressed down by a contraption that bore down evenly until it reached the circular notch keeping the barrelhead in place. Then the two hoops at the top were forced down, so that the barrelhead was held tightly in place; the name and grade of the apple, the name of the grower, and the name of the warehouse were painted on the cover; and the barrel was rolled away ready to ship. It was an assembly line at its best. At lunch-time there were often tests of strength, such as lifting a barrel of apples up over one's head or lifting a barrel of apples off the floor by the chimes.[9]

The town was the centre of an apple-growing district and one saw the farmers pruning, spraying, dusting (a form of spraying), ploughing, and picking. One saw all kinds of apples – from delicious eating apples such as Gravensteins (red and yellow), Cox's orange pippins, ribston pippins, and bishop pippins, russets and northern spies, to apples shipped to England to form the base for jams and jellies such as greenings and fallowaters, starks, etc. There were thirty to forty varieties. All apples were barrelled, not boxed as they are today, and the principal market was England.

Canning also had a sawmill, a cooperage, which made apple and potato barrels, and a blacksmith shop. Above all it had a shipyard, which built four three-masted schooners while I was young. I missed no stage of the work – laying the keel, fashioning, and placing the ribs, planking and caulking, laying and caulking the deck, and erecting the tall masts of Douglas fir, which came from British Columbia; rounding, smoothing, and placing and, finally, the stepping of the masts; then putting up the crosstrees, erecting the topmasts, and mounting the rigging.

How wonderful it was to watch the riggers. And the blacksmith shop making and galvanizing all the fittings. But above all the shipwrights – those skilful carpenters who formed the master's cabin out of teak and mahogany. Then there was the installation of the rudder, the painting of the ship, and finally the launching. Thousands came from all over the county seeking vantage points in order to watch the vessel go down the ways and into the river basin, shooting out into the water and being restrained from crashing into the dykes by huge hawsers. Twice I was on board vessels when they were launched. One knew the ship from stem to stern, having crawled up the rudder-hole, climbed the ladders to the crosstrees (usually on a dare) and watched the young men who shinnied up the hawsers from the crosstrees to the top of the topmast and carved their initials on the ball at the top. One knew every nook and cranny of the vessel and imagined oneself sailing on it to foreign lands.

The regular blacksmith shop (as distinct from the one at the ship-yard) was a fascinating place to go to watch the smithy take the old shoes off the horse, peel off a part of the hoof, select the shoe in its rough form, heat it white-hot, bend it, try it on the hoof, and watch it burn, then finally fit it and drive the nails into the hoof. How he handled the horse – his back to the horse's rear, putting the horse's leg up through his split leather apron while never letting the horse back away from or kick him.

For those who wanted to fish or hunt there was trout in the little river and in the streams up on the North Mountain. There were also in the big river eels and tommycod and the occasional flounder or flatfish. Three miles away, at Kingsport, there was fishing for tommycod, eels, smelts, and flounder – not to mention a nice sand beach and swimming when the tide was in. In the woods around the town were weasels, rabbits, skunk, and racoon. On the dyke-lands there was muskrat. I remember trapping my first muskrat. One set the trap near the hole at the side of the stream, then placed a carrot on a stick protruding from the bank directly over the trap. The animal caught his leg in the trap but its fur was unharmed. Coming down to tend the trap, I was excited to see the chain drawn into the hole; I pulled it out and there was the rat. I flung it up the bank and hit it over the head with the side of my hatchet and killed it. When I got home I skinned it, turned the pelt inside out, and put it over a board to dry and cure. Later the buyers came and haggled over the price.

In the winter there was skating on outdoor ponds – which was enjoyable until one tried to pull on the lumberman's rubbers or moccasins, only to find they were frozen solid. Later the town fathers built a rink, which was a great improvement, for there was a room with a stove in it where one could change. This brought hockey to the town.[10] Canning built up a hockey team, which com-peted with teams from Wolfville, Kentville, and Windsor in what was known as the Valley League. The town produced teams, which, though they never won the league or a championship, on many occasions carried Windsor (who became Nova Scotia champions) into tie games or close games with scores of 1-0 and 2-1. There were no seats in the arena – one tried to find a place "along the boards" – and the rink was always packed.

On one occasion, when the larger towns got into faster company, Canning put together the Beavers, a junior team, which performed well and played teams from all over the province. In summer there

was baseball and Canning always had a pretty fair team. Unfortunately, the school grounds were just large enough for an infield; the
outfield was the public highway. But they played baseball anyway.
These were the only team sports in my day – no football or basketball. Occasionally, we saw a game of football or basketball by
going to a match at Acadia University in Wolfville.

The town also had a brass band, with a Professor Gordon as
bandmaster. It played during intermission at hockey games and also
in the rink other nights for skating. In summer it played Thursday
nights in the bandstand and people came from all round the countryside to hear it. I played in the town band for some time, until I
entered Grade XII and then just did not have the time. I started on
the alto horn but did not enjoy it much because one did not play a
tune. Later I switched to the cornet, a small instrument of the trum-
pet class. My great moment came when I was to play a few solo
bars at the rink. It was a very cold night and, while I was waiting
for my solo, the valves froze. Fortunately, my fellow cornettist
noticed, and he carried on without me. I learned that one placed
one's mittens over the instrument and kept moving the valves. Later
I tried the trombone and took it home to practise, much to the
annoyance of our neighbours; it was then that Grade XII saved them.

Employment for youngsters was varied and sporadic. I worked
in a grocery store, a hardware store, a butcher's shop, the Post
Office and, once in awhile, in Mother's drugstore. I picked straw-
berries for one and a half cents a box, potatoes at two and a half
cents a bushel and apples at ten cents a barrel. For a week I shov-
elled coal out of a railway car into a dray, and then from the dray
into people's cellars – $1.50 a day for hard, dirty work. I hoed
potatoes on a farm in Kingsport where the rows were a mile long.
We worked from 7:00 to 12:00 and 1:00 to 6:00, walked there and
back (six miles), brought our own lunch, and were paid $1.00 a
day. My brother Harold, who was a year older, would be doing
one and a third rows to my one, then one and a half and, by the
end of the day, nearly two, but he got the same pay. I also worked
in the post office, six days a week in summer from 8:00 to 6:00,
with half an hour off for lunch, and from 6:30 to 10:30 or 11:00
on open nights; the pay was $8 per week. All the stores in town
had open nights – Tuesday, Thursday, and Saturday – for the benefit
of shoppers who came in from the country, bringing their eggs and
butter for sale and do their shopping at the stores. It made a long

day for the clerks. The town would be very crowded on open nights, especially Thursdays and Saturdays.

On one occasion, when I was working in the grocery store, a customer came in on Band night and ordered a jug of molasses – about two gallons. I went in and turned on the spigot in the hogshead and put in the first gallon; then the customer went out, saying he would call back for it later. I put the gallon measure under the spigot again and went out to listen to the band. Another customer came in and I forgot the molasses. Then the owner came back from an errand and went into the molasses room – the molasses was all over the floor. Of course I had to clean it up and tell him how it happened. He was angry at first but he did not fire me, nor even dock my pay. But he did say, "Never leave it running again; turn it off and go back to it."

The butcher's shop where I worked had a charge system known as the McCaskey system. Each customer had his slips placed in a slot, where they accumulated. The proprietor was busy, fell behind, and said he would have to take the chits home to update and check for errors. I enjoyed arithmetic, so I offered to do the work in my spare time during the day and at nights. It was duck soup; I arranged all the chits in alphabetical order; then checked, verified, and updated them. The proprietor was very pleased and paid me in salmon and back bacon, two expensive luxuries in those days.

One would hear apple-farmers discussing the blossoms, the set, the spot, and then occasionally the August gale, as it was called. I shall never forget the gloom and doom of the morning after an August gale that swept from one end of the Annapolis Valley to the other. I was in the butcher's shop when a farmer came in. The proprietor asked what it had done to his orchard. He answered, "Not enough apples to buy my wife a new hat." And so it went. Of course everyone had borrowed in order to buy spray and fertilizer, had pruned, and bought apple barrels – and now there was no crop with which to pay the bills. It should have been a great lesson to me but, years later, I, along with two farmer friends, bought a farm in Kingsport, where I had hoed potatoes. By then I was practising law and thought we had got a great bargain. I happened to be in Wolfville in a car with Roy Jodrey listening to the radio. All of a sudden it started to hail. Hailstones as large as marbles or mothballs bounced off the hood of the car. I heard Jodrey say, "My God the apple crop." I was so interested in the baseball game I paid little or no attention. Suddenly he said, "They're yours too." To make a long story short, our entire crop of thousands of bushels of apples was ruined. It cost me $3,333.34 in less than ten minutes. My partners bought me out, after first trying to persuade me to go into the chicken business. I turned them down, because a client of mine had lost 10,000 chickens from the pip[11] a few days before. It takes guts to be a farmer.

CHAPTER TWO

Home and School

Father was away for two years during the First World War[1] and
when he came back he was not well. I think he was diagnosing
himself. Because he was ill, Mother used to take me out of school
to accompany him on his trips in the car in summer, the wagon in
early spring, and the sleigh in winter. This was to make sure he did
not fall asleep, which had happened twice, once in the sleigh (the
horse came home without him) and once in the car (which went
off the road).

This was really the beginning of my education in a manner not
provided for by the schools. First, Father told me I would find that
"only part of what you earned was yours." At that time income
tax was not a serious problem. In fact, it was not a problem at all
to my father who delivered babies at $2.50 to $5.00 apiece and
who travelled over the North Mountain, stayed all night, put me
up at a neighbour's house, and came back the next morning. It was
not income tax but subsistence – the butcher, the baker, and the
candlestick maker. In other words, one had to pay out money for
the essentials of life.

Secondly, the more one earned the more one spent; there were so
many things one wanted that one could end up having nothing. So
it was essential to save a portion of one's earnings. This would not
be easy, especially when one was young, so the best method was
involuntary saving. Father told me about life insurance, which
served me well over the years. It gave me a borrowing base and
enabled me in the 1970s to borrow at five per cent.

Thirdly, Father told me it was easy to form bad habits but more
difficult to form good ones. So it was important to get into the

habit of forming good habits, for example, punctuality, routine, and daily planning. He started me off by making me report each day on the temperature at given times, 8:00 am and 6:00 pm; he gave me a scribbler in which I recorded the information and reported it to him. Thus I formed the habit of being in a certain place at a certain time each day. Then every night before going to bed I prepared an agenda for the following day.

Fourthly, Father told me that the two greatest inventions of man were democracy and free enterprise. He described democracy as government by the people's elected representatives and warned me that, unless the phrase "government of the people, by the people, for the people"[2] was properly understood, the day would come when people thought they should have a part in governing. He went on to tell me that, in order for democracy to succeed, there should only be two parties and that it was equally important they both be strong.[3] If they were, then they could produce strong candidates, so that no matter which party was elected, the people would have good representatives and consequently good government. He told me that over the years both parties would in the main be similar; if not, then one of them would be wrong. He told me I would live to see the day when every province west of Ontario would elect other than Liberal or Conservative governments; bearing in mind that he died in 1922, that was an astute prediction.[4] When I asked why the West would vote that way, he told me Westerners were a "polyglot" people, who had no loyalties to the Liberal or Conservative parties, having brought with them ideas from the continent of Europe. Father also told me that Quebec was the rock on which this country would stand or fall and that Quebec would understand, better than Ontario, problems in the Maritimes. I asked him about Quebec. He told me that just as Ontario had broken its promises to the Maritimes, so too had it deceived Quebec. He then told me that we English are very difficult people (his paternal ancestors were Loyalists who settled in New Brunswick, his father a Church of England minister[5]). He told me of English stubbornness with the Boers,[6] their treatment of the Irish,[7] and the treatment of their own people in New England;[8] he warned that one day, if we did not watch out, the French in Quebec would want to secede as we did in Nova Scotia at one time.[9]

Fifthly, Father told me it was important for intelligent people to take a part in politics, to join a party, work for the party, and *never* desert it. I asked him, "What if the party is wrong? What if your candidate is not as good as the other one?" His answer was, "That, my boy, is when the party needs you most." Then he went on to explain that there will always be people who change their minds, always people who think they know enough to "vote for the man," always people annoyed at what their party has done (perhaps it will be they who change the government, which may be good). But if there are not faithful party workers come hell or high water, then the party will grow weak, the other party will always win, and one's own party will not be able to attract strong candidates. This will breed the third party, which will lead to minority governments and gradually to a stronger and more powerful civil service – government no longer by the elected representatives. Father told me he did not care which party I joined,[10] provided I never quit it. He did give me a lecture or two on the histories of both parties, Liberal and Conservative; I always felt he was reasonably fair, but it seemed that most of the good things were done by his own party.

Fortunately, I began writing a diary in 1920[11] and I have done so faithfully every day for 60 years. In it are the recordings of what I have set out above. As a result, I have read and reread this advice. I have also lived to see everything my father told me come true. Unfortunately, Father died when I was only fourteen and he only fifty-two. I have often wondered what it would have been like to have had the opportunity to discuss university education with him, and if he had been alive in the 1940s. I wanted to be an engineer; Father approved and planned that I should go to McGill, which was his alma mater.[12] He told me that McGill had the finest engineering school.[13] After he died, however, everything changed. Mother left the family in charge of a nanny[14] and went to Dalhousie University to take a course in pharmacy so that she could run Father's drugstore and support the family.[15] She *decided* I was to be a lawyer, then talked me into studying law; as a matter of fact, she changed the course of everyone in the family, to put us all on what she called the right track. Things worked out reasonably well, which only confirmed her opinion that what she had done was in the best interests of all. She wanted my brother Harold to go to the Maritime College of Pharmacy[16] (he wanted to be a farmer); my sister Julia graduated from Acadia University, became a school-teacher, and then married a farmer.[17] Mother talked him into selling the farm and he became an insurance salesman.

I used to tease her and say how often I wondered what it would have been like to have been an engineer. She just looked at me and said, "You might not have been a good engineer." Mother was a remarkable woman. She was the one in Canning to whom everybody in trouble came for advice. Once in a while, after I became a lawyer, when she wanted legal advice she came to me. If she did not agree, she would simply say, "Frankie, you don't understand," and then see a much older lawyer in Kentville. If he confirmed my advice, she never told me. She just cut me "down to size." Mother lived to be eighty-two; she had broken her hip and was recovering, when she contracted pneumonia and died – still to the day of her death[18] as bright as a silver dollar.

One of the most amusing incidents involving Mother occurred in 1957. I had already been appointed to twenty-one directorships[19] when Peter Newman[20] wrote an article in *Maclean's* about the 100 busiest directors in Canada.[21] The formula Newman used was to calculate the assets of the companies of which one was a director and then list the top 100 directors in descending order of "assets directed." If one was on the board of Royal Bank, as I was at that time,[22] one had a big head start. This startled me considerably, as I knew I had no *power*. I wrote Newman telling him it was ridiculous; if one company were taken away I would not be on the list, so the addition of that one gave me no power. Newman, who was not impressed, wrote me a letter in reply, stating firmly that he did not believe his formula was wrong; Canada's 100 busiest directors had all kinds of power. The day after receiving Newman's reply I had an envelope from Mother enclosing the article with a note pinned to the top saying, "Frankie, I don't believe a word of it. Love Mother." I sent it along to Newman with a covering note, which said, "You may fool some people but you can't fool Mother."[23]

Canning had a four-room schoolhouse with four teachers: one for the "Blackboard Class" (Primer) and Grades I and II, one for Grades III, IV and V, one for Grades VI, VII and VIII, and finally the principal, who taught Grades IX, X and XI. One was expected to enter Primer class at age five. I went but was incorrigible and was sent home until I was six; then I did Primer and Grade I in one year. My teacher in Primer and Grades I and II believed in a thorough grounding. My teacher in Grades III, IV, and V was my favourite in all my years at school. Then through Grades VI, VII, and VIII I again had the same teacher. The great advantage of this

arrangement was that the teacher got to know the students, with
their individual capacities and weaknesses. In Grade VI my teacher,
like myself, was from Loyalist stock. At our first geography lesson
we were given scissors and instructed to excise the map of the
United States. I never did learn American geography. Father was
furious; he said only the English could do that. But that teacher
taught us to draw from memory the boundaries of every province
of Canada and fill in the locations of the capital cities. For Nova
Scotia, we learned to draw in the boundary lines of each county
and locate the shire towns; for Kings County, the principal towns
and the mountains; for Canning itself, we drew a map showing
every road and street, the location of the industries, and the course
of the Habitant River winding through the town.

The student in Grade VI got a preview of Grade VII, while the
student in Grade VII got a review of VI and a preview of VIII.
When I finished my third-quarterly examination in arithmetic and
turned it in, I noticed the Grade VIII exam on the blackboard so I
wrote that and turned it in also. I made 100 per cent, so the teacher
persuaded Mother to let me try both sets of final examinations. I
did, and passed into Grade IX. I shall always be grateful to that
teacher for recommending that I take the two grades in one year –
imagine a whole year in Grade VIII when one already knew enough
to pass it well. The same was true in high school, except that the
principals all only lasted one year. But each year was easier because
one was getting previews. In all my years at school, and this
included the Kings County Academy in Kentville for Grade XII, I
never had a poor teacher. ·

Mother sent me to the Academy for Grade XII so that I could
enter second year at Dalhousie University.[24] In order to get to
Kentville I took the train, a distance of only six or seven miles. Stops
along the way resulted in our always being a little late for school;
at apple-picking time in autumn we would often be an hour late.
At Canning School they had not taught Latin or French, so when
I got to Kings County Academy I had to take four years of Latin
and four of French. The teacher, Winnifred Webster, who had
also taught Mother, volunteered every recess to teach me four years
of French, while the principal, J. Logan Trask, came back early from
lunch to teach three students four years of Latin. Of course, while
I was learning the rudiments, the rest of the class were ahead of
me, reading Molière and Caesar. When the final examinations came

round, it was all sight translation for me. Looking back, I am amazed that these two teachers, for no extra pay, volunteered of their free time to teach me. I was only fifteen, so there were not very many outside attractions; I worked hard and absorbed fast. Mother indulged me during examination week in June 1924 by having me board at a friend's home in Kentville, so I could study more and not lose any time travelling back and forth to Canning.

At that time one wrote what were called Provincials, nine standard examinations prescribed by the Superintendent of Education in Halifax. All senior high school students, wherever they were, wrote the same exams. They were also marked in Halifax, which meant that one day a letter would arrive and in it would be the news: Grade or No Grade. I passed and had just got through the door to tell Mother when the phone rang. It was Winnie Webster, asking "Did you grade?"

"Yes.

"How did you do in French?"

"I got 76."

"Not bad."

Having taught me algebra, geometry, and trigonometry, she asked me about these; I received 100 per cent in each of them, so she was happy. I thanked her – I expect casually. It was not until years later that I appreciated all she had done for me. Mother then made me phone Principal Trask to tell him how I had fared and to thank him; oddly enough he was more interested in my marks in solid geometry, which he taught. He was pleased, though not overjoyed like Miss Webster.

I was through school. Mother said, "First you must find a job to earn money to go to college." I suddenly realized that gone were the days of trapping muskrat and weasels, working in the local grocery store, and hoeing potatoes at a dollar a day. I would have to make real money. I saw an advertisement: "salesman wanted" by a publishing company, John C. Winston, to sell cookbooks, Bibles and dictionaries (there was another called Ropp's Ready Calculator).[25] My uncle – Mother's brother, Blake Clarke – said there should not be a house that would not want at least one of these. So over the summer of 1924 that is what I did, apart from selling a few apple trees. I earned more money than I would have done hoeing potatoes, but still not enough. So Mother helped me a little, then spoke to my uncle in Dartmouth, who took me in.[26] I shall never forget the days I lived with my uncle, Walter Harold Covert. For five years I grew up with this family of eight: Uncle Harry, Aunt Mary, and their six children – three daughters and three sons – three younger and three older than I. It was a great education for me just to learn how to live with a family other than my own. I suppose it was my wonderful Aunt who really made it possible and fairly smooth. She was full of love for her family and made room for me too. I worked very hard at my studies and tried to do my share of the household chores. My male cousins' outside interests were different from mine. I worked most of the time and when university examinations were over, I left to get a summer job.

Uncle Harry was head of his law firm[27] and a prominent corporate lawyer.[28] One of the great delights for me were the Sunday dinners when he used to hold forth, telling stories and discussing the topics of the day. If ever there was a man to whom the definition of gentleman applied, it was he. Every year, when I came back to university, the whole family welcomed me; indeed, when I finished my last year in 1929, they coaxed me to stay on. I resisted the temptation, as by then I had begun to realize what a tremendous thing they had done for me. I changed from being a hot-tempered, argumentative boy to a calm, more reasoning, though still somewhat dogmatic young man.

I doubt whether anyone greener and more a country bumpkin ever entered Dalhousie University. I was in short trousers and very conspicuous, being the only undergraduate so clad. I wrote Mother about it, but she told me all the boys would be looking at the girls and most of the girls would have boyfriends and never give me a thought. Aunt Mary, however, guessed, asked about it, took me over to Page's[29] in Halifax, and bought me a suit with long trousers.

On registration day I wandered round the campus to listen to what people were saying. I heard some asking others what classes they were taking. I heard one fellow talking about History 5 and Government 5 and thought it meant he had been there for at least five years. Finally, at nearly noon I went in to register for English 2, French 2, Latin 2 and Mathematics 2. Then I started looking through the curriculum to see what else I could take to fill in the hours. Unable to make everything fit, the first thing I knew the registrar[30] was saying, "Come on young fellow, it's getting to be lunch time, what's the trouble?" I presented my sheet showing the hours filled and the hours still vacant (there were eight classes, including Physics with its laboratory time.) He perused it, then with a quizzical but kindly look on his face asked, "How many classes were you planning to take?" I said I would take ten the first year, just as I had done in Grade XII. Then he asked what I planned to do; "I'm going to take law" adding that I wanted to get a BA and affiliate so that I could take both the BA and the LL B in five years.[31] He told me that first-year students were only allowed to take five courses; I replied that would never do, as I could not finish in five years. He asked me why I was taking Mathematics 2,[32] which I told him I liked. Then he got out my file and saw that I had four 100-per cent exams in mathematics. It turned out that the university registrar was also the professor of mathematics. In the end Professor Macneill allowed me to take eight courses; afterwards, he even permitted me to call History of English Law (a first-year law class) an arts class in order to form a group of three history classes. To form the second group of three, he called three classes in first-year law, "Law I, Law II, and Law III." This enabled me to take another class in mathematics from him in second year. Murray Macneill was one of the greatest teachers I have ever known.[33]

Lectures began I believe the very next day and brought some sharp shocks. I walked into French 2 to find a new professor, René Gautheron, from France and only recently appointed. Unfortunately Winnie Webster, from whom I learned French, did not know and accordingly did not attempt to teach French pronunciation. I was in this class over a week, not understanding a word that was said. One day the student next to me jabbed me in the ribs and said the professor was asking for the student by the name of Covert (he pronounced it *Co-vair*); he had called my name every morning and I had not answered. He stood over me speaking in French. I told him I did not understand. He told me to go to his office after classes were over, when he advised me to drop back to French 1. I explained I could not do so, told him my history of French study, my career plans, etc. He started us on the *Fables* of Jean de La Fontaine to teach us pronunciation. To this day, fifty-six years later, I can still recite the story of The Crow and the Fox:[34] "Maître corbeau, sur un arbre perché, / Tenait en son bec un fromage. / Maître renard, par l'odeur alleche ..." The professor and the class were kind as I recited again and again, gradually to Dr Gautheron's satisfaction. He just did not believe it was possible.

The second week brought Latin 2, with the professor of classics, Howard Murray.[35] I was in the front row because my surname began with C; suddenly he asked me to read a passage from the poet Ovid. When I stood up and started to translate, he roared at me, "I said *read, not* translate." I had never been asked to read Latin before and it had never occurred to me that one would recite the Latin. I had not got beyond two words when again he roared at me, "Say the Latin alphabet."[36] At this stage I did not even know there was such a thing. He wrote *A* on the blackboard and asked me what it was.

"An AYE," I answered.

"No," he said, "it's an AH."

Next he said, as he wrote down *B*, "What's that?"

"BAH," I answered, almost triumphantly.

"BAY," he said, still roaring.

He took me through the alphabet for the full fifty-five minutes. I was still in short trousers, still felt very conspicuous, and was so miserable it was all I could do to keep from crying. I nearly quit university.[37]

But I was enjoying mathematics, as well as both physics and the physics laboratory, so I soon forgot Latin 2. The first day in class the professor, J.H.L. Johnstone, said that some of us would see the atom split and spoke of the tremendous power that that would generate.[38] I was captivated immediately; but it was the laboratory I loved. Unfortunately, I had another class which prevented my arriving at the physics lab on time; however, I could stay at the other end and did so until they kicked me out. As a result, I did double the number of experiments required; Dr Johnstone tried to get me to give up law for physics, but I turned him down.

I was also enjoying history for the first time in my life – thanks to the wonderfully interesting professor George Wilson. And Government 2 (general political science) under Henry F. Munro.[39] I think I learned more in that class in one year than in any other in three years. I liked English 2, given by the Professor, Archibald (Archie) MacMechan, but not the "themes"[40] we had to write every week. Though I never received a D, I did receive C–, C, and C+ for weeks, then B–, one B and, on my final theme, B+. Realizing I just could not write led me to take two classes from MacMechan, the final one being English 10 (advanced English composition), which was really for intending authors. There were only eight students in the class and they were good, at least in my opinion. I did so badly that after two weeks MacMechan called me to his office, suggested

I quit the class, and added that he would see to it I got my money back. I told him I had paid my money, wanted to learn to write, and thought I had a right to stay. He shook his head, saying, "I can't stop you." He was easy on me for the rest of the year, and I noticed the class were generally less critical of my essays and short stories. Early in the second half of the year (1926–27) MacMechan announced we all had to write something and submit it in early April. It had to be at least 10,000 words and would account for sixty per cent of the grade while the exam for only forty per cent. I decided very quickly that the only thing I knew enough to write about was my own home town of Canning. I wrote under the title Apple Tree Landing, which was the name the New England Planters gave it about 1760.[41] I wrote something every day for weeks on end, polished it, shined it, corrected it, and finally rewrote it in my very best and neatest handwriting. Then I decided to turn it in about two weeks before it was due.

Taking it up to MacMechan's office, I announced, "Here's my essay."

He looked at me; "You have two more weeks at least to polish it, you know."

"I've done that over and over and neglected some of my other studies."

"Very well." The next week he asked me to stay after class; I went to his office and was told – "I know the town you wrote about; you must love it. It's a beautiful piece of work and I just want to say I'm glad you didn't take my advice. You have learned a lot." He gave me a distinction grade in his class, without my writing the distinction exam.

Some of the English classes were among the few I liked in the arts course, though mostly it was a chore. I disliked Latin, French, logic, psychology, and biology but enjoyed mathematics, physics, and history. I particularly enjoyed government, or political science as it was later to become known. My first year in arts was so dreadful that if it had not been for mathematics, physics, and government, I should have wanted to quit. I could hardly wait to get to law school. For the summer months I had a job bellhopping at the Hackmatack Inn in Chester,[42] which was not only remunerative but also tremendously exciting. It took seven years of practising law before I earned as much per month as I did as a bellhop – and board and lodging were included, not extra. The result was that, in my junior year (1925–26), I had money enough to take a girl out and I did so for three years. Bellhopping taught me about people; that the job was important; and that, even if one were not tipped, one should do the job well and give the same service to all. It taught me that if a man was successful, he was usually courteous and pleasant. It taught me what the help expected of guests and, in later life, how to treat the so-called help. I enjoyed the experience greatly and was offered many jobs.

Finally, in the autumn of 1926, I arrived at the law school. It was a dingy little place – three rooms and a library tucked away in the corner of the Forrest Building, which also housed the medical and dental schools.[43] There were three full-time professors. The first was the dean, John E. Read, who in 1929 became legal adviser to the Department of External Affairs and in 1946 a judge of the International Court of Justice. It was Read who in later years tried to entice me away from my law firm to join him in External Affairs, at a considerably higher salary than I was earning.[44] The second was Angus L. Macdonald, who in 1933 became premier of Nova Scotia and who later tried on two occasions to recruit me as a minister in his government. The third was Horace Read, who later taught at Minnesota Law School, before returning to become dean of law at Dalhousie and chair of the Nova Scotia Labour Relations Board. In addition, there were several downtown lawyers who came up to lecture on subjects such as shipping, bankruptcy, probate, mortgages, and practical statutes.

I was still as green and shy as could be. I remember months later hearing the boys talking about being "articled" and I too bashful to ask them what it was. Finally I spoke to my uncle, who was horrified that he had not told me about it. Then he did one of the greatest things, which would affect my life forever. He said, "If you article with me and do poorly, people will say, 'He couldn't even do well with his uncle's help;' if you do well, they'll say, 'Why wouldn't he, with his uncle behind him?'" So in February 1927 he took me over to meet a young fellow by the name of James McGregor Stewart and I became articled to him. The delay in time resulted in my call to the bar almost a year late.[45]

Stewart had already achieved a great reputation as a corporation lawyer and was soon to be recognized throughout the country as a prospect for directorships such as Royal Bank, Montreal Trust, and Canada Cement. When he became head of the firm in 1927 he was only thirty-eight and the firm third in size in Halifax. But he was a great builder of the firm and under him it became number one. Having had polio as a youngster, Stewart was lame and used crutches. A man with a tremendous broad frame and a large head, he had a very kindly face and a completely disarming smile. A brilliant student, he was Governor General's gold medallist at Dalhousie in 1909 and a junior professor of classics. He was also a respected philatelist and an authority on stamp valuations. From childhood he read Rudyard Kipling and gave his collection of Kipling books and manuscripts to Dalhousie University before he died in 1955 – it was reputed to be the second finest in the world.[46] He followed sport and did his best to take part in it. He seldom missed a Dalhousie football game and was in my time made honorary president of the Dalhousie Amateur Athletic Club. Stewart seemed to be able to solve with the greatest ease any problem presented to him. A judge told me that in his early days Stewart was an excellent advocate; that when he appeared before the Supreme Court in Banco,[47] the judges used to fight to sit on the bench to hear him. Another judge told me that on one occasion Stewart's opening sentence was, "My client is a liar and he lied consistently in this case; I don't ask you to believe a word he said, but, nevertheless, he must win this appeal." Stewart captured the imagination and ear of the court immediately; so much so that, when counsel for the respondent rose to reply, he was interrupted again and again by the court saying, "But Mr. Stewart has admitted that." The lawyer was completely demoralized; Stewart won the appeal. Unknown to him, however, his client was in the courtroom listening.[48]

Stewart had also been a downtown lecturer at the law school, where, for the first time in all my years at school and university, I felt a sense of purpose; that at long last I was on course, building the ship, and learning to become its captain. I was fascinated by the case-method of studying law. It was like reading novels instead of studying. On the first day of company law Angus L. Macdonald told us about *Salomon v. Salomon*,[49] which established the principle that a company was an entity separate and distinct from its members or owners. When one incorporated a company, it was like the birth of a new baby with an existence separate and apart from its parents, the company promoters. That to me was sheer romance and I saw the possibilities. Macdonald also taught partnerships, crimes, and procedure and made them all interesting. When you asked him a question he used to drawl, "Well now, I don't know, what do you think?" Soon he would have the whole class debating. Then he would sum up both sides of the argument and state what the law was or how it was applied. I thought him an excellent teacher.

Though a Rhodes Scholar with an outstanding record as a student, Dean Read was very shy and, as a result, often bullied his students with his brilliance. First he would beguile them into taking one side of an argument, then have them take the other side. Finally he would ask, "having seen both sides *so clearly*, which do you *now* choose?" Dean Read taught contract, constitutional law, and procedure. For procedure he divided the class into law firms, three in each firm; we would draw pleadings and appear on motions before him as a judge in chambers. He was a stickler for form and insisted on full compliance with the Rules of Civil Procedure. At the beginning of second year, in 1927, Dean Read approached five students, saying he wanted to conduct an honours course in Roman law, which would meet every Saturday afternoon from 2:30 to 5:00, to listen to papers prepared and read by one and criticized by the others.[50] I had grave doubts about the additional work and was about to say no when I thought of the other four – Charles Gavsie, T.H. (Tom) Coffin, Duncan MacLellan, and Herbert Frederick (Fred) Brooks-Hill Feaver. Discussing it with them and finding they were all for it, I went along. It was a superb class. Though I did not like the subject, I learned a lot and it was a great experience to listen to the dean and watch the workings of the minds of my fellow students. It was then that I really began to appreciate the sheer brilliance of Duncan McLellan and Charles Gavsie. The group of five all graduated with honours.[51] Unfortunately, McLellan, who I have always thought was the most brilliant member of the class, died a year or two after his graduation. One can only wonder to what dizzy heights he might have ascended. Coffin became a justice of the Supreme Court of Nova Scotia in 1961 and in 1968 a justice of the Appeal Division.[52] Charles Gavsie became general counsel to the Department of Munitions and Supply[53] (and its successor, Reconstruction and Supply), deputy minister of the Department of National Revenue, and president of the St. Lawrence Seaway Authority. Then he returned to private law practice in Montreal.[54] Fred Feaver abandoned law and joined the Department of External Affairs as third secretary, reaching ambassador rank in 1956.[55]

The assistant professor, Horace Read (no relation to Dean Read), was young and had just finished his Master's degree at Harvard Law School. His were beautiful, studied lectures and there were few debates in his class; his selection of cases, coupled with his lectures, ensured that, if one studied, one had an excellent grounding in all his subjects. Read taught property, trusts, bills and notes, conflict of laws – subjects both tedious and difficult.

In my class there were only thirteen, but occasionally we would join first year for a class, and likewise for another we would join third year. This enabled one to get to know everyone else in the law school well. Every year there was a Mock Parliament in which the speaker of the legislature usually acted as speaker. Our legislature was modelled on the House of Commons and dealt with matters of federal jurisdiction. Very seldom did a person choose as his party one that he was not to espouse in later years. I was still too shy and there were so many skilled debaters in the House, that I attended, watched, and listened, envying the brilliance of my classmates.

There was also Moot Court, something in which everyone had to take part. In first year one appeared as junior counsel, along with second-year students who were king's counsel, before a court of three judges, who were third-year students. Thus, over the three years, one acted as junior counsel, king's counsel, and judge. The cases were devised by the professors and the facts agreed, while counsel prepared a factum and delivered it to the judges. As junior counsel, one helped one's senior but did little more at the hearing of the case than present the facts and rough outline of the argument after which senior counsel took over. Some weeks later, the court would hand down its decision. Everyone took it seriously. The professors attended each hearing and chose four students from among the king's counsel who would compete for the Smith Shield, a trophy given in 1926 by a former professor, Sidney Smith, who in 1929 became dean of law.[56] The Moot Court finals case was heard by three judges: two real ones from the Supreme Court of Nova Scotia and the third usually the president of the Nova Scotia Barristers Society. The students involved were all in their third and final year.

It was a tremendous thrill to be selected and I recall my own case vividly.[57] The four of us[58] selected tossed coins for appellant and respondent respectively and for partners. I drew as partner a great friend of mine, Duncan MacLellan, while we were opposed by two whom I thought were the most brilliant in the class. We won the toss and chose the appellant's side. We worked on preparing the case for about six weeks until finally the night arrived. Leaving home over an hour early, I stopped at a restaurant, then walked the two miles to the law school. Despite walking very slowly I arrived early, my heart pounding as I opened the door. I put on my wing collar, bib, and gown and still the clock ticked slowly. I worried whether my mouth would open to let out the words. Finally the court came in and took their places: Justices Joseph A. Chisholm and Stuart Jenks of the Supreme Court and T.W. Murphy KC, president of the Nova Scotia Barristers Society.[59] There were no opening words of welcome. Justice Chisholm, presiding, asked who appeared for the appellant. I was the first speaker so I opened, oblivious to the law students who were there watching. All I saw were the three judges. The words flowed, the court asked questions, I fielded the answers with ease, and, when finished, sat down and listened to the other three. When I started up to reply the court stopped me. "We do not need to hear from you, Mr Covert; we have decided that the appeal should be allowed." We had won the case. Then two minutes later they announced the winners of the Smith Shield: F.M. Covert and Duncan MacLellan. For the first time the courtroom was no longer silent, as applause rang out. It was 26 February 1929, a night to remember.

When finals were over in April, I reported to the law office. I was in Windsor searching titles for the Canadian Pacific Railway Company, when the results were posted and announcement made that I had won the university medal in law. I was so excited for Mother, who came down for convocation, that when I went up to receive my diploma I walked right on past; the crowd roared with laughter. I had to go up again for high honours in jurisprudence and the crowd was still laughing. Then a third time, to accept the university medal in law, for which the audience was generous in its applause. It was a great day for me but an even greater one for Mother, highly amused though she was by my missing the diploma on my first ascent.

Before every exam I had always worried that there might be questions I could not answer; apart from mathematics, where one could prove the answers, I used to worry until I saw the examination paper. But every time I wrote an exam in the second and third years of law school I always knew not only that I had passed but also that I had achieved a first. It was a very enjoyable change for me, which I attribute first to hard work and secondly to loving the study of law. Compared with other schools or the arts course, I enjoyed law school. Though a little slow compared with my classmates, I worked harder than any of them. When finished writing finals, I threw my book in the air and exclaimed, "That's the last exam I'll ever write." The joke was on me. Thirteen years later, I joined the RCAF to study to be a navigator and in less than one and a half years wrote more exams and tests than I had written in all my college days.

CHAPTER THREE

At the Bar

At the end of second year in April 1928 I had planned to bellhop again, but Stewart insisted I spend the summer working in the law office under my articles. He said I would be paid $11.50 per week and that that was the first time an articled clerk had ever been paid. So, of course, I articled. There was a political campaign in progress,[1] the lawyers were busy politicking and, consequently, left all kinds of work for me to do. I searched titles, drew wills, incorporated companies, drafted leases, and generally was very busy. Best of all, Mersey Paper Company Limited[2] was being formed and I was in the midst of it, actually drawing the incorporation documents and serving for months on the board as a provisional director. Not only was this a great lesson in corporate law; it also made the third year of law school much easier and more interesting. I had gained confidence and discovered how to use my time to better advantage.

When I became articled in February 1927, the firm name was Henry, Stewart, Smith & McCleave; when I started working under articles in the summer of 1927, William Alexander Henry[3] was still alive and he gave me two tasks. The first was how to draw a clause in a will to keep a grandfather clock in the family for the longest time possible. I had just finished lectures on this and proceeded to tell him. He asked me to write it out. I did so and gave the case, "Life or lives in being of the heirs of Queen Victoria." Having done this, I was then asked to outline completely the differences and similarities between *dower* and *curtesy*.[4] Again I knew them by heart; again he wanted them in writing. A few minutes later I gave them to him with the authorities. I thought nothing of it until a few days later Stewart called me in and told me that Henry had been singing my praises. I told him I had just had lectures on these subjects; "I thought so," he said, and laughed. He gave me some work to do, then said, "Let this be a lesson to you; never accept an old man's judgement of a young man. He is first surprised that the young man knows anything and then astonished when he finds that the young man knows something that he, the old man, doesn't." I never forgot that – the first of many pearls of wisdom Stewart passed on to me.

In the summer of 1928 I was beginning to learn how a law office operates, but of course I could not do much except prepare briefs, conduct title searches, and draft company incorporation documents. After graduation in 1929 I was finishing out my articles and learning as much as I could. I tackled everything, because I realized that, in February 1930, I would be on my own. When I was called to the bar, Stewart asked me where I was going to practise; I said I did not know but thought I might go up to Kings County. He said that was too bad, that they could use a lawyer. I said, "If you mean that, you've got a boy." Even though 1929 had been a year of articling, it was nevertheless important, because in 1928 I began working on the memorandum and articles of association of Mersey Paper Company. I believe that that was when Stewart first began to take notice of me. First, he asked me whether I could find out anything about no par value shares.[5] It happened that I had seen in Dalhousie law library a little book on no par value shares, which aroused my curiosity.[6] Having summarized the advantages and disadvantages, I recited them to him. Stewart was impressed, so I gave him my handwritten summary and he had his secretary[7] type it out.

Next Stewart asked me to look at the draft memorandum and articles of association of the Mersey Paper Company. The memorandum was a rough draft, composed by his secretary.[8] I got out some precedents and completely revised the memorandum, rearranging the objects clauses, so that the important ones appeared first and in better order; then I thoroughly reworked the articles, using Palmer extensively, as the firm library had the latest edition.[9] Stewart was so delighted that when the articles were duly printed and the day came for them to be signed, he asked whether I would like to be one of the incorporators. Naturally I accepted. After I had signed, he suddenly exclaimed, "You're not 21 yet are you?"[10] When I answered no he said, "I guess we'll have to get someone else." I asked him to wait while I went into the firm library to look up an English case,[11] which said an infant could sign. When I assured him I would also sign a share certificate in blank and a resignation as provisional director, he laughed. I was in. When Mersey's paper mill was officially opened, in December 1929, I travelled on the special train from Halifax to Liverpool to attend the ceremony.

The firm, when I joined it in February 1930, was infirm. W.A. Henry had died in 1927; Robert David McCleave, the youngest of the senior members, in 1926. Henry was not young but McCleave was and undoubtedly a brilliant career lay ahead of him.[12] Our competitors called us The Half Dead Firm. One lunch hour I was alone in the office; everyone out except the accountant and the office boy. The telephone rang and the caller asked for Mr Henry – "He's dead." Then he asked for Mr McCleave – "He's dead too." Then for Mr Stewart, who was in England. Finally for Mr Smith, who was in Ottawa. Then he asked whether anyone was in – I told him I was; he asked my name and whether I was a lawyer, to which I replied that I had graduated but had not yet been called to the bar. He told me he was a farmer selling apples in the City and had to pay a licence fee – I think over $100 – and asked whether there was any way to avoid it. I told him that if he leased a room in a cellar for a few dollars a month, he could become a taxpayer and not have to buy a vendor's licence. He asked whether I was sure, I told him yes and then he said, "Now I'll give you some advice. You don't know my name or address so you can't bill me. You can't live that way." Three days later, a big barrel of apples arrived at the office, with an anonymous note addressed to F.M. Covert: "Your fee; your advice works."

The lawyers at the time were Stewart (who succeeded Henry as head of the firm), Charles Breckon Smith, Henry Poole MacKeen, William Marshall Rogers, Joseph Patrick Connolly, and Clyde Winston Sperry, who had graduated a year ahead of me. I was at the bottom of the totem pole. C.B. Smith was a lawyer's lawyer and an all-rounder; a great pinch-hitter, a great student, a bulldog on cross-examination. He did not believe in being smooth but a fighter. He could quote by the paragraph the leading cases, which he could find by just taking the book from the library shelf; he had an extraordinary memory. But he never delegated. One might go to court with him and plan to present some of the argument, only to have him monopolize it. All the times I went with him he never called on me, so I started avoiding him. He knew the case so well

he was sure he could do it better and truth was he could. Many a
battle he fought. His greatest triumph was in the Judicial Committee of Privy Council[13] and he argued that case again and again.
Smith was a great and fearless trial lawyer.

H.P. MacKeen was one of the most painstaking lawyers I ever
met. Pleadings, briefs, and even opinions were done over and over,
polished and shined until the prose was perfect. While Smith was
in his prime and doing the trial work, however, MacKeen was held
back. It was only after the war ended in 1945 that he came into
his own and soon was the leading trial lawyer in Nova Scotia.
MacKeen was really in a class by himself. His cases were won by
sheer preparation, studied cross-examination, and compelling jury
addresses. It was probably his success in criminal conspiracy trials
that first brought him to public attention. First he acted for the
crown and obtained convictions against the rum-runners. Then,
years later (after first asking the RCMP, whose methods he had
learned, for permission to act), he defended many of the same
accused and obtained acquittals. MacKeen was one of the most
popular lawyers at the bar; his porridge parties at the Nova Scotia
Barristers Society's annual meeting were legendary.[14] In 1963
MacKeen became lieutenant-governor of Nova Scotia and Halifax
gave him the keys of the city. His vice-regal speeches were gems. It
was he who resumed the tradition of the lieutenant-governor's
receiving new queen's counsel appointed by government.

Marshall Rogers was a brilliant student – winner of the university
medal in law – and a painstaking lawyer. Unfortunately, when his
father died[15] and left him money, Rogers began playing the stock
market and did so well at it that he practically gave up the practice
of law, while his secretary did most of his work.[16] Rogers could
have been a great lawyer, but his love of the market left no room
for love of the law. He died, aged sixty, of a brain tumor.

Joseph Patrick Connolly was an enigma. Once an office boy in
the firm, he served in the First World War as an Army private and
won the military medal. After the war he studied law at Dalhousie
(which gave him the LL B in 1929), wrote the bar examination,
and began the practice of law. Connolly was a flamboyant character,
a great raconteur who embellished everything, including the truth.
He directed musicals, even comic operas like *Mikado*, and was in
constant demand to direct at the Dalhousie Glee Club. During the
Second World War, having become director of special services in

the Royal Canadian Navy Volunteer Reserve, he produced *Meet the Navy*. The official Navy show was a tremendous hit on the London stage; in 1946, when the revue was made into a film, Connolly served as assistant director. If he had gone to Hollywood in his youth, Connolly would have made a fortune. Law was not his forte. He never completed a task and someone always had to step in to finish it. Connolly served as chief pensions advocate after the war and later worked for the National Film Board. Unfortunately, Stewart persuaded him to give up his job in order to run as a Conservative candidate in the federal election of 1949, a year when it was hopeless to be a Conservative. Connolly was a lamb led to the slaughter; he lost the election and had no job to return to.[17] He died in January 1955, two weeks before Stewart.

Clyde Winston Sperry was an all-round lawyer but eventually handled nothing but real estate; he may have been the most competent real estate lawyer Nova Scotia has ever seen. Though small in stature – he did not weigh 150 pounds – Sperry was an outstanding athlete and did well in basketball, football, badminton, and tennis; in the latter two he was always in the top ten in the province. A thorough gentleman, loved by all who knew him, he died following a simple hernia operation on 30 December 1974. It was ironic, for he had decided to go easy and take up golf, a game he had never played. Sperry did not have a mean bone in his body, never criticizing anyone or gossiping.

In January 1931 the firm became Stewart, Smith, MacKeen & Rogers. Connolly was a member, but three of the four seniors balked at including his in the firm name, which delayed for several months the formation of the new partnership. Stewart and Smith each had his own secretary, while MacKeen and Rogers shared Susannah W.A. Almon, who had been with the firm longer than any of the lawyers.[18] Connolly had no full-time help; he got whatever he could but required little in any event. The third secretary worked for the rest of us. Sperry and I both had a full-time secretary by 1930, but if at any time Stewart's or Smith's secretary required help, our work waited. Though the Depression had set in, we still had a full-time switchboard operator and accountant (bookkeeper), and an office boy. The staff was small but extremely efficient and turned out an amazing amount of work. Office hours Monday through Friday were 9:00 to 1:00 and 2:00 to 6:00, while on Saturday 9:00 to 1:00; the only break was at 4:00 pm, when everything stopped for tea, prepared and served by the switchboard operator. The firm occupied a part of the third floor in the Roy Building,[19] which at that time commanded a beautiful view of the harbour and seawards – a view since mostly cut off by taller buildings between it and the harbour. Though small by today's standards,[20] the firm was closely-knit; everybody knew every client the firm had and almost used to cheer when new clients appeared. Under Stewart they came thick and fast.

When I started working in 1929, I was not a member of the bar, so my name could not show on the firm's letterhead; I had to wait for over ten months for that to occur. Nor even then was there an office for me – only a corner in the library, which did not impress my clients. Stewart eventually had the landlord move the door out into the corridor and gave me a room next to his. This room was to my liking, for it had a door opening on to Stewart's office. But it was not to be – I would have had an office larger than Connolly's. Stewart asked whether I would mind exchanging offices with Connolly. I was so glad to have an office of my own that I readily agreed and was given the little office at the end of the hall, which had been Connolly's, while he moved into the new one. I also just acquired a secretary, M. Isabel Carruthers, who was a beginner like myself but learned very fast and was a stickler for neatness. I once corrected a letter she had typed and was going to send it out when she retyped it, warning me that I must never send out a letter corrected in ink. The next thing I knew she insisted that the outside window, which was cracked and dirty, should be covered with opaque paper. Miss Carruthers remained with me until I went to Ottawa in September 1940; then she began to work for Stewart.

The first month after my call to the bar in February 1930 Stewart was retained by the Town of Liverpool to contest seventeen mechanics' lien actions against it. Even the town solicitor had abandoned his client and accepted some of the cases against the town, while the only other lawyer in town took the rest of them. Stewart asked me to prepare the pleadings and the briefs and said I could go with him to Liverpool to try the cases. I went down to Woolworth's, purchased two loose-leaf binders with paper, and prepared the seventeen defences and briefs, together with an outline of how counsel for the town should attack as well as defend. I worked day and night and, when ready, presented Stewart with the two binders containing the statement of claim on the left and the statement of defence on the right, followed in each case by the brief. They formed a pretty massive tome, which Stewart took home with him. The next day he told me to file the defences. The trial dates were set. The day before, I asked him when we were leaving; he said he had decided I should go alone and that, if I got into trouble, to call him. I could hardly believe my ears; I was almost frightened. I took the train to Liverpool, where the first person I saw was the town clerk, Seth Bartling.[21] He took one look at me and, when I told him Stewart was not coming, said simply, "This will never do." He telephoned Stewart, who told him to let me try the small one first and that, if he were not satisfied, Stewart would come down. Thus I learned for the first time what a persuasive man Stewart was. In the end, I tried all seventeen cases and won them. The town clerk was very pleased, of course, but so angry at the town solicitor that he invited me to come to practise in Liverpool and promised me the town solicitor's job as incentive. Of course I was not interested; I would never have left Stewart for triple the money.

A few days later, on 1 April, I appeared with H.P. MacKeen before the Supreme Court in Banco for the respondent.[22] Though disappointed that we were not called upon, I remembered what Dean Read had said: "Don't be disappointed – you've won – if you did speak you might lose it." Despite what anyone says, however, when one prepares for a hearing and then does not get the chance to make the arguments, there is a let-down even in victory.

My first criminal case was in the Police Court,[23] where I defended a black woman, Mary Howe, accused of stealing coal from S. Cunard & Co. Ltd. After the crown finished presenting its case, I received a note from someone behind me, which read, "Move for dismissal – they haven't proven ownership of the coal – it might be her own." I looked at it for about ten seconds and suddenly thought, "That's right." I so moved, the stipendiary magistrate dismissed the case, and I turned round to thank my adviser, who had disappeared. I afterwards learned he was a reporter from the Halifax *Chronicle*.[24] The afternoon newspaper on page three carried a small headline: Lawyer Wins First Case By Calling No Witnesses. I wrote the reporter a note, to which he replied, "I was afraid you might blow it." Defending several small criminal cases in the Police Court, I won them all and learned what a tremendous advantage the accused criminal has – proof beyond a reasonable doubt and no cross-examination, unless he takes the stand to give evidence on his own behalf.

The main event of my first year at the bar was American Telephone & Telegraph's starting to build a telephone cable across the Atlantic, which involved the construction of a special line along the eastern seaboard from New York and New England through New Brunswick, Nova Scotia, and Newfoundland. The intermediary was a wholly owned Canadian subsidiary with a parliamentary charter: Eastern Telephone & Telegraph.[25] The cable had to be distant enough from other telephone and telegraph lines to prevent crosstalk, yet near enough to highways to be readily accessible for repairs, if necessary. Thus it kept changing direction, in a zigzag manner, all because the line had to be perfect on land, while the undersea cable was to be of a length never before imagined. This limitation, of course, prescribed where the line could go. If the company had to purchase, then laying the cable might be held up. Nova Scotia gave the company the power to expropriate after a hearing before a commissioner appointed by the government.[26] The legislation also provided for value determination by an arbitrator who was the County Court judge for the district where the lands were situated. The company was very successful in its purchases, but there were some holdouts, especially among those who discovered that ET&T was a subsidiary of the great AT&T.

In September 1930 I had four expropriation cases in Truro before a commissioner appointed under the act. AT&T sent up a lawyer, Albert S. Marzo,[27] to help with the proceedings. I met him when he got off the train in Truro. He asked where Stewart was and I told him he was not coming. Like the Liverpool cases, the response was, "This will never do;" Marzo called Stewart, who persuaded him to let me try the first small case and if it were not satisfactory, he would attend. I do not think I ever saw anyone as nervous as Marzo during the hearings; he was always pulling at my gown during cross-examination. He need not have worried; I won all fourteen cases.

Towards the end of November 1930 I handled four arbitrations in Amherst to determine the value of lands successfully expropriated. Marzo came again, again he wanted Stewart to come up, and again Stewart persuaded him to let me try the little one first; in the event of trouble, he would come up. We had paid insurance into court to cover all the cases, but, as none of the awards exceeded the amounts paid in, there were no costs against us. This was particularly important, for news of our success spread along the bush telegraph. On 9 December I got a raise; Marzo had written a complimentary letter to Stewart. In Eastern Telephone & Telegraph I found a new client, who never consulted anyone else first but came direct to me – all because of Stewart. It was to lead to many things.[28]

In my first year of practice I argued thirty-nine cases and won thirty-eight, worked 134 nights, received a raise, and took out more life insurance. All was right with the world. In my second year the first big job was the winding up of Stanfields Limited, textile manufacturers, whose surplus had been accumulating since the days of the Klondike gold rush.[29] On the winding up of the company, this surplus, which amounted to over $1.5 million, could be distributed to the shareholders as a non-taxable accretion to capital. I was very proud to be managing a transaction as large as that, which involved incorporating a new company and transferring the assets of the old company to it, then changing the name of the old one to something innocuous and formally winding it up.[30] Stewart let me handle it all. The final day, when I was to appear before the judge in chambers, I was in bed with a temperature of 104. I got to court, made the application, then went back home to bed and called a doctor.

In April 1931 I defended a doctor, Patrick Mockler Kirwan (a nephew of the chief justice of Canada),[31] charged with break and enter of a pharmacy and stealing morphine. The crown proved that Kirwan, who had been blacklisted for being a drug addict, called at the pharmacy the evening in question and ordered morphine, but was refused. When the shop closed, he was observed to be loitering near the pharmacy. Shortly afterwards, the police noticed the door was broken in; they called the pharmacist, who observed that morphine was missing – all the phials being numbered. He told police about Dr Kirwan and they went to the boarding house where the doctor lay in bed – "his eyes like pinpoints." Finding two phials of morphine in his bedroom slippers, they arrested and charged him. Though not one witness testified as to the numbers on the phials, when I asked the crown attorney whether his case was closed, he answered yes. I moved for dismissal on the grounds that a chain of evidence was no stronger than its weakest link. The pharmacist knew which numbered phials he held and which were missing, yet no one identified the phials from the accused's bedroom slippers as those missing from the pharmacy. The judge, Walter J.A. O'Hearn,[32] who had been once a great criminal defence lawyer and briefly attorney-general of Nova Scotia, called on the crown attorney, who argued nobly but to no avail. The judge reiterated my point: maybe the doctor bought the phials from some other drugstore. Discharging the prisoner, Judge O'Hearn told him he was fortunate to have a lawyer who knew when to keep his mouth shut. My old friend the reporter carried a banner headline on page three of the afternoon newspaper: YOUNG LAWYER WINS ACQUITTAL BY KEEPING HIS MOUTH SHUT[33] – followed by an account of the trial. I wrote him a note of thanks to which he replied, "You're learning fast."

That same month I acted for Philip Hooper Moore,[34] promoter of what later became one of Nova Scotia's most successful summer resorts, White Point Beach Lodge.[35] Moore had entered into a ten-year employment contract at $10,000 per annum to act as president and managing director of the company, which went bankrupt long before the contract was to expire. Moore came to see Stewart, who handed the case over to me. I filed two claims on Moore's behalf, one for $57,090, the commuted value of the contract; the other a smaller claim for $10,587.93. The trustee[36] having disallowed both claims, I appealed the disallowances and the case came on before Mr Justice Hugh Ross of the Supreme Court, sitting as judge in bankruptcy.[37] I merely exhibited the contract and the company minutes; there was no need to call a witness, because a section of the Nova Scotia Companies Act declared the minutes and a contract prima facie evidence. The trustee, however, called three witnesses, the first of whom was Dr John George MacDougall,[38] the leading surgeon in the province, who had operated on my two sisters for appendicitis, as well as on my father.[39] He gave evidence that the contract was for five years and $5,000 per year. When I started to cross-examine him, he was very upset that I should doubt his word and started to lecture me. The judge told him I was only doing my duty. Then followed another doctor, Harold Edwin Killam, who had courted Mother before she met Father; then the dean of the bar, Thomas Reginald Robertson KC, solicitor of the bankrupt company. Though all gave evidence to the same effect, I cross-examined them to see whether they could have made a mistake. The answer was no – and none of these men would have lied; I was dumbfounded. The judge having adjourned the hearing at 4:00, I went to his chambers and told him I wanted to retire. He told me I had no business coming to see him, that I was prejudicing my client's case, and that I had better talk it over with Stewart. Finally he said, "You want to be lawyer, judge, and jury." I saw Stewart, who told me I must continue. I had no right to judge; having gone thus far, I must assume my client is honest. So, with my tail between my legs, I went back to court the next day. Against my advice, my client took the stand and was torn to shreds. What Moore had done was replace a page in the minute-book and a page in the contract, which contained the true amount and the term. It was incredible that he should have thought to get away with it. I won the second, smaller claim but of course lost the first, the big one. For over a year, every Monday morning I received a letter from Moore showing how I could have presented the case better and diagonally across it in red ink "$50,000 over the dam." Stewart told me not to reply and finally he stopped writing.

Especially worthy of note that year was the reorganization of John H. Emmett Limited.[40] Emmett had been a small butcher who achieved an excellent reputation – so enviable that he could not handle it. An investment house[41] financed the building of a new store and the purchase of machinery and equipment. Then the Depression set in and it was obvious Emmett's was going under. The investment dealer came to Stewart, who turned the file over to me. There were debentures, a mortgage, the bank's secured debt, creditors preferred and common, stock preferred and common, etc. I worked out a scheme of reorganization, further to which the court ordered meetings of all classes of creditors. The scheme involved both increasing and reducing capital, arrangements with creditors, etc. I read three textbooks while conducting the reorganization, supervised the meetings, and had everything completed and ready for the judge's final order; in the meantime, however, the company was losing more money and was petitioned into bankruptcy. All my work went for naught, while the firm had paid out quite a lot of money in disbursements. Stewart consoled me; he told me I probably knew more about company reorganization now than any lawyer in the province and said, "You didn't work for nothing. You've learned a great deal. It's the firm that's lost the money but they now have a pretty fair corporate lawyer they didn't have before." Small wonder that with Stewart and me it was hero and hero worship.

One day an elderly man called Morrison came in to see me with his son, Malcolm, a fine-looking young man in his mid-twenties, who walked with a limp; both were coal miners. Malcolm broke his leg in a mining accident and it had been improperly set so that it was shorter than the other. When he went back to the mines his leg caused him so much pain that he was unable to work. The Workmen's Compensation Board[42] at first declined to assist. A friend of mine, Dr W. Alan Curry, who was a leading surgeon, agreed to see Morrison and concluded that his leg should be re-broken and reset. Curry also agreed to go before the Board and give evidence. It was difficult persuading the Board to reverse their earlier decision; I assailed them with Curry's professional reputation and a final plea that this young man's future hung on the decision. The board acquiesced, the operation was successfully performed, and the old man brought Malcolm in to see me and proudly had him pull up his trouser leg. Malcolm afterwards went to work on a ship. One day his father came in with tears in his eyes; Malcolm had contracted malaria and died. I too shed some tears, so very grateful had he been to me.

My third year of practice, 1932, saw one case of considerable interest – *Cross v. Dares et al.*,[43] which I successfully argued both at trial and on appeal. The Supreme Court in Banco decided that the client was bound by the statement of his solicitor; it became the leading case. I also argued two cases for Mersey Paper Company, one in Truro and the other in Amherst, both against leading counsel. The latter was appealed, but the Supreme Court in Banco divided evenly, so my client prevailed.[44]

We were serving notice of expropriation on behalf of Eastern Telephone & Telegraph in a small community on Cape Breton Island up in the Highlands. It was February and the roads were bad. We went to the owner's house and talked to him, explained that he could appear and oppose the application, but again tried to buy the right of way. He simply answered that no one was going to take his land; I explained we were just asking for a right of way – that the land was still his – but he would not relent. So we left and had only gone a few yards when our automobile became stuck in the mud. We went back to his house and explained our plight; he imme-diately brought a pair of oxen and pulled us out of the mire. We tried to pay him; he refused but invited us back for tea spiked with rum. We accepted. As I was thanking him, I said how grateful we were and how kind he was to help the enemy; then I suggested he should think of the telephone line over his land (and a long way from his house) as his participation in the great experiment of actu-ally telephoning across the Atlantic Ocean for the first time in history.

I concluded by saying, "Think it over, see a lawyer, and ask him whether you really have any chance of success in opposing us and we will pay the lawyer's bill." He saw a lawyer in Sydney[45] and sold us the right of way.

In October Stewart suggested to me that I might become a partner in 1933, but there had to be unanimity; he did not discuss it further, so I knew there could not have been unanimity.[46] But there were consolations. I started going steady with my younger cousin Mollie Covert.[47] The whole world was suddenly wonderful – not just the practice of law. By 1933, my fourth year of practice, the Depression was so severe that the practice of corporate law began to change. I was scrutineer in what became almost an annual battle for control of Moirs, the chocolate manufacturers;[48] our firm was acting for one faction, while Burchell, Smith, Parker & Fogo[49] for the other. C.B. Smith and his brother F.D. (Frank) Smith, an equally brilliant lawyer with the other firm, were opposing counsel. It was a sight to watch the two brothers fighting like Kilkenny cats.[50] But these were signs of the times – the company survived.

There were crucial meetings of Fred C. Manning's holding company, United Service Corporation, whose bankers gave Manning forty-eight hours to raise the money to pay off their loan. Manning flew to Akron, Ohio, where he was able to raise the money from the Goodyear Tire Company, paid off the Canadian [Imperial] Bank of Commerce, and switched to the Bank of Nova Scotia. He became one of its biggest Maritime customers and in 1947 a director. Fred Manning[51] had started as a car salesman and gradually built up a conglomerate consisting of a chain of service stations serving the Maritimes, a bus company, four car dealerships, a tire retreading plant, and a car accessories company – all wholly-owned subsidiaries of United Service Corporation Limited.

During the depths of the Depression Manning's friendly rival, Roy Jodrey, who was struggling to make a ground wood pulp mill[52] profitable, had built a hydroelectric power plant to ensure cheap energy and then a moulded-pulp products factory to use the waste product of the paper mill. In July 1933 I incorporated Jodrey's Canadian Keyes Fibre Company Limited,[53] which made paper plates out of the waste product of the ground wood pulp mill. Jodrey always maintained it would be the tail that wagged the dog; CKF Inc. became a very successful company and many years later I became a director of it.[54] Both Jodrey and Manning had been born poor and left school and both became leading industrial entrepreneurs in Nova Scotia. It was amazing to see how they worked their wonders in completely different ways. The one common thread was hard work and a detailed knowledge of their businesses.

My first Supreme Court jury trial was exciting, because halfway through the presiding judge, Humphrey Mellish, had a heart attack and was out for two months. Coming back, he resumed the trial at the very point where he had left off.[55] Every juror was present and apparently ready to go again. I protested that the plaintiff's case was now stale, while the defendant's would be fresh in the jury's mind. Mellish was severe with me, but the jury I think sympathetic. Counsel for the defence was Laurence Arthur Lovett KC, the leading litigator at the bar,[56] who handled me roughly. It was nerve-wracking waiting for the jury to return; after four hours' deliberation they could not agree. Eventually the action was settled out of court.

I bought Mollie's engagement ring from Birks and the engagement was officially announced on 31 July, Mollie's twentieth birthday. Two weeks earlier, the legislature had been dissolved and a provincial election called for 22 August. The Conservative Party of Mollie's father (then lieutenant-governor) was in power and facing the electorate for the second time. Apparently they expected a hard fight, because, when the voters' lists were published, thousands of names of eligible voters were missing; nor were there enough revising officers to enumerate them in time. The Liberal Party applied to the Supreme Court for a mandamus to appoint extra revising officers. The writ was granted, I was appointed, and we sat from early in the morning until late at night, day after day. People stood in line for hours to get their names on the list. I worked continually for over ten days, finishing on 16 August. The election, on the 22d, saw the Liberals swept back into power under the leadership of Angus L. Macdonald, who had been a teacher of mine at Dalhousie Law School.

My fifth year of practice, 1934, started out with a loss in the Supreme Court but, two days later, a forty per cent pay raise; my diary says, "See the possibility of getting married." The big case was *Kendall v. Maritime National Fish*, a company that was a good client of ours.[57] Stewart called me in and asked how I was getting along with it. I told him I had no worries, that the lawyer on the other side was a police court lawyer.[58] Stewart put his glasses down on the end of his nose, looked over the top of them, and said, "Oh! You don't think much of Police Court lawyers, eh?" He picked up the phone, called H.P. MacKeen and said "Harry, this young man needs some Police Court work. Give him those Automobile Legal Association cases for a year or two." And MacKeen did. It took some of the conceit out of me and gave me respect for the ability of the police court lawyer.

Having lost the Kendall case, I decided to appeal. Stewart called me in and said that C.B. Smith[59] did not think I could win on appeal and should abandon it because the trial judge had made findings of fact against me. I started to argue the case but he stopped me, called Smith in and said, "Convince Charlie." I argued; Smith began to interrupt; Stewart stopped him, then after awhile cut me off too and said, "Charlie, we'll let him learn a lesson and if he loses, the firm will charge the client nothing." I won the appeal. When I went in to tell Stewart he laughed and said, "I knew you would."[60]

Early in July I appeared for one Moors, who asked me to bring an action against two spinster sisters, the Misses Taylor, who had built a double garage without getting a permit and had leased it to some rum-runners, whom Moors alleged were keeping him awake at all hours of the night. The garage was built in an area where the ladies could not get a permit. So I brought an action to compel them to tear down the garage. L.A. Lovett acted for the defendants. I applied to the court to strike out his defence and succeeded. He appealed and then abandoned the appeal and down came the garage. Lovett talked me into agreeing on costs because of "these poor old ladies."

Mollie and I had set the date for our wedding. We hunted many days for a flat and in June found one at 113½ Morris Street – an upstairs apartment. In July we worked on a budget and selected the wedding ring. I obtained a driver's licence and a marriage licence. We bought more furniture, moved it into the flat, and finally, on 25 August 1934, were married in St Paul's Church in an evening ceremony. Mollie looked beautiful. We drove to Chester for our honeymoon at the Lovett House, owned by a friend of mine. We played tennis, swam, went yachting, played bridge, and visited an old teacher of mine in Mahone Bay. We dined at the Hackmatack Inn, where as an undergraduate I had bellhopped. Then we drove up to Mother's in Canning to spend the last two days and so back to work.

There was another case opposite L.A. Lovett. I brought an action on behalf of two architectural engineers against the Nova Scotia Association of Architects, which in 1932 had secured an act of the legislature whereby any architect who satisfied the association's executive council that he was an architect could be given a certificate entitling him to practise. H.B. Pickings and Clifford St John Wilson were well-known civil engineers who had designed many buildings. The Architects Act set a date when the satisfying of the council had to be done. The Depression had suddenly caught up with architects as well as engineers. So Pickings & Wilson wrote a letter to the association about two days before the deadline, listing some of the buildings they had designed. The association let the date pass, then advised Pickings & Wilson that satisfactory evidence had not been provided and their application was dismissed. They consulted me. I told them I would apply for a mandamus on their behalf but thought it would not succeed because of the wording of the section; the council had to be satisfied and said they were not. Pickings died in September 1935, before the case came to court, so I discontinued the case in respect of him. Then I argued the case and lost. I tried to bargain with Lovett over costs on account of Mrs Pickings's poor situation and Wilson's not getting a licence. But Lovett insisted on taxing costs, even though I reminded him of *Moors v. Taylor*. It made no difference; he just said, "That was your privilege and decision." Angry, I had the unmitigated gall and rudeness to say to him, "Mr. Lovett, you're an old man[61] and I'm young and I'm going to meet you and fight you [so that] you never forget this." He looked at me, smiled, and said, "That's the way I like it." Knowing Attorney-General MacQuarrie well, I showed him the correspondence and the decision and asked him to introduce a bill to amend the Architects Act.[62] I appeared before the legislature's law amendments committee, where the architects association was raked over the coals; to avoid the amendment they admitted Wilson, who in 1939 became president of their association.

In 1935 there was much less litigation, but an increase of company creditor arrangement work – a sign of Depression times. I handled a few probate cases, an occasional case in the Police Court, several small cases in the County Court, two in the Supreme Court, and one before the Pension Appeals Board.[63] There were two company creditor arrangement cases, one for Ungars Laundry, in which I was bitterly opposed by my arch-enemy Lovett. I had never worked so hard and success for my labours was a sweet reward. The second was an application under the Companies' Creditors Arrangement Act, 1933 on behalf of Canadian Keyes Fibre. I conducted the meetings and made what was the first application in Nova Scotia under this act. At the meeting the arrangement was opposed by a creditor whose claim was large enough to have defeated the proposal. I persuaded him that if he could not vote for it, then (for the benefit of the community) to refrain from voting at all. The company issued preference shares to cover the debt and eventually every creditor was paid dividends for each year they held the shares and then 100 cents on the dollar when the shares were redeemed.

One Saturday morning in April 1935 I had a call from Mrs H.J.B. Marriott, co-executor and beneficiary of the will of William Henshaw Newberry, whose housekeeper she had been for many years.[64] Newberry had died the previous night, having bequeathed his body to Dalhousie Medical School "for anatomical purposes." Newberry's family told Mrs Marriott that there must be a funeral and the deceased buried "properly." As Newberry had left his entire estate to the Marriotts, Mrs Marriott was having a difficult time and called me for advice. I consulted the Anatomy Act and found that no one had the power to dispose of his own body.[65] Then it occurred to me that if the family were to consent, I could accomplish the testator's object. I called Dalhousie to find out whether they would accept the body if the family consented. Then I called the deputy attorney-general, Fred Mathers, and asked whether he saw anything wrong with my proposal to have a closed empty coffin and to conduct a funeral while giving the corpse to the Medical School. He said that was alright. I met the family and pointed out that they would be complying with Newberry's wishes that his body be used for anatomical purposes and that, as far as the public was concerned, there would have been a "proper" funeral. They agreed.

After the provincial election of August 1933 swept the Liberals back into power, the former Conservative premier, Gordon S. Harrington, was given an office in our firm for a couple of years. Among his clients was E.D. Rudderham, a strong Tory, who consulted Harrington on what proved to be a very interesting case, which Harrington invited me to handle. Rudderham had leased for a period of years a shop he owned in Guysborough to the Nova Scotia Liquor Commission for use as a liquor store. When the Conservatives were defeated, the new government decided to terminate the lease. Rudderham refused to accept the decision, put a padlock on the door, and protected his property with a shotgun. As the store was full of liquor, the government's solution was to prosecute him for "having liquor in his possession in excess of ... imperial gallons not purchased from the Commission." Though the literal meaning of the words covered the facts, this was obviously not what the section was meant to address. Rudderham, who met me when I arrived in Guysborough, took one look and said, "I don't know – I want a man who can come in here fighting." I told him not to worry. The hearing before the stipendiary magistrate, Aubrey H.H. DesBarres, lasted most of the day. The crown attorney and I did tremendous battle over objections and arguments and concluded with fairly long speeches. When we had finished addressing the crowded courtroom, the magistrate (a gentleman farmer) said, "We've heard long, learned, and elongated speeches from counsel and I would like to make a 'spiel' myself, but it's getting time to feed the chickens and milk the cow so I'll cut it short." He quickly summed up the facts: "This section was never meant to cover this kind of situation. The crown is trying to use a criminal prosecution to settle what is a civil matter. This is a prosecution which I must dismiss and acquit the accused." The crowd roared its approval. Rudderham drove me down the main street, yelling at the top of his voice so that all could hear, "Acquitted, Acquitted, Acquitted."

Late in 1935 I had a letter from an arts classmate of mine in Montreal, whose father, Arthur Francis Dentith, was an Anglican priest in the Diocese of Nova Scotia. The Reverend Dentith was having difficulties with the bishop, John Hackenley, and his son wanted me to see what could be done about them. Dentith was a older man with an excellent reputation who had been honoured by the King for his work with the Boy Scouts. The moment I saw him I knew I would hear the truth, the whole truth, and nothing but the truth. He had retired as rector of Spryfield[66] and was to turn over his books, the rectory, and everything else to the new incumbent.[67] All Dentith wanted was an audit and a receipt for what he was turning over; then he would vacate. Bishop Hackenley, who "demanded" immediate "obedience" to his "orders," had not reckoned with Dentith's stubbornness. Having called a public meeting of the parishioners, the bishop first berated Dentith for engaging a lawyer, saying "No innocent man needed a lawyer." When I rose and interrupted, he roared at me, "Sit down!" I refused and said I would insist he withdraw that remark and I would continue to interrupt him until he did. I turned to the parishioners and asked whether there was anyone who doubted the integrity of Dentith. The parishioners started to clap, soon they all joined in. I turned to Hackenley and lectured him on the right of any person to counsel, stating that Dentith was simply asking for the audit as a precautionary measure; when he got his clearance and receipt (though not before) he would turn over the property. When someone in the audience remarked, "That's fair and just," the bishop in a fit of anger adjourned the meeting. But Dentith got his way.

Later that December, I was playing bridge at the Halifax Club with Mr Stewart when he announced that on 1 January 1936 I would become a partner in the firm. All of the partners[68] made me feel welcome. January, February, and March were mostly taken up with work for Manning and Jodrey. Manning's United Service Corporation (USC) and its many subsidiaries kept me busy supervising corporate meetings, drafting resolutions, and keeping minutes. Manning asked me to join USC, offering more than I was earning, but I told him I could not give up the practice of law. Jodrey kept me busy travelling to Hantsport to prepare a bond issue and working for both Minas Basin Pulp and Paper Mills and its subsidiary Canadian Keyes Fibre. I learned a great deal attending these meetings and seeing how directors conducted their business. It was the beginning of a superior education, which fitted me for what would constitute a major part of my life's work.

In April 1936 I appeared for my friend, the aviator Harley Goodwin, who was being sued for damages to an aircraft he had hired and then crashed in New Brunswick. L.A. Lovett was my opponent and the jury brought in an adverse verdict, which we appealed successfully on the grounds that it was perverse.[69] Goodwin had to wait seven months before getting a favourable decision; an unfavourable one would have ruined him.

On 18 May 1936 our son was born, whom we called Walter (after Mollie's father), Michael (the name of our choice) and Stewart (after Mr Stewart). He has never been known by any name other than Michael or Mike. Mother and son came home from the hospital on 30 May.

The following month there were several meetings of the Manning group of companies. I started work on another bond issue for Super Service Stations Limited. The company was issuing serial bonds at $100,000 each, in denominations of $100, $500 and $1,000; Manning incorporated the Nova Scotia Bond Corporation to wholesale them. Between that little company and Roy Jodrey, Manning sold the bonds, which enabled Super Service Stations to build all over Nova Scotia and eventually in New Brunswick and Prince Edward Island. Five days after Michael was christened, on 7 August, Jodrey invited me to join the board of Minas Basin Pulp and Paper Mills (Minas Basin Pulp and Power Company). It was my first real directorship.

One Saturday morning I was laying a flagstone walkway from the front steps of our house to the sidewalk on Fraser Street, when along came a handsome young man in overalls who enquired, "Are you Frank Covert, the lawyer?" I said yes; he introduced himself as Charlie MacCulloch and asked me to look at a contract drawn between one Donald Hogan and himself, which was a fixed-salary contract over five years for him to build houses. He asked whether the contract was legal and binding. I told him it was but advised against signing it. When he asked why, I said that if he had any hopes for the future he should not expect to work for five years without a raise. He answered, "I asked for legal advice, not economic advice." Reminding me of this forty years later, while driving me downtown from a Dalhousie Investment Committee[70] meeting, MacCulloch told me he had provided for annual adjustments in salary. By then he was Nova Scotia's leading real estate developer.[71]

The Canadian Bar Association held its 1936 annual meeting in Halifax and for seven days in August work in the law firm just about ceased. Stewart was Nova Scotia vice-president of the CBA and so we were turned loose to do our part in making the meeting a success. There was near tragedy at the end of it; H.P. MacKeen's wife, Alice (Al), and their daughter Judith[72] were aboard a yacht in Halifax Harbour when there was a gasoline explosion and fire, in which both Al and Judy were badly burned.[73] Their recovery was complete but it was a long, painful process; poor Harry was like a lost soul for weeks on end.

On 30 December 1936 Stewart called me in and told me that Mersey Paper was going to buy approximately 176,000 acres of timber limits[74] from two elderly gentlemen in Boston, Neal Rantoul and S.H. Fessenden.[75] They were willing sellers and Mersey Paper willing buyers. The only problem was price and they had agreed to appoint a famous cruiser, James W. Sewall of Old Town (Maine), to appraise the area, determine the number of cords of accessible timber, and advise on the prices for each of the species (spruce, fir, pine, hemlock, etc.). Stewart asked me to try my hand at the agreement. I drew a simple, standard form of sales agreement in which, for price and payment I merely noted that Sewall was appointed sole arbitrator of how the price was to be calculated "in accordance with the terms set out in Schedule A, payment in accordance with Schedule B and the lands described in Schedule C." All three schedules were blank. Early in January I took the agreement in to Stewart, saying he would have to negotiate Schedules A and B in Boston. He took it home with him. I did not then realize what an experience awaited me.

On 4 January 1937 Stewart called me in and told me he was not going to Boston; he grinned as he said *I* would have to negotiate Schedules A and B. He had earlier told me the amount involved was over $1 million, so I was nervous. The following day I went to Liverpool, from where, accompanied by Ralph Seaborne, manager of the woodlands department of Mersey Paper and C.H.L. (the Colonel) Jones, president and managing director of the company,[76] I sailed to Boston via Saint John on the Yarmouth ferry. I expected to be in Boston two or three days; we were there for eight.

The vendors' lawyer, Walter Powers, provided my first introduction to American legal draftsmanship. Day after day we worked on the agreement and when we were through it was six times as long; we had probably amended every paragraph and clause and sub-clause dozens of times. Though the sessions with Powers were tedious, I remembered an injunction of Stewart's: "Don't fight with the lawyer on the other side as long as it takes nothing away and it's not ambiguous. This way you are more apt to get what you want." So I stuck to my guns and, when the agreement was done, I was happy with it. The negotiation of the schedules was instructive. Sewall was a tremendous fellow, the soul of integrity, and fair to both sides; Seaborne, my technical adviser, won round after round with Powers. We concluded the agreement on the 12th and were to meet at the offices of Fessenden and Rantoul to secure their consent. Then, at the last moment, Powers said he had a few changes to make. I thought Jones would have a fit. But they were only punctuation changes. At one stretch in the drafting of the agreement, Powers and I worked thirty-six hours without sleep. I was exhausted when, at 7:00 in the morning, we went out looking for a place to eat breakfast, but none was open.

The next day Izaak Walton Killam arrived from Montreal. He had conceived the idea of Mersey Paper and was president of Royal Securities Corporation, which controlled it. Nova Scotian by birth, in his youth Killam had sold newspapers, but he went on to become one of Canada's greatest industrial promoters and financiers. Because he owned about ninety per cent of Mersey's common stock, he came to Boston to vet the agreement. Jones put Seaborne and me in the adjoining room, while Killam read the contract, so that we would be available if Killam wanted information or explanations. There was a very long silence unbroken except by the sound of turning pages, as Killam digested the contract. After more than one and a half hours Killam said to the Colonel, "That's a fine contract. Where's Jim?" (meaning Mr Stewart).

The Colonel replied, "Jim didn't come down."

Killam asked. "Then who drew the contract?"

The Colonel answered, "A young fellow by the name of Covert. Would you like to meet him?"

Killam, without a second's hesitation, replied "No, don't bother."

So I did not meet the great Killam, whom I had seen again and again entering the firm's offices. He was always ushered into Stewart's suite at once and remained closeted with him for hours.

Late that afternoon I was feeling so unwell that the Colonel told me to stay in bed until the last minute. Then I could get a taxi and bring to the boat everybody's luggage, which would all be in the porter's hands downstairs at the hotel. I finally arose, got into the taxi with all the luggage and said to the driver, "The Boston boat for Yarmouth."

"You haven't left enough time."

"I have to make it."

"If I'm fined you'll have to pay the fines."

After an exciting ride, we arrived at the pier to find the Colonel pacing up and down the wharf. He asked what the hell kept me and I told him I had no idea it would take over half an hour to go anywhere in one city. He looked at me and said, "Frank, you'll always be a country boy." He had persuaded the captain to hold the vessel for a few minutes and all was well. But the Colonel told me that if I had not made it with the luggage, I would have been through.

Returning, I began work on a $7 million bond issue for Nova Scotia Light and Power, which meant I had to prepare and record trust deeds for seven or eight subsidiary companies.[77] There was also a reduction of capital for Fred Manning's Super Service Stations Limited. January through April, I served on the executive committee of the Civic Reform League, which involved numerous meetings at night, trying to persuade people to run for mayor or alderman on Halifax City Council. At the elections held on 28 April 1937 every one of our candidates was elected.

In February 1937 I attended my first meeting as a director of Minas Basin Pulp and Power. I also went on Mersey business to Montreal, where we were to meet officials of the Chicago Title & Guarantee, which owned timber limits in Annapolis and Digby Counties. The Colonel had negotiated a verbal agreement, so Seaborne and I accompanied him to Montreal to close it. We had not been with the Chicagoans more than fifteen minutes when they started to talk about renegotiating the price. C.H.L. Jones was very angry and said there was a deal; Chicago said it was verbal and not binding. Jones quickly called the whole thing off and told me to go home, which I did. Coincidentally, over thirty years later I negotiated the sale of Lincoln Pulp Company, which had bought the lands, and then prevailed upon the new owner to sell half of them to Minas Basin Pulp and Power and half to Mersey Paper.

In April I appeared in Juvenile Court, incorporated a Dominion company – Maritime National (1937) – and did a bond issue. In the partnership division, my share increased and I was given a bonus. In June Nova Scotia was in the midst of an election campaign and I gave political speeches at Musquodoboit, Grand Desert, Lawrencetown, East Preston, and Head of Jeddore.[78] I enjoyed it immensely; of course, one usually has a friendly audience and one begins to believe that one is an orator. On 29 June the provincial Liberals won a sweeping victory, 25 seats to 5. I really got a dangerous taste of politics. The political speeches on the hustings were exciting and tempting.

Apart from arbitrations for Mersey Paper and some appearances before the Public Utilities Board, the sum total of my work as a barrister in 1938 was a case in the Probate Court, one in the Juvenile Court, an exciting jury trial with H.P. MacKeen,[79] a divorce case, and an appeal in the Supreme Court in Banco. I spent four days in Boston in June, representing Mersey in arbitrations under the machinery set up by the agreement. Sewall was the sole arbitrator and the arbitrations were very successful; Seaborne made a magnificent witness.

On the solicitorial side I drafted a modern set of company articles of association, which became the standard. I lectured at Dalhousie Law School on the winding up of companies and read two books on corporate accounting, balance sheets, and financial statements. I gave opinions on bond issues, including one for the government of Prince Edward Island. On one day I supervised and wrote up the minutes of sixteen meetings for the Manning group of companies. I supervised many meetings for the Manning group and finally recommended to Manning a young lawyer to do this kind of work.

I acted for the underwriters, Pitfields,[80] as well as for the company on a Super Service Stations Limited bond issue. This is a practice frowned upon in many jurisdictions. Many argue that there is a conflict of interest. I believe that by having two sets of solicitors, all one does is double or triple the time and more than double the cost. Once the parties have agreed on the terms, then, as solicitor for the company, one makes sure there is complete disclosure; really the interests of both parties should be identical. In addition to acting for Pitfields and Super Service Stations on a preferred share issue, I also did bond issues for Super Service Stations and United Service Corporation and held meetings of bondholders about amending the existing trust deed. I introduced to Manning a friend of mine, Percy John (Perce) Smith, who afterwards became the Halifax manager for Pitfields. From then on, Pitfields did securities issues for all the Manning group of companies, which in later years included not only Super Service Stations and United Service Corporation but also a private investment holding company, Great Eastern Corporation, of which Smith and I in due course became directors. When Manning died in 1959, I was elected president.

I appeared before the Legislature's law amendments committee on the Conditional Sales Act Bill,[81] was sent to Liverpool by Stewart to supervise the legalities of the annual meeting of Mersey Paper (which he could not attend), and met Walter P. Zeller, who owned a chain of discount department stores, Zellers – Retailers to Thrifty Canadians. I handled the purchase of a downtown Halifax commercial property for Zeller and had another little battle with L.A. Lovett over a tenant who maintained he had not received proper notice to quit. This threatened to hold up demolition of the existing premises and the building of the new. I persuaded Lovett to agree on a statement of facts, with the notice to quit attached, and to appoint the taxing master, Charles Frederick Tremaine KC, to act as sole and final arbitrator with an unappealable decision. Zeller's Montreal counsel were highly worried, but I had a case right on the nose, which I showed Zeller. He let me go ahead and we got a decision in two days. Zeller, who was very pleased, was in my office when I instructed the contractor to go ahead and start tearing down the building as soon as the tenant, one Valensky, informed me he had moved out. It was a great moment for me when Zeller phoned his Montreal counsel and told him work had started.

In November 1938 the appeal court handed down its decision in *Coxe et al. v. H.T. Warne Limited*.[82] This was an action brought by the proprietors of Lour Lodge in Digby against one Warne, the owner of a sawmill that scattered blackened cinders all over the hotel property. The plaintiffs having sought an injunction, the defendant gave jury notice. The trial took place in the Supreme Court at Digby and was a cause célèbre in the town. H.P. MacKeen carried the burden of the trial, but he let me examine a few witnesses and cross-examine one. He gave the jury address. In the midst of their deliberations, the jury asked to discuss a matter with the judge; they enquired in open court whether they could, as part of their verdict, find that the mill owner had to do something about the stack (chimney) on the mill – for example, heighten it to abate the nuisance. Justice Carroll, presiding, said no; they could only answer the questions put to them. So the jury retired again and later came back with a finding of no nuisance. Plaintiffs moved for a new trial on the ground that the verdict was perverse; the jury wanted to recommend that the chimney stack be heightened to abate the nuisance. The Supreme Court in Banco disallowed the appeal, which in my view shows the real value of a jury. They were more interested in preserving the employment of the townspeople than protecting the American tourists in the summer hotel from inconvenience. When the plaintiffs threatened further appeal, Warne lengthened the chimney.

By 1939, my tenth full year of practice, I really had ceased as a barrister and was a solicitor. My only trial work was a case in the Supreme Court and one in the Police Court; corporation work occupied most of my time. When Mother came to town I took her to see Stewart, who told her I had given him a five-year vacation. I lectured on company incorporation at Dalhousie Law School, went to Boston again for more arbitrations under the Mersey agreement, and was retained by seven companies to appear before the Legislature's law amendments committee to oppose Bill 105, which would have imposed additional taxes on corporations.[83] There were numerous Public Utilities Board rate hearings involving subsidiaries of Nova Scotia Light & Power: Chester Light and Power (Chester), Milton Hydro-Electric (Brooklyn), and Barrington Electric (Clarks Harbour). I attended several directors' meetings in Hantsport of Minas Basin Pulp & Power and spent a great deal of time on the reorganization of Acadia Sugar Refining, which included supervising meetings of shareholders.[84] I worked on a bond issue for Minas Basin Pulp and Power and on a preferred share issue for Best Yeast Limited, also doing the prospectus. I handled another bond issue for Super Service Stations and did one for Eastern Light & Power. I appeared before the Public Utilities Board on a water rate case for Maritime Fish (a subsidiary of Maritime National). There were numerous chambers applications relating to companies' winding-up, approval of reorganizations, etc.

Legally, the highlight of 1939 was deputizing for Stewart as legislative counsel for Famous Players Canadian Corporation. The Liberal government had introduced Bill 92 to amend *The Theatres, Cinematographs and Amusements Act.*[85] The bill was aimed at what the independent exhibitors called the Famous Players monopoly of the better films and would have given the Board of Censors full powers to regulate motion picture distribution. Famous Players retained Stewart (who was about to leave for England)[86] and he handed it over to me. I got in touch with Laurence M. Graburn, manager of the flagship Capitol Theatre in Halifax, and Famous Players' senior official in Nova Scotia. I went over the bill with him, and he told me it could not work.[87] For weeks Graburn tutored me in the practical business of operating a film exchange. It was a fascinating lesson and I a willing pupil. I had him go over my brief and then ask me all kinds of questions to see whether he could stump me. Finally he agreed I was ready – it had been nearly four weeks' preparation.

Down to Halifax from Toronto came Messrs Nathanson and Bragg.[88] Graburn took me to the train to meet them. Bragg took one look at me and asked where Stewart was. I told him England. They went up to the hotel room and called a lawyer, Colonel Cooper,[89] whom they asked to charter a plane and fly to Halifax. The Colonel came and appeared next day before the law amendments committee. The crowded chamber heard speech after speech by the independent exhibitors. Finally, Cooper started his presentation. He had not had time to prepare and the committee tore him to shreds. I saw Bragg lean over to Graburn, who then whispered to me, "Frank, are you ready to go on?" I answered yes. When Cooper finished, I rose. I described how movies were distributed, e.g., a Deanna Durbin film would have its premiere in Winnipeg (where she was born) and always in the largest theatres.[90] *Pygmalion*[91] would go to highbrow theatres, a Tom Mix[92] film to where it would be best appreciated; some films paid a percentage of the gate or take and so on. I introduced the committee to all the problems and then dissected the bill, showing that it would not work. I argued also that it was ultra vires under the power of Parliament to regulate trade and commerce.[93] Yet it was obvious there were problems to be solved. I suggested that a board of arbitration be set up, consisting of one representative from the independent exhibitors who knew the business, one from the big interests such as Famous Players and 20th Century Fox, and an independent as chairman. The amending act passed, but with a proviso that would not come into force until proclaimed. After the hearing, the independents and Famous Players got together and it was agreed to hold some arbitrations that very night. A board was quickly constituted and we tried case after case, in no time achieving unanimous awards in every one – to the complete satisfaction of the independent exhibitors. The procedure worked so well that precedents were established, as a result of which the problems ceased and the board of arbitration itself was wound up shortly afterwards.

Early the next morning I had a call from Premier Angus L. Macdonald, who asked me for a report on the arbitrations and the basis of my ultra vires argument. I gave it to him; he chuckled and said, "You are probably right." He asked me if I could bring Bragg and Graburn down to see him within half an hour. We did so and Macdonald, who had been my teacher at law school, told my clients I had been one of his star pupils at law school and that I had apparently satisfied the law amendments committee that the law should be passed but not proclaimed, which would encourage all the parties to act reasonably. He told Bragg and Graburn that if that was satisfactory, that was what would happen. He shook hands with us as we were leaving and said to me, "Frank, if I can ever be helpful, just let me know." The act was never proclaimed. My clients paid 250 per cent of my bill, and for years afterwards sent free passes at all Famous Players theatres for Mollie and me and two guests.

On 3 September 1939 England declared war on Germany and the Cunard liner *Athenia* was torpedoed. There was scarcely a Cunard liner I had not boarded to note the master's protest on an admiralty court libel and *Athenia* had been a frequent caller at the Port of Halifax. It was a sad day, on which I noted in my diary, "This war will be a bad one." Before the end of January 1940 Canada was in the throes of a wartime election campaign. I spoke at political meetings in Berwick with James Lorimer Ilsley, MP for Digby-Annapolis-Kings, who was minister of national revenue and a Kings County native. This was followed by speeches in Waterville, Wolfville, my own hometown of Canning, and Kingston – all in the space of eight days. On 26 March the Liberals won an overwhelming victory at the polls.[94]

Two days earlier Perce Smith called me, saying he could not disclose the name of his client, but could outline the facts using fictitious names and companies, state the problem, and find out whether I could help him, which his client's lawyer had been unable to do. For three evenings we worked on it and the last evening we came up with a solution, which appeared to be foolproof. We consumed half a bottle of rum and I forgot about it. Then I had a call from Fleming Blanchard McCurdy,[95] president of Eastern Trust, who asked me to come down to see him. I accepted with alacrity, wondering what it was all about. When I entered I saw Smith, L.A. Lovett, and McCurdy, who outlined what Smith had told him of my plan. I immediately assured McCurdy that Smith had gone to great pains to conceal the client's identity (I still had no idea what company was involved.) McCurdy accepted that, asked a few questions, and then asked me first whether I was sure of my opinion; I said yes. Then he asked whether I could work with Lovett. I replied, "Yes – if he can work with me." Lovett nodded assent. I worked with Lovett four nights in a row, always at his office. The first night he called me Covert; the second night he called me Frank; the third night, every once in awhile he would say, "Well now, my son, what do you say about this?" We got along famously and at the end of it all he asked me what I was going to charge. I thought in view of the amount involved and the four times I had met with him, I would charge $750. He told me it was ridiculous, that McCurdy would bargain me down anyway and finally told me his bill would be at least $7,500. I sent my bill and the day it went out I had a call from McCurdy. I said to myself, "Oh, oh, here comes the haggling;" never having had a complaint in my life, now I was worried.

"I have your account. Is that your whole bill?"

"Yes, sir."

"And I have your opinion. Are you still as sure of it?"

"Yes, sir."

"A cheque will be in your hands within the hour."

"Thank you, sir."

I expect McCurdy received Lovett's bill first and was delighted with mine.

At the same time I was retained by counsel for H.R. Bain & Company, Toronto investment dealers, to defend one of their salesmen, R.S. Newbury, who had been arrested and charged with securities fraud. One of the prosecution witnesses fared badly on cross-examination, so I did some plea bargaining, several charges were dropped, and Newbury pleaded guilty and paid the $5,000 fine. In April the firm increased my share in the partnership – retroactive to January – and awarded me a $500 bonus.

CHAPTER FOUR

Munitions and Supply

In August 1940 I had a phone call from Henry Borden KC (in Ottawa), who was general counsel in the Department of Munitions and Supply.[1] Borden wanted me to come to Ottawa and work as a solicitor in the legal branch. He told me it would be a real contribution to the war effort and that I should report by 2 September. On the 21st I started preparing to hand over my files; I worked night and day for four days, getting the files in shape and dictating memoranda for each file. Mollie and I relaxed at White Point Beach Lodge for six days, then back to Halifax. I worked hard on the 30th and 31st to clean up the rest of my files and on the following day, 1 September, I left for Ottawa on the Ocean Limited;[2] Mollie and Mike came down to the station to see me off. Though I would negotiate contracts with lawyers from all across Canada and begin learning the art of draftsmanship in a way I had not known before; though it seemed to satisfy me that I was doing a useful job in the war effort, I often look back and wonder how I could have walked out of the firm with such little notice and not have given a thought to what the firm would do by way of replacement. It was a pretty thoughtless thing for me to have done, but the firm never complained.

I arrived in Montreal on 2 September and proceeded by train to Ottawa, got a room at the Alexandra Hotel, and went over to the Department to meet John de N. Kennedy, director general of the legal branch.[3] Kennedy introduced me to two of the lawyers in the branch, Thomas Z. Boles and Henri-Paul Lemay. I told him I hoped to report for duty the following morning. On 3 September I reported for work and met my law classmate, Hugh H. Turnbull and John A.F. (Jack) Miller, another expatriate Nova Scotian and Dalhousie graduate.[4] I only just managed to meet Henry Borden, who was headed back home to Toronto. My friend Turnbull had found room and board for me with a Mrs Scott at 25 Oakland Street.

My first four days at the Department were dreadful. Kennedy would pass me a file and say prepare a go-ahead letter for his approval. Now I had no more idea what a go-ahead letter was than the man in the moon. I asked some of the lawyers for samples, which they provided, and tried to draft one. I took it into Kennedy, who just handed me another file. The next day I got the first draft back, slashed all to pieces. This routine continued for nearly a week. I went in to see him, telling him that the approach, in my view, was ridiculous. He told me sharply there was a war on and that he did not have time for discussions of this nature, handed me another file, and dismissed me. I then began to collect from the other lawyers go-ahead letters and contracts of all kinds, took them home with me to study at night, and began to design specifications which could be printed.

Henry Borden returned from Toronto and told me Kennedy was complaining that I did not seem to want to work. I got out my files and showed Borden what had happened and what could be done to improve the preparation and speed up the completion of contracts. He said, "You're just what we need here." Borden afterwards made me assistant general counsel and *then* I began to get interesting work. I worked on the Bren gun contract[5] and on the Atlas Steel plant extension; met Sir James Dunn and worked on the Algoma Steel contracts; and met Wilbert H. Howard, a Montreal lawyer[6] with whom I was to become great friends. Mr Stewart, dominion coal administrator, came to Ottawa quite often and I had dinner with him. I spent several days on the rubber contract, working with Sir John Hay, one of those Englishmen who can make one feel like a colonial, but he had a tremendous capacity to draft with great clarity.[7] In October I began work on the Montreal Locomotive contracts to build tanks.[8] These occupied me fully for days at a time. The tank and rubber contracts involved over $100 million each.

On 19 October Mollie moved out of our house, which she had let to a group captain in the Air Force who was a doctor. On 24 October I found a house, 106 Strathcona Avenue, fully furnished, which we could rent for $50 a month. The next day I had lunch at the Rideau Club with J.L. Ilsley (minister of finance) and Thomas Alexander Crerar (minister of mines and resources). On

9 November I signed the lease for the house and the next day phoned Mollie to come up – we could have the house by the 15th. I had been away seventy-one days and had written her every day;[9] on the 13th I had a wire she was on her way. On the 15th Mollie, her brother Jack, our son Mike, and our Newfoundland maid Irene arrived in the family car. Jack stayed a few days and left by train on the 18th. Two days earlier I went down to the boarding house on Oakland Street, said my goodbyes, and brought my belongings to our new home. I now resumed work in earnest; Mollie used to pick me up at nights at the Department.

Work at the Department of Munitions and Supply ("M&S") was fascinating; people brought from all over the country had given up their normal lives, moved away from home and been melded into a team of dedicated professionals whose only thought was to get the job done speedily and well. It took a great deal of planning; everyone had to learn that government systems and safeguards were not the same as in their own businesses and not necessarily ruled by red tape. Sometimes companies had to do things they did not like and became angry at the minister's powers. Sometimes it took so long to finalize a contract that people threatened to call the whole thing off. Sometimes the members of Parliament wanted so much information that the question became how to give them enough without trenching on the secret and confidential. In my first full year at M&S – September 1940 to September 1941 – I ran into all of these problems.

Fortunately I met the minister, C.D. Howe, by sheer accident early in 1941.[10] We were in the men's room and, of course, I knew who he was. He asked me my name, where I was from, and what I was doing. When he found that I was a lawyer from Halifax, he asked whether I had gone to Dalhousie. I answered yes; he remarked he had taught engineering there.[11] I replied that I knew. Howe had a problem, which everybody was saying could not be satisfactorily solved,[12] and invited me to his office to discuss it. He explained the problem; I went out, bought a sandwich and chocolate milkshake, and sauntered up to the Supreme Court library, where I found the answer quickly. Returning to the Department I prepared three memoranda: one about two pages long, setting out the facts, the answer, and the authorities; the second, a summary about half a page long; and the third, seven typewritten lines, setting out briefly the answer. I went to Howe's office immediately after lunch and handed him first the two-page memo. He started to peruse it and stopped. "Tell me the answer shortly," he said. I handed him the briefer memo. He glanced at it, saying "Just tell me." I handed him the seven lines, which he read. Then he said, "In future see if you can keep it to four lines." He summoned his secretary, told her to see that the file was turned over to me, and asked me to see it to a conclusion. That chance encounter altered the whole course of my work at M&S; I was called directly to Howe's office on many, many occasions.

While Howe was away in England,[13] M&S orders in council had not been going through with the usual speed; one in particular, dealing with a gun plant to be built by Canadian Westinghouse Company, had been completely held up.[14] Deputy Minister G.K. Sheils made arrangements for me to appear before a committee of the Cabinet on 13 January 1941 (my 33d birthday) and told me not to come back without the approval. I was in the midst of explaining to the committee that the approval was urgent, because Westinghouse said they were stopping work until the order in council passed, when a pageboy entered the room and said, "Gentlemen, Prime Minister King is ready." It was as if a bomb had been thrown; I was nearly knocked over in the rush, as they all went to the Cabinet room. I went down the hall to see Arnold Heeney, clerk of the Privy Council, and tell him what had happened. He laughed, looked at his watch and said, "In about two minutes your independent three musketeers from Nova Scotia will be coming along the hall." I went out and just moments later J.L. Ilsley, Layton Ralston, and Angus L. Macdonald appeared.[15] I stood in their path; Macdonald said, "Tell me, what's the trouble?" I told him. He said, "Go back to the Department; I'll have Mr. Heeney telephone you when it's through." I went back to the Department, where Sheils saw me enter, then waited for me to call. When I did not, he phoned me; I told him I did not have the approval yet but that I had great faith in Macdonald. Sheils was annoyed, but about ninety minutes later the news we were waiting for came through.

In the winter of 1941 the steel plants were being enlarged. That February I worked on the Algoma Steel contract with Sir James Dunn and his lawyers, E. Gordon McMillan KC from Toronto and Wilbert Howard from Montreal. The day we were finishing up, I suddenly broke out with German measles. When the M&S nurse so diagnosed me, Dunn got up and left, but Wilbert Howard stayed on. I was bedridden for five days, while Howard sent me books to read. Howard and I worked together often; I learned a great deal from this corporate lawyer, who was a superb draftsman and a very fair and honourable man.

I also worked on the Steel Company of Canada (Stelco) contract. M&S wanted to build a plant squarely in the middle of company property. Stelco's lawyer was Glyn Osler KC, reputedly a very difficult man. The company became difficult, so much so that I had to draft a telegram setting a time limit and threatening to take over the plant if they refused. That brought them to Ottawa and I was present when Howe met them. He was magnificent, telling them that if they had any faith in the future of Canada after the war they should welcome this opportunity and that they could not lose. Finally they accepted it and Osler and I ironed out the contracts. He was tough but we stuck to it until we were finished, whereupon he wrote Deputy Minister Sheils saying he would like to deal with me on all future contracts, because I would not delay matters but would see it through. Sheils took Osler's letter in to Howe, who showed it to me saying, "I hope this doesn't mean you were soft with him."

Next came the Atlas Plant Extension Limited contract, which was time-consuming. The company lawyer, Lynn B. Spencer KC of Welland, was a bulldog, but we got along well and years later became great friends. In effect Atlas converted a 400-yard-long plant into one almost a mile long – and the plant only had to close for twenty-four hours.[16]

In March 1941 I was sent to Washington on Borden's recommendation and was there over ten days working on contracts for tank engines and transmissions. I made the acquaintance of F.T. (Fred) Smye, who was later to come to Ottawa and work as executive assistant to Ralph Pickard Bell, director general of aircraft production branch in M&S. Fred knew his way around Washington; when I told him one of my main problems was that the American companies were always afraid they would have no recourse if the government did not pay, Smye arranged interviews for me at the Office of Production Management and the Treasury. As a result, I wrote Henry Borden that we should enter into some kind of an arrangement with the American government to overcome the problem. This was done later.[17]

In May 1941 Army procurement sent Colonel McAvity to Washington and M&S sent me along to accompany him. The Americans, not yet at war, were offering for military use machine tools, etc. When these were shipped and arrived at the border, Customs intervened and there was a great deal of criticism. Early in September I was instructed to draft an Order in Council to overcome the problem.[18] This involved hours of meetings with the deputy ministers of national revenue, finance, and M&S. The matter seemed so straightforward that I just could not understand the delays and waste of time. In the evenings I wrote a short play with the following dramatis personae:

His Majesty represented by the Minister of National Defence
His Majesty represented by the Minister of Finance
His Majesty represented by the Minister of Munitions and Supply
His Majesty represented by the Minister of National Revenue
His Majesty represented by the Deputy Minister of National Revenue
　　for Customs and Excise.

In the play I had His Majesty talking with His Majesty and explaining to himself what he wanted to do and asking why he could not do it; and the coup de grace: "after all, it is only I dealing with me." I sent this comedy of manners to my friend the minister of finance and to each of the deputies concerned. Ilsley was not amused and the deputies were furious; Howe got a big kick out of it. But the mission was soon accomplished.

In September there was a strike at the automotive parts factory of McKinnon Industries[19] in St. Catharines, which had contracts to manufacture parts for the twenty-five-pounder gun, for tanks, and for other weaponry.[20] Worse, a strike at the plant would have tied up three war programmes. There were provisions in the Defence of Canada Regulations[21] that if police could not handle the situation, the Army might be called in. Howe give me the problem late Friday afternoon, 12 September, the day after the sixteen-day strike began. I worked late into the night, got the papers ready, and on Saturday called on the deputy minister of justice Fred Varcoe. He had a golf match arranged and wanted to defer the discussion. I told him we planned to call in the Army that afternoon. I telephoned Henry Borden, who came over and prevailed on Varcoe to get the minister of justice, who controlled the RCMP,[22] to sign the documents; the RCMP had advised that they could not handle the situation. It was nearly noon. I went to see Ralston, minister of defence (and a lawyer). He started to read the documents, got down some law books, and took out his pen to amend the text. I brazenly took the pen from his hand and begged him to listen to me first. Then I called Howe, who was also out golfing. He caught a taxi back and asked Ralston what the trouble was; then he said, "Layton, forget you are a lawyer and just be a minister." Ralston eventually signed at Howe's urging and I phoned the radio station. Everything was set in motion. The Army, which was already near the plant, moved in. The picket lines were dispersed and the plant put back in action.

Later in September Henry Borden's old office was given to me. At the end of that month I went on a fishing trip with Borden to Echo Beach Lake, near Buckingham, Quebec, to a lodge that had been owned by his uncle, Sir Robert Borden, prime minister of Canada during the First World War. The real purpose of the trip was for Borden to discuss with me the reorganization of M&S, which was growing so fast it was running into organizational problems. Borden, who had a remarkably original mind, came up with potential solutions over and over again. If any one of them was analysed and rejected, he just came up with another. He told me I had great powers of analysis and that he wanted someone to reject his answers until the right one came up. We made some progress.

In November there were labour problems at the gun plant of Sorel Industries, where the workers had set up the Sorel Control Committee. Howe called me in, and I met the Simard brothers, shipbuilders extraordinaire, with one of whom, Edouard,[23] I became great friends many year later. I also worked on contracts with the Aluminium Company of Canada, which were so difficult that Charles Gavsie had to help me. The climax of the year came at the end of it. On 30 December Hugh Turnbull and I were within fifteen feet of Winston Churchill in the House of Commons when he delivered his famous "some chicken, some neck" speech.[24] He held the audience in the palm of his hand.

On 1 January 1942 I was promoted from solicitor to assistant general counsel. Then on the 26th our first daughter, whom we named Mary Jane after Mollie's mother, was born. On 29 March she died.[25] The bottom seemed to have dropped out of the world.

Henry Borden ordered me to take three weeks' leave; but before two weeks were up, I could not stand the idleness and the thinking. On 1 May Borden invited Mollie and me to come to his farm for a few days; then L.B. Spencer invited us to Welland, where I visited the Atlas Steel plant extension and we stayed with the Spencers in the countryside outside Welland.

On 11 May I went back to work and a few days later appeared before the financial controls subcommittee of the parliamentary select committee on war expenditures. The subcommittees were composed of MPs from all parties, though the majority of members were Liberals and the chair of each subcommittee was also a Liberal. Each of the chairs eventually became a cabinet minister. Lionel Chevrier,[26] the deputy chief government whip, who had been appointed chair of the financial controls subcommittee, said I should make all the arrangements to have the proper persons in M&S prepare briefs for presentation to the subcommittee. I was upset when Chevrier phoned me and told him I did not have time. He said, "Speak to C.D." I did; Howe told me it was very important to see that the briefs were well prepared and also that only proper information be disclosed. For example, we had to keep confidential those contracts entered into on behalf of the British government. So I worked night and day, appearing as counsel for M&S, when tank production, shipbuilding, aircraft production, gun production, etc. came under investigation. I had twenty appearances in twenty days before this subcommittee. Everything went well; the chairs were pleased, the subcommittees were pleased, and even Deputy Minister Sheils was happy.

On 10 August Mollie's brother Robert Laird Borden Covert, a lieutenant in the Army, was killed in an accident at Camp Debert.[27] Bob was Mollie's youngest brother and a fine athlete. His death came as a terrible shock to his aged parents. Eight days after Bob's death, I spoke about enlisting to Howe, who told me he would not permit it. On 11 September, when Howe was in England,[28] I went down to the RCAF recruiting office, only to find I was too old to join an aircrew.[29] So I came back to the Department, saw W.J. Bennett (Howe's executive assistant), and arranged for him to call the secretary of the minister of national defence for air, C.G. (Chubby) Power, to see what he could do about it. They had me medically examined – ran all the tests, physical and mental – without my age ever being asked; it was guessed at twenty-one (I was in my thirty-fifth year).

The Air Force regulations, which provided for an age limit of thirty, were suspended for fifteen minutes while my application was accepted, on condition that I apply only for the grade of Navigator. I agreed, met with Air Marshal L.S. Breadner[30] and Air Vice-Marshal R. Leckie,[31] and was ordered to report 29 September. I worked hard right up to the 26th, saw Howe, told him I had someone to replace me who was a far better lawyer than I – Charles Gavsie – and brought him in.[32] Gavsie replaced me as assistant general counsel, later becoming associate general counsel, and finally general counsel of the Department of Munitions and Supply. The previous day M&S held a farewell dinner, at which Howe addressed the gathering and I was presented with a gold watch and commemorative photograph album.[33]

Frank.

Please keep this as a memento of 1940-42 at ~~Mr. Henry Borden, K.C.~~ M.S. + with best wishes for Christmas + good luck

Henry.

BORN AT MIDNIGHT

Under the green roofs of sprawling temporary buildings in Ottawa lies the Department of Munitions and Supply, the nerve-centre of Canada's industrial war-effort. Here is administered the nation's biggest business, the business of producing ships and tanks, planes and guns, ammunition and explosives for use by the United Nations on battle fronts the world over and the business of purchasing all the requirements of the Dominion's Armed Services, from buckets to boilers, from candles to carpets.

The Department was created by "The Department of Munitions and Supply Act" passed at the special session of Parliament September, 1939, and brought into force at midnight, April 8-9, 1940. The Department carried on and extended the work of its predecessor bodies, the Defence Purchasing Board and the War Supply Board, in the mobilization of the resources of the Dominion for the prosecution of the war.

This vast wartime organization has employed, at one time, as many as 4,700 men and women, has harnessed Canadian Industry to war production and has trebled the industrial output of the Dominion.

Frank Covert's "M&S" commemorative photograph album, September 1942

We have had a hand in history, you and I and the million men and women who work in the war plants of Canada under our direction.

Whether you have been in the Department of Munitions and Supply for four years or four months, you have helped speed the work of war. You have shared in the immensity of our industrial revolution. Today, Canada ranks fourth among the United Nations as a producer of war goods. Tomorrow, her great, new productive capacity will make her a giant in peacetime production.

C. D. Howe

C.D. Howe, minister of Munitions and Supply

G.K. Sheils, deputy minister of Munitions and Supply

S.G. Gumm

1 Lionel Chevrier, 2 W.J. Bennett, 3 T.M. Bryson, 4 Lt. Col. W.A.
Harrison, 5 R.A.C. Henry, 6 E.P. Taylor

1

2

3

4

5

6

1 H.H. Turnbull, 2 R.W. MacLean, 3 R.T. Donald, 4 M.C. Tillotson,
5 Col. F.F. Clarke, 6 J.U. Fletcher

1 K.B. Palmer, 2 C. Gavsie, 3 J. de N. Kennedy; 4 F.M. Covert,
5 G.M. Jarvis, 6 G.R.B. Whitehead

1 W.E.P. De Roche, 2 F.F. Waddell, 3 R.J. Brennan, 4 T.Z. Boles,
5 E.G. Arnold, 6 D.M.S. (Legal Staff)

1

2

3

4

5

6

1 R.P. Bell, 2 J.A.D. McCurdy, 3 F.T. Smye, 4 A.K. Tylee, 5 C.E. Elliott, 6 E.S. Dixon

1 R.C. Berkinshaw, 2 Henry Borden, 3 J.G. Godsoe, 4 J.G. Fogo,
5 W.T. Patterson, 6 R.L. McCrea

1 W.C. MacEachern, 2 J.M Kitchen, 3 T.E. Arnold, 4 J.E. Gibson,
5 Miss V.V. Mallory

Offices of the Department of Munitions and Supply,
375–385 Wellington Street, Ottawa

Wartime civilian transportation

CHAPTER FIVE

On Active Service

On 29 September 1942 I was sworn in to the RCAF as Aircraftsman
A/C 2 No. R188884 and left for Toronto. I sat up all night – there
were no sleepers – and arrived the following day at the Manning
Depot on the Canadian National Exhibition grounds.[1] There were
over 8,000 of us. At lunch the first day we passed by hatches
through which we handed in our plates. As I got to the one opposite
the gravy I said, "No gravy please"; the fellow looked at me and
shot back, "Oh, à la carte, eh?" while dumping two ladles full of
gravy on my plate.[2] I was no longer on Civvy Street. The first night
was unforgettable; over 2,000 in one room (the horse palace), sleeping
and snoring.[3]

In November I was chosen for the Precision Squad, preferable to
cold guard duty or tarmac patrol. The Precision Squad was trained
to drill in unison – three "flights," performing twenty minutes of
rifle drill without a single command – truly a sight to behold. The
physical training, marching, drilling, and studying were intense, but
one wore a white flash in one's cap and was regarded with a little
more respect than the ordinary AC2. On the debit side, we had
been handed over from the kindly corporals to the drill sergeants
and especially the sergeants major. I recall missing the order to
remove the bayonet from my rifle; it was the only one of 120 stick-
ing up in the air. After the drill, I was ordered to do push-ups,
encouraged by the sergeant major, who pressed the butt-end of the
rifle in the small of my back, making it difficult to come up and
speeding my way down. I did not miss that order again. Though
not over-impressed by three months of Air Force life, I was more
physically fit than I had been in years. And I realized by their quick

reaction to orders how well-disciplined a group of 8,000 young men could be.

The year 1943 began with a party for the Precision Squad in a downtown Toronto hotel. Apparently one of the rites of passage was a trip to New York on a war bonds promotion. That year, however, they needed to send us sooner to the Initial Training School (ITS) – so no junket; only the party at the Oxford Hotel, where we were treated to beer, sandwiches, and three strippers who really stripped. We were warned in advance that we were "not allowed to lay a hand on the girls." A dull evening, but a lot of the younger men enjoyed it, or seemed to.

On 8 January we were notified of our posting to No. 5 ITS at Belleville, Ontario; two days later we boarded a train and arrived at night. Thus began the spit and polish, though coupled with being able to wear work clothes, or khaki drill. There were daily lectures on everything from mathematics to Morse code, Air Force law to meteorology, aircraft recognition to gunnery. There was something for everyone – pilots, navigators, gunners, bomb aimers. At the end of the course we were vetted and sent on to Elementary Flying Training School (EFTS), if it was thought one would make a good pilot; Air Observer School (AOS) for training as a navigator, and Bombing and Gunnery School (B&GS) for bomb aimers and gunners.

Of course, every one of the young lads wanted to be a pilot. Among the first hurdles was the Link trainer, a small plane-like vehicle in which one sat while the instructor manipulated the controls and the "pilot" had to react.[4] My first trial in the Link trainer occurred the third day after my arrival. I was hapless; the officer said, "I suppose you'll cry when I tell you you'll never make a pilot." I replied I could only be a navigator. He looked at my papers and then at me quizzically and finally said, "Thank God." I was *not* insulted. There were a few more sessions in the trainer but, I have no idea why, each was as bad as, or worse than, the first.

Perhaps the worst ordeal at ITS was the decompression chamber, in which a group of airmen were seated with two instructors wearing oxygen masks. Gradually the air was withdrawn from the chamber and measured to simulate flying at high altitudes. Without an oxygen mask, one's fingernails turned purple; one's neighbour had purple lips and looked ridiculous; and one was given simple arithmetic, spelling, and writing exercises and had grave difficulty doing them. One by one the men began to pass out and were given oxygen masks, while the rest of us went higher and higher. I did not pass out but, coming down, as the air was reintroduced, my ears pained excruciatingly. When shown the exercises done, one almost doubted one's own handwriting. Nor was it pleasant having to watch the men faint. But the experience taught us what happened at great heights and the necessity of wearing and taking care of one's oxygen mask; not to mention the symptoms of hypoxia– the blue nails, the blue lips, and the distorted countenance. I was to observe them again in training in England.

On my first leave, in Ottawa, I became ill with an infected ear. I went down to the Medical Inspection Board and queued in zero-degree weather, waiting to get in to see a medical officer. Finally, sensing the blood in my ear and unable to stand the pain, I dashed past everybody and into the office, telling the orderly I thought my eardrum was bursting. An officer came out, looked at it, then took me in to where four officers were drinking tea. They improvised a mask, administered ether, and operated on my ear, which was so badly infected that pus squirted over one officer's uniform; he was still grumbling about it when I regained consciousness. Then I was sent to the RCAF Hospital at Uplands, where for three days I suffered pain so excruciating I could not sleep. It was so severe that when Mollie came to see me, I could not even hold her hand. She called Henry Borden, who summoned a civilian doctor to examine me. He raised such a furore that I was transported to Ottawa Civic Hospital that very night and operated on again early the next morning. I remained there for thirty days. For awhile it was difficult, but as I began to regain my strength, I made many friends in the public ward and studied hard. All my friends from M&S visited me and, of course, Mollie came every day. Finally, on 10 March, I was sent by train back to Belleville and thence to Trenton for further medicals. The officer was going to put me into the decompression chamber, until I referred to my thirty days in hospital and two ear operations. When he heard that, the interview lasted thirty seconds and I was sent back to Belleville. I had only just returned when all my class graduated and I had to make new friends all over again.

In April one of the instructors asked whether I would like to be an instructor. He was surprised when I said no so emphatically, but I was always afraid that that would happen. If the Link trainer weeded out the non-pilots, then the exams weeded out the non-navigators. Many of my friends actually cried when they did not make the grade as pilot. In May our flight graduated and we were given a big party at the local country club. Then we were given flying suits, helmets, and goggles; it seemed as though we were finally getting somewhere. I was posted to No. 1 AOS in Malton, where I arrived on 6 June. Two days later I received a letter from a friend of mine, Bill Finseth. Bill, who was eighteen or nineteen years old, had been posted to the EFTS and his letter described his first solo flight, his first intentional stall[5] and loop-the-loop.[6] It had all the enthusiasm that youth can give and was so vivid that one lived the experience while reading it.

I studied extremely hard and was soon flying in Avro-Ansons,[7] as second navigator, then first navigator, then navigator on night flights. I had never felt so incompetent. Seldom did I ever suffer to such an extent from the fear of failure. It spurred me to work harder and harder, but no flight ever satisfied me and some were nightmares. Once I was flustered and nearly panicked. Once I was lost. My logged-flight marks went from bad to fair to good to bad. I almost despaired.[8] Even after two months I had a "ghastly" trip, according to my diary.[9] As late as 20 August my diary states, "I didn't keep a proper log;" I questioned whether I had the right to endanger an aircrew. On 29 August I got a mark of 73 per cent; my diary states, "Don't think I deserve it." Four days later, 76 per cent; "I didn't deserve it." By the middle of September I began to get 80s and on the 24th an 84, but I was "far from satisfied with my work." Of a flight on the 27th: "I was lousy."

Finally on 12 October I had a "magnificent" flight and said to myself, "I think I can navigate." On that date we received our final marks; my average was 76 per cent. We were given our Sergeant's hooks and proudly went downtown to a tailor to have them sewn on to our battlejackets. We walked through the streets of Toronto certain that everybody noticed we were sergeants. I could not have believed that at age thirty-five I would be so proud of sergeant's rank. On 14 October we had our wings parade; one by one our names were called, we marched up to the Wing Commander, saluted, had our navigator's wing pinned on, backed up, saluted, and about-faced – turned and, almost with tears of joy, marched back into our flight with our precious wing. My great friends Henry Borden CMG[10] and Bill Kelley,[11] together with their wives Jean and Isobel, came out to Malton to see the ceremony. It was one of the proudest moments of my life. Afterwards they took me to the Park

Plaza Hotel for roast duck, after which Borden drove me back to
Malton. Such was their many kindnesses to me throughout my
training. Again and again, when I had a twenty-four or forty-eight-
hour pass, I was invited to their homes for weekends. Out at Borden's
farm in King City I shot the stars with my sextant, which I had
smuggled off the base. If it had not been for the Bordens and the
Kelleys, I would have been a very lonely man. When I was posted
to Malton in June, Mollie had returned to Halifax.

On 15 October I was called in to be told I had received a
commission as Pilot Officer and was now J-36828. The instructor
said he had recommended me as instructor; I told him that if I did
not get an immediate posting overseas I would leave the Air Force,
that C.D. Howe would have me released. I got the posting. The next
day I went to Quebec, where Mollie met me and we stayed at the
Chateau Frontenac. Then by train to Halifax, where the whole family
(including Mike, now 7) met us at the station. From the 19th to the
31st I saw everybody I could, including, of course, Mother in
Canning. Then on 1 November we marched through the streets of
Halifax to the ship, the new *Mauretania*.[12] Mollie followed the
parade with Mike, who every time he saw me yelled, "Hi Dad." This
brought roars of laughter from everybody around me and a great
deal of ribbing. None of them was probably old enough to be married. And so a ship with at least 7,000 people on board pulled out
of Halifax Harbour about 10:15 the following morning, 2 November
1943. Eighteen months would pass before I saw Halifax again.

We crossed the Atlantic in a week without incident, except that
6,000 of the 7,000 on board were seasick the first day out. I survived without being sick and actually enjoyed the last five days of
the voyage. On the 9th we docked in Liverpool, boarded a train at
night, and the following morning arrived in Bournemouth – to roses
in bloom and palm trees.[13] Taking up residence in the Royal Bath
Hotel, we were to have fully fifty days until the end of the year to
see England. We motorcycled, bused, and bicycled around the countryside. I fell in love with England almost from the first day. Lady
Ryder's organization[14] encouraged members of the Commonwealth
armed forces to register with it, select the places they would like to
visit and state what they would like to see and do while on leave;
then the organization found families who would accept the service-
men as guests. It was a magnificent idea, magnificently executed.

Early in December 1943 my friend Mus Henson and I went to
Salisbury to see the Cathedral, which my father wrote me about
when he saw it during the First World War. Though we had been
taking lectures, I was beginning to worry again about my knowledge of navigation. The first two weeks of 1944 passed quietly
enough in Bournemouth. Through Lady Ryder's organization I met
an English family, the Sheltons, who invited Henson and me to join
them for bridge. On 14 January we were notified of our posting to
Filey in Yorkshire on, of all things, a commando course. The following day we went by train to London, York, and Scarborough
and thence to Butlin's camp at Filey, where we lived in cold,
unheated rooms for 33 days. The commando course was a disaster
– not meant for aircrew. A broken ankle here, a broken wrist there
and it was soon stopped. Aircrew were too valuable to train for
commando raids. So instead we were sent on paperchases and long
hikes and played some soccer. A colonel in the Army was brought
up to keep us occupied and show us how ack-ack guns[15] worked.
The boys, thinking it a waste of time, were not as attentive as they
should have been, so the colonel lined us up in three flights – we
were a combination of Australians, New Zealanders, and Canadians (even one pure Maori) – and proceeded to lecture us about
being sloppy. He made the great mistake of saying he had always
heard that colonials were all officers but not gentlemen. It was the
word colonials that caused the eruption. Someone called out, "You
lousy penguin."[16] He dashed down demanding to know who said
that – it was repeated at the other end of the flight – then ran up
and down threatening us; everybody began yelling at him and we
broke up. The first thing I knew I found myself with the other
eighty-nine, pulling up fences and then, with a rock in my hand,
about to follow the example of everyone else and heave it through
a window. I suddenly realized this was a small riot and that riot
fever had gripped me. I dropped the rock and grabbed my room-
mate and together we went to our cabin. The next day two Canadian officers came up from London to investigate. When they found
out the cause, that was the end of it, except for a slight lecture.
From then on we had long hikes and paperchases to keep in condition but no more English officers. On one of these hikes I saw a
little store with russet apples in the window. I went in and asked
whether I could see the barrel in which the apples had come. They

were from a company in Kentville, Nova Scotia, six miles from my hometown of Canning!

On 21 February we were posted to Dumfries in Scotland, where there was an Advanced Flying Unit (AFU). The day we arrived we formed part of an honour guard for the funeral of three airmen whose aircraft had crashed in the fog on Snaefell.[17] It was a stern warning that one had better know where he was when flying in this country. Four days after arriving in Dumfries we started flying; I flew on 25, 27, 28 (twice) February and, on 5 March, three times. Then on 7, 8, 9, 11, 14, 15, 17, and 30 March. I enjoyed it, though it was bitterly cold, especially at night. I started to play chess with the Church of England padre. It was an excellent way to occupy the mind before a flight. On the 13th the mail arrived and in it a letter from the attorney general of Nova Scotia advising me that I had been appointed king's counsel;[18] it came as a complete and very welcome surprise.

On 3 April we were posted to No. 22 OTU (Operational Training Unit) at Wellesbourne Mountford; at long last an aircraft other than the Avro Anson. We arrived on the 4th and the following day at least 100 of us were put in a room and told to "crew up," i.e. pick our crew mates. Not knowing anyone, I did not think to take off my gaberdine,[19] so, of course, nobody knew my trade. Finally, when no one approached me, I took off my coat. Immediately a tall, thin, blue-eyed, good-looking pilot came over and asked whether I was crewed up. He told me his name – Wib Pierce – and I told him mine.

"How about being my navigator?"

"Sure."

"Do you know anybody here?"

"No."

"Well, we need two gunners, a wireless operator, and a bomber."

We looked around. I saw a bomb-aimer, Ted Hutton, whom Wib asked whether he was crewed up. Hutton joined us without question and found two gunners whom he knew, Don MacLean and Des McMurchy, who in turn found a wireless operator – all within five minutes.[20]

The skipper, Wilbur Clark (Wib) Pierce, age twenty-two, was from Reston, Manitoba and a true westerner, a gentleman in every sense of the word. He was calm and cool in emergency; his best landings were under stress, as on our first return trip still carrying a full bomb load. Wib's coolness was such that when the aircraft was caught in the cone of searchlights and chased by night-fighters over Bonn and one could hear everyone else breathing through their microphones he said, "Jesus Christ, what a hell of a way to make a living; Navigator, give me a course to the target." The tension was immediately relieved. His decision to go on to the target on three engines and against his better judgement, was probably the correct one.[21] We were offered a chance to train as Pathfinders[22] because of our record. The skipper was enthusiastic – that was the kind of fellow he was. I told him that if he agreed he would lose most of his crew. I was sure I was not good enough to be a Pathfinder and concluded we would end by splitting up. He decided to say no, which was a blessing for us all. Pierce became flight commander[23] and gained the rank of squadron leader.

Ted Hutton, the bomb aimer, also age twenty-two, was a native of St James, Manitoba and the only other person in the crew who could fly an aircraft; he had washed out of pilot training. A quiet, shy man but very capable, in many ways he was the all-rounder. He could fly the aircraft but not land it. He was a good assistant navigator and had an excellent record as bomb aimer. He was of tremendous help to me and kept his feet on the ground (so to speak) at all times.[24] Don MacLean, the mid-upper gunner, age nineteen, was a big, broad-shouldered youngster who could only just fit in the upper turret. Always helpful and concerned, Don was an optimist, always laughing. He loved to eat and enjoyed the pub crawls. He was strong enough to break me in two and treated me as delicately as a piece of precious china. Des McMurchy, the rear gunner, also age 19, was slim, dark-brown-eyed, and slick-looking. He was a crackerjack with the guns and could nip off the drogue[25] inch by inch in gunnery practice. Des was quiet and moody and I never really got to know him as well as the others.

On 15 July 1944, during a seven-hour training flight, McMurchy (who had complained of stomach pains before the flight) had a severe attack in the air. Foolishly, he crawled out of the turret, took off his oxygen mask and passed out. When the skipper, who periodically called each crew member, did not get an answer from Des, he asked Don to check; Don went back and found Des on the floor, unconscious. We dropped height, put Des back on oxygen and radioed to base that we had a sick man on board – suspected acute appendicitis – and to have the ambulance at the end of the runway. This was done and Des was on the operating table at Northallerton hospital within the hour.[26] During Des's recuperation, we had a spare gunner, Sanderson, take his place; when Des got back, he flew with us as well as other crews to catch up so that he could be screened[27] with us.

Apart from the wireless operator, Campbell, whom we lost the day we joined the squadron,[28] that was our crew from the beginning to the end of the tour, except that later at the HCU (Heavy Bomber Conversion Unit), we acquired a new member, flight engineer Frederick J. (Freddie) Haynes, also age twenty-two, the only Englishman in our crew. It was not until ops (operations) were nearly over that I learned from the skipper that Freddie was airsick nearly every flight. Freddie always used to have me calculate on my computer[29] the air miles and mileage per gallon of fuel. Freddie had a fine sense of humour and was a general favourite of the whole crew. Of the wireless operators, at the end of our thirteenth op Smitty[30] finished his tour of duty and from then on we had different wireless operators whom I hardly ever saw (the last was Eric Willey). We never had any trouble finding a rear gunner or a wireless operator; we had a reputation as a Gen Crew (seasoned veterans).[31]

Two days after crewing up we faced the dreaded decompression chamber again. Then, for two weeks, lecture after lecture where, most importantly of all, I was introduced to Gee, a radio aid to navigation invented by Sir Robert Alexander Watson-Watt.[32] I knew immediately that this was the instrument which would guide me through my tour of duty and was determined to master it. I even had the ground crew teach me all they knew about it and they went out of their way to help me. Study at Wellesbourne included wet dinghy drill at Royal Leamington Spa. Then on 3 May we started flying, eight times in eight days. I was not happy with my first flight; the Vickers Wellington, though not a fast aircraft, was over 50 per cent faster than the Avro Anson. The first thing I found out was that I was kept very busy; so pressed that I had to plan my fixes better.

On our third trip we finished early and the skipper asked me what I would like to do. I told him that as a child gone fishing on the little river I used to think how wonderful it would be roaming around up in the clouds. He told me I would be disappointed but that we would go. So up we went roaming through the alleyways hither and yon among the clouds. After a little while there was a noise like a siren, growing louder and louder – a balloon barrage[33] – and we were heading for it. By now darkness had fallen and we could not see it. I gave the skipper a reciprocal course to the one we were flying, and still the noise grew louder. It was frightening, but gradually began to subside. We had escaped the City of Bristol balloon barrage! The skipper remarked, "That is one good lesson. This aircraft is not a toy to play with." He swore us to secrecy and then asked me to give him a course to base. Such was the beauty of Gee. You could plot the aircraft's position with more accuracy than the width of the pencil with which you plotted it.

The second flight later, on 7 May, was a nightmare. Each day before a flight the navigator was handed a beautiful watch with a sweep-second hand. I put the watch on my wrist and was handed a parachute, which I dropped and which opened when I picked it up. This meant I had to pay a fine and, of course, endure the horse laugh from everybody. After we were airborne for a little while, I found my speeds were all fast and winds strong. Finally, when I gave an estimated time of arrival (ETA) to the skipper, he queried me; we checked the times and found I was many minutes slow. What happened was that I had not wound the watch, which had nearly become completely unwound and was slow; thus all my calculations were wrong. The trip was a disaster until I settled down for the last leg. The logs were being marked, so the next day I was asked to explain – I did – no comment. I could see the skipper was worried; the crew said nothing. Finally, on 10 May, we were sent on a cross-country flight – it was my best trip ever.

On 21 May we began night flights – my first as second navigator. The first navigator was having a very difficult time, so I went in to ask whether I could help. Noticing that his fingernails were purple, I advised the skipper who sent the bomb aimer to investigate. Apparently his oxygen mask tube had a leak in it. The skipper reduced height and I carried on until the first navigator was better. But the skipper aborted the flight and returned to base. (I did not relish flying with another crew.) We practised night bombing and fighter affiliation both night and day. A fighter would chase us, come in parallel and then turn to put his guns on us. We would dive towards him and downwards, while at his faster speed he would evade us and then come at us from the other side. Then we would turn towards him and drive upwards while he passed under us. This manoeuvre was known as the corkscrew; it was to serve us well on operations one night.

We flew nine times between 21 and 29 May and eight times between 2 and 10 June. Then a high-ranking officer came to the station, raised hell at the high concentration of flying and sent us on leave. On 26 May, a beautiful, sunny day, we were all out after lunch watching a Spitfire chasing a Miles Magister.[34] Speed-wise the Miles was no match for the Spit but was continually ducking. Gradually, however, the Spit began forcing the Miles down lower and lower until the Miles pilot made a manœuvre which ended in his crashing and being killed. The next day the CO summoned all personnel to the briefing room to say, "These are weapons of war, not toys to be played with," and forbade all "horseplay." It was a sombre gathering.

On 4 June, late at night, we took off on a cross-country flight, crossing a weather system on one leg of the trip. I had a wind and applied it; getting off track, again and again I applied it. What happened was that I was applying an average wind and, when doing so, was flying in an entirely different wind on a different front. I had never experienced this before and did not know the reason. Finally back on track, we got home, but to me the trip was a disastrous failure. Completely discouraged, I watched the skipper smoking a cigarette in bed and fall asleep and burn his lip. He was obviously worried about my competence. The next day I saw the navigation officer who said, "Everyone is entitled to one bad trip." As I was going out the door he added, "Everyone who passed through that front had trouble." The next night, 5 June 1944, we went up again and were called home. The whole sky was filled with aircraft – the long awaited Second Front[35] had come to pass.

On 7 and 8 June we achieved a bullseye,[36] – a great trip even though my Gee was unserviceable for four of the five hours and ten minutes we were airborne. Two nights later, we had another bang-on trip. Every day during the first half of June, I went down to the Navigation Section, where almost every day one of our class washed out. By the 9th there were only two of our class surviving; the other was a young French-Canadian, Emil Lefebre. He and I shook hands and wished each other luck. On the 10th we did fighter affiliation for only an hour, and came back to find that our assessments were up; I scored above average. Soon afterwards news came that we were posted to 1659 HCU at Topcliffe,[37] where we would be trained on four-engine bombers like the Handley-Page Halifax. From 16 to 20 June the whole crew visited York, Thirsk, Ripon, Fountain's Abbey, and Ripon Cathedral's famous old crypt, built in 670. Then to Harrogate and finally Topcliffe, where we saw dozens of Halifaxes coming home from ops and landing at nearby stations.

On 27 June 1944 I received word of my promotion to Flying Officer, still only one stripe but a little thicker than the Pilot Officer's. We flew circuits and practised landings in daytime, daylight bombing and air-to-air firing. Then the same exercises at night. Then two-engine flying, never dreaming we should have to do so operationally one day. Then, finally, on 15 and 16 July we had two bull's-eye flights, which were long and tough but went beautifully. The next day we did a fighter affiliation followed by a night cross-country and then another fighter affiliation. We were asked to turn in our logs and again I received an "above average" rating. I suddenly felt I could navigate. On the 18th Wib and I went on a picnic with Wib's brother, George, who was education officer at RCAF Topcliffe.[38] Just as we sat down to eat after a long bicycle ride into the country, I passed out. The skipper tended me like a baby from then on; secretly we both went into Harrogate, gave assumed names to a doctor and had a physical for which he charged one crown.[39] I was pronounced fit. We told him what happened and he said it could not happen in the air if I were wearing an oxygen mask. After that Wib made me put one on as soon as we took off.

Three days later the whole crew went into Harrogate to a big dance at which we had a marvellous time. We knew the next step was posting to an operational squadron. On 23 July we were posted to Squadron No 433[40] at Skipton-on-Swale,[41] which lay close to Topcliffe. Then on the 24th July we lost Lyle Campbell, our wireless operator, who had tuberculosis. Hutton, the bomb aimer, and I were immediately sent to Leamington to take lessons on a new kind of radar – H2S.[42] It was a magnificent instrument. On the bottom of the plane was a big blister in which turned a scanner that generated a map, like a relief map of the ground above which the plane flew. The map appeared on a little round screen, about seven inches in diameter, on which one could recognize a city; by adjusting knobs one could fix the direction and distance of that city from the aircraft. One thus had an instant fix, whereas with Gee one had to work it out. The problem with H2S, however, was that while it was turned on, the aircraft could be plotted by the enemy, because of the signals the scanner was sending out, whereas with Gee the signals came to the aircraft from towers sending out signals which the aircraft picked up. Hutton became an expert on H2S and I also taught him to operate the Gee box, so that he could almost act as second navigator. When permitted to operate H2S we could get fixes

on both machines; while I was working on calculations, Hutton
could either get me a fix on H2S or hold the Gee signals for me.

From 2 to 4 August we flew our Halifax Mark III and worked
on radar. Then on the 5th we did our first op, to St-Leu-D'Esserent.[43]
We had just arrived at the target and I was working out the final
settings for the bombsight, when something happened and we lost
height.[44] The skipper told us, "Prepare to jump;" I suddenly
thought, here I am, all that training and I'll either be killed on the
first trip or become a POW for the rest of the war. It was my job
to lift off the door of the hatch through which we were to jump
and hand it to Hutton, the bomb-aimer, who would place it in the
nose of the aircraft. I did this and looked at Hutton's eyes – they
were like glass. (He later told me, "So were yours.") The next thing
I knew the skipper was saying, "We are too low to jump." In the
meantime, our new wireless operator, Smitty, had pulled his ear-
phone cord and was trying to shove me out of the hatch. I did not
even have my parachute on. I shoved him back into his seat and
pointed to the earphones. The skipper asked me to give him a course
to a station on the south coast of England. I was so glad we were
not going to jump that I was all thumbs. I estimated a course, then
worked it out on my computer and gave the skipper the course to
the airfield.[45] We jettisoned some gas crossing the Channel and flew
on to England; the latitude and longitude of the airfield was marked
on rice-paper,[46] which we were supposed to eat if crash-landing in
enemy territory. We kept losing height as we approached the coast
of England, flying on two engines and with a full bomb load. When
we approached the station and stated our plight, they told us to go
round again. The skipper said he could not, so in we came – all of
us (except the pilot and bomb-aimer) lying down in the crash position. Wib made the best landing he ever did, – just "greased her
in." It was a relief to walk on land. Within a few hours an aircraft
was sent for our crew and we were flown back to base at Skipton.
We were later advised that our first trip did not count, because we
could not drop the bombs.

The next day we were sent out again on a night operation, an
army co-op[47] south of Caen (time 4:50).[48] We attacked again on
the 9th; the target was the V-1 flying-bomb site at Foret du Croc;
and again on the 12th, another army co-op, at Falaise (time 3:55).[49]
These were all night flights and I actually enjoyed them. After coffee

laced with rum, we went in to debriefing with two other crews. We heard the questions, "What was the flak like?"

"Heavy."

"Accurate?"

"Bang on."

"Close or far below?"

"Close."

Then our turn, the skipper's answers a little different but not much.

Then came a gen crew. The same questions, the answers: "Light flak, not very accurate and far below us." All three crews left together; ours learned a lesson. I thought the flak was heavy and close, as I ducked at every explosion, finally stopped looking, and just kept busy. Flak reminded me of driving a car in a snowstorm when every snowflake funnels right in.

On 15 August we did a day op to Soesterberg in T for Tondelayo,[50] which could not make height or the required speed and earned a few holes from some sharp flak. I was glad to get home; I did not like daytime raids. On the 18th there was a night flight to Connantre[51] (time 6:10), on the 22nd three hours' night practice with radar and bombing, and on the 25th an op on Ferfay.[52] Between 27 August and 3 September the whole crew was on leave in Edinburgh – the first and only time we tried that; our wants and desires varied too much. We resumed flying on the 5th; the 21st, on the way back, we were diverted to an American aerodrome at Ford on the south coast of England. We had to report for debriefing. The Americans, who always flew by day, could not understand why we flew at night and were astonished when we told them we had not been attacked by, or had even seen, an enemy fighter. In the morning, having breakfasted on orange juice, corn flakes, and bacon and eggs, we hated to leave for home.

We flew five times in the first two weeks of October. There were practice flights – formation flying, etc. – but also operations against Emden, Le Havre, gun emplacements southwest of Calais, Domberg, again gun emplacements near Calais, Sterkrade, Cap Gris Nez, and a submarine base at Bergen. There was a night raid on Dortmund,[53] another on Bochum, and then on Duisberg, where we went in at H-4 to help mark the target.[54] We had completed seventeen ops and I had the best record as a navigator in the whole squadron, bombing on time and on target. I was enjoying it, though still fearful of making a mistake.

We were due for leave and already packed to go on 14 October, when our crew was summoned to go on the Duisberg raid, because a crew due back from leave had failed to return. The boys were extremely angry. So when briefing was over, I took two of them (the air gunners) up with me to see the CO[55] and said we were packed to go on leave; "If we don't get back and miss our leave we're going to raise hell." He looked at me – I winked – and he said, "I don't blame you. I'll help you raise it." Thus we were on leave from 15 to 21 October. I went alone to Edinburgh and Aberdeen and from there up to the RCAF station at Dyce, where I took some photographs of the grave of Bill Kelley's brother.[56] It was a beautiful autumn day and there was some colour in the leaves, which, though nothing like their colour in Nova Scotia, reminded me of it. Bill's brother had been aircrew. After all the kindness Bill had shown me, I thought it was the least I could do. The photos, though not in colour, showed the grave clearly and I also took some shots of the surrounding countryside and wrote a note to Bill. I returned from Dyce to Aberdeen but did not stay long. Two things struck me: first, the many buildings of pink marble or granite and, second, the women. They wore rouge, lipstick, and silk stockings and did not look as dowdy as women in the south. Aberdeen was a seaport and the sailors brought the women there things in abundance, which women in the south could not buy. From Aberdeen I boarded a train for Middleham and Leeds and had a wonderful time seeing shows and the sights of Leeds.

I arrived back at the station on the night of 21 October to another series of ops interspersed with crew practice flights, Gee and H2S practice and bombing practice. On the 23rd there was an excellent night op against Essen (time 6:20); on 1 November a night op on Oberhausen (time 6:25), and on 6 November a day raid to Castrop-Rauxell (time 6:00).[57] There followed three weeks of cross-country flights, API (air position indicator) homings, Gee practice, and wind-finding. Then on 30 November a night op to Duisberg (time 6:35) – one fighter attack – and on 6 December a night op to Osnabruck.[58] Our own aircraft, "Y" Yokum, had a flat tire going down the runway, so we had to get another aircraft – all our gear out, by jeep to the other aircraft, queuing for take-off. Then the second aircraft had a "mag" (magneto)[59] drop and we had to get into a third aircraft, QB-J. We were 61 minutes late taking off, 21 minutes later than the "last time of take off." Of course the flight plan was useless (except for the trip home), so I set a course across the Channel towards the Zuider Zee. Having run out of Gee range,[60] I looked for the second Gee box, it was not in the kite.[61] So it was to be dead-reckoning navigation. I asked the skipper to let me turn on the H2S when I thought we were near the Zuider Zee. (We were not supposed to activate H2S until about six minutes from targets because it would enable the enemy to plot our flight path.) The skipper gave permission, but we were on the wrong side of the Zuider Zee. With the bomb-aimer's help, I got two fixes in one minute, turned off H2S, calculated the wind, and set a new course to the target. We bombed within 4.7 minutes of the original time on target.

On 26 December all hell broke loose. We did a day op in foggy weather to the St-Vith area.[62] German troops under Generalfeld-marschall von Rundstedt had broken through American lines and American troops were hemmed in. American pilots, not trained to fly at night or in fog, were of no help, so we were called to do an army co-op and bomb the German troop positions. The danger, of course, lay in the possibility of bombing our American allies. We were briefed by an American colonel who gave us a real pep talk – the briefing was entirely different from our own. Our aircraft having encountered some trouble, we were twenty-four minutes late setting course. I cut corners, however, caught the main bomber stream, and we bombed dead on time. As a precautionary measure a line was drawn on our charts, and until we reached this line and flew sixty seconds – measured by a stopwatch – beyond it, the switch which permitted the release of the bombs was off and the bombs could not be released. Crossing the line was logged (time and fix), the stopwatch started, logged, the switch pulled on and the time again logged. Then we navigated to the latitude and longitude of the target. Before arriving we were supposed to (and did) see traces of bullets of a prescribed colour. Again the stopwatch and sixty seconds beyond the line before the bomb aimer could press the tit.[63] Everything went beautifully and we headed back to base, only to find it fogged in; we had to fly away up to Leuchars,[64] where there was a seaplane base operated by the RAF. It was now night-time, the runway had a cliff at one end and a mountain at the other, and there was very low cloud. I wanted a practice run with Gee to find out how long it took to come down and break cloud. Haynes, the flight engineer, said we were running low on gas – only a cupful. We had the practice run and then out to sea and back; we broke cloud, just at cliff edge, and came in. The skipper's landing was not his best and we bounced several times. My log read: "landed 18.51 – airborne 18.51.02 – landed 18.51.04 – airborne 18.51.05 – landed 18.51.07." Later, when the skipper saw the log, he was not amused. By the time we reached the end of the runway, Haynes' cupful of gas had run out and two of the four engines sputtered and died. The next day we flew from Leuchars to Skipton-on-Swale in 1:15; I used the trip for Gee practice and homing.

Three days later, on 30 December, we did a night op to Cologne. My diary says, "Set course on time for a change, good trip, bombed on time." It was a seven-hour flight and I was tired. Since it was our twenty-eighth op, we would ordinarily have had only two more to go. At first, based on the fact that five per cent of the aircrews were lost on each trip, twenty ops constituted a tour. As the ratio improved, the number of ops per tour was increased; twenty-eight when we started, it was afterwards raised to 30. The problem with our crew was that the skipper became squadron flight commander and, as a result, bent over backwards to give the short trips, etc. to other crews, so that he could not be criticized.[65] This meant that crews which had come to the station long after us, finished their tours before us and were screened. Then rumours started about crews who had "gone for the Burton"[66] on the first extended tour and our crew became a bit jittery. The skipper, I think, welcomed the extra flights on the simple theory that that was what we had come over to do. I do not think we shall ever know how close we were to mutiny. At the request of the crew I drafted letters to No. 6 Group Headquarters at Allerton Park but never mailed them; we were always waiting for a reply, which, of course, never came. During the year letters from home made life much easier. The war seemed to drag on. And then it was announced a tour would be thirty-two ops. It seemed to me the brass thought the war would be over soon and so were not bringing on replacements as fast; or, possibly, they wanted experienced crews for what were becoming longer ops.

We did not fly again until 7 January 1945 and then it was just practice bombing, timed runs, and gunnery. Wib was making sure his crew would not get rusty. The crew did not enjoy practice; I, being much older, welcomed it because it would be deadly to slip. On 10 January there was a heavy snowfall and we were all out with snow shovels. Then finally some ops: 13 January (No. 29), a night op on Saarbrucken; 14 January (No. 30), to Grevenbroich; 16 January (No. 31), to Oslo Fjord (laying mines). Three trips in four days and only one more to go. No. 29 to Saarbrucken (time 7:20), an all-Canadian raid, was one of our best. Two days later we saw photographs of what we had done; I do not think there was a roof left on any building in the whole city. The next night we started out to Grevenbroich but, over the base, developed a fire in one engine. The fire was extinguished but we were left with only three engines. The skipper said we would go out and jettison our bombs in the North Sea. I asked him whether we could not just follow the route for awhile, for practice. Then I took a shortcut and found we were on track and on time. Wib kept asking where we were and finally I suggested we could easily make the target. He said he was not going to fly over the target area on three engines and at a lower height than planned. I pressed him and kept reporting progress. The skipper polled the crew, first stating he would make the final decision. The crew, hungry to complete the op, voted unanimously to go on if I said we could make it on time. The skipper kept us in suspense, asked for a final ETA, and then said okay. At the last run in, he stuck the nose down and we bombed 1.5 minutes ahead of time. This was to ensure that no aircraft was bombing above us and likely to hit our kite. The trip lasted 6:30 hours. The next day Wib was awarded an immediate Distinguished Flying Cross (DFC). I was to learn later that he recommended me. The very day I got back to Canada, I received notice that I had been awarded the DFC as well.

Two days after the Grevenbroich raid we went gardening – laying mines in Oslo Fjord. The mine floated down by parachute which dissolved in the sea water. Nobody liked gardening. To begin with, there were only six aircraft on the trip. It was low-level flying and the rate of return was not good. We took off on 16 January at 1825 in our own aircraft, "Y" Yokum. Though the met (meteorological) staff had predicted winds of 20 to 25 mph, we had not been out long when we were getting winds of up to 80 mph, with tailwinds to boot. So we were getting there too fast. This meant "wasting time," which was done by flying 60 degrees off track for, say, three minutes, then switching back towards track by altering course 120 degrees for

three minutes, then 60 degrees again on track. The flight path formed
two sides of an equilateral triangle, the base of which equalled a
three-minute side on track. This meant one had flown six minutes to
do three minutes on track and had then "wasted" three minutes. As
a result, one could do legs of six minutes but had to watch in order
not to get too close to enemy territory. Going north, then south, then
north, then south kept one very busy and was very tiring. Of course
I not only had to keep taking fixes to see that we got back on track
but also to keep recalculating the estimated time of arrival. Finally
we were able to activate H2S and see the rocky coast and try defi-
nitely to position the entrance to the Fjord; then to work out the
wind and the course which would take us up the Fjord against an
80 mph crosswind, which would blow us right on past the Fjord.
We missed the first run but had a perfect second run, though met by
severe anti-aircraft fire; it was apparently not close because my diary
says, "No excitement but met badly out." However, the trip was not
over. We now had to fly back against the 80 mph wind; the return
trip seemed endless, with the flight engineer warning us about fuel
levels. We flew down low and close to sea level, where the wind had
less velocity, and made it back to base at 0150 (time: 7:25). Thence
to intelligence (debriefing) for our report of the trip, helped by coffee
laced with rum. From there to the mess hall for bacon and eggs
– the only time we feasted on this delicacy was after an operation –
and was it good!

Two days later, we received a fine letter from the American colonel
telling us how successful the 26 December army co-op at St-Vith
had been; at the same time the Navy advised us that the minelaying
in Oslo Fjord had been a complete success. On the 17th the skipper
took us up for an air test, wind finding, gun practice, and homing
with Gee. We used to blindfold the skipper, then I would set the
coordinates of the base on Gee and bring him in right over it. I
always blessed Watson-Watt for his invention and never failed to
give the Gee box a pat as I left the aircraft. On that occasion the
skipper let us off with a mere 65-minute practice.

On 18 January 1945 Fred Smye from M&S arrived in his chauffeur-
driven automobile, got me time off, and we drove to the RCAF
station at Middleton St. George, in the hope of seeing our mutual
friend Jack Miller, but he was on leave. While there the commanding
officer showed us round the station and tried to demonstrate Gee,
but he had the signals reversed and it would not work. I pointed

that out, so Fred asked him to let me operate it; I got it right and, of course, both Fred and I were very pleased. Fred drove me back to Skipton-on-Swale and then had to leave but not without filling me in on all the dope at M&S.[67] From 27 January to 3 February I had another wonderful leave – Middleham, Harrogate, Leeds, Manchester, and Knaresborough – bicycling through as much of the English countryside as possible and seeing every play I could.

And so back to base, where the news was startling. First, the squadron was going to convert to Lancasters,[68] which meant not only a lot of practice flying but also losing our old friend Y- Yokum.[69] Secondly, the tour had been increased to thirty-six ops, which meant we had five more to go, instead of just one. The crew (except the skipper) were angry as hornets. On 6 February the pilot of an aircraft on our station attempting to land saw that he was overshooting and tried to lift off, aborted, and crashed in the little village, taking a piece off the roof of a house where a children's birthday party was in progress. The children were unhurt; the crew were mostly killed. I served as pallbearer at their funeral. On the 9th and 10th we had five practice flights in Lancaster "Y"; during the last flight most of the instruments, including the API and the H2S, were u/s (unserviceable). So most of the three hours were spent operating Gee. None of this induced in me any great confidence in the Lancaster, which was hard to get into, hot, and uncomfortable. It was a pilot's plane, not built for the navigator like the Halifax. However, it could carry a ten-ton bomb.

We all thought that that was enough training, but it was not to be. On the 16th I secretly went into Harrogate for a medical (fee one crown) from Dr Sharp, who gave me the all-clear. On the 22nd a fellow navigator, Rusty Manning (also from Reston, Manitoba), got word that his father had died; I helped him draw up an application for compassionate leave.[70] On the 23rd and 26th we had two more training flights, one 6:00 hrs the other 3:10; then finally, on the 27th, op no. 32, in Lancaster "T"– a daylight raid on Mainz (time 7:20). It was a gaggle (formation), our first follow-the-leader; all I had to do was navigate to the first concentration point and then the skipper joined the stream. I made fixes, plotted the courses, and kept a log just as if it were a regular flight. The Gee box was unserviceable; fortunately, it was a gaggle and daylight. Thus the month of February passed with only one op, which was very bad for crew morale.

In March there were five missions. The first, on the 2nd, in Lancaster QB-B, op no. 33, was a daylight raid on Cologne (time 5:40). We set course seventeen minutes late and bombed 2.3 minutes late; otherwise, the trip was uneventful. The second, on the 7th, in Lancaster S, op no. 34 to Dessau, was our longest trip thus far.[71] At one point we had a wind velocity of 120 mph which, with our air speed of 240, gave us a ground speed of 360 mph – 6 miles per minute. We bragged for a week of the speed. On the way home we were diverted to the USAAF aerodrome at Ford, near Plymouth, arriving at 1:18 am; the flight had taken 8:30 hrs. Again the intelligence officers, unused to night flying and night bombing, marvelled at our report that, though there was flak, there were no fighters. On the 8th we spent the morning at the American base, where we breakfasted on oranges, corn flakes, and bacon and eggs, and bought cigarettes at ten cents a pack. Then we flew home in 1:25 while I practised Gee and "bombing."

On 11 March, in Lancaster T, we did op no. 35 to Essen (time 6:25), taking along the CO of the station, Group Captain H.H.C. Rutledge[72] – always considered bad luck. Unknown to me, the skipper handed over the controls; almost every time I took a fix we were a bit off track, so I began watching the compass and checking with the skipper. Finally I said, "Skipper, you've never done this before, but you keep getting away from the course I gave you." The skipper immediately got back on track but then, a few minutes later, I complained rather testily "You're off again." G/C Rutledge then said, "Navigator, it's not your skipper, it's me and I'm handing it back." I felt embarrassed but from then on every course was bang on; we had such a good trip that the G/C congratulated the crew. I told him we were due to be screened long ago and that I hoped the thirty-six ops would not be increased. The skipper was terribly embarrassed, but the crew were very pleased when the G/C said he would look into it.

The skipper put us down for op no. 36 on 15 March, a night flight to Hagen in Lancaster T. Though Hagen was a hot little target and we had a few flak hits, it was on the way home that the excitement occurred. We were near Charleroi,[73] when, all of a sudden, ahead of us we could see aircraft being shot at and firing off rockets – the colours of the day – to identify themselves as friendly. We were over territory that the allies had captured and were at a loss to understand why there would be enemy fire. The skipper asked

me to check my fixes and also wanted Hutton to double-check on
H2S. We did; we were on track and where we were supposed to
be. The skipper asked me to head 90° north of track. I gave him
the course, we diverged from the route and arrived back at base at
1218, after 7.5 hours of flying. The debriefing reminded me of the
noise of a cocktail party at its height; one could not hear oneself
talk. Other aircraft in our squadron had been shot at. Apparently
allied troops on the ground at Charleroi had not been advised of
the raid or of the colours of the day and those who showed the
colours only exposed themselves the more readily to anti-aircraft
fire. We later heard that our troops on the ground had shot down
six[74] of our own aircraft. That was the last trip; our first and last
flights were the worst – or at least the closest calls.

On leave from 16 to 24 March, I went to Leeds and Manchester,
then Chester and then over to Llandudno (in Wales), where I
climbed to the top of Great Orme's Head. Then, via Manchester,
back to base. Having just finished op no. 36, and believing it would
be the last, made the leave extra special for me. There was no
tension, no urgency. Whereas on previous occasions I had tried to
pack in as much as possible, because there was always the chance
the leave would be the last, now I felt completely relaxed; I often
slept in, stayed up late, browsed around, walked, saw plays, went
into pubs, enjoyed Chester with its Rows[75] (covered sidewalks, two
storeys), the wall around it, and the canal with the small boats
poled along it, and the wildness of Wales. I wished it would go on
forever. Though notified that we must always keep in touch with
base and be back for sure on the due date, I did not bother to do
so; I was damned if I would let this leave be spoiled. But I was
home to base immediately I was supposed to be, on the 24th. The
next day we were advised our crew had been screened; no more
ops for six months. It was a great relief – I had done what I set out
to do, was desperately tired, and had reached the stage where I
feared that extra trips would be our downfall. They were extremely
bad for morale. The skipper, however, would have been delighted
to fly on and on and on.

On the 29th the aircrew and the ground crew invited me over to
the sergeants' mess, where they had saved for me a full glass stein
of Scotch. We sat in front of a big grate fire and sipped away,
reminiscing, telling jokes, and offering toast after toast. When my
liquor was all gone, they led me in to the dance next door. I made

them promise, before I started to drink, that they would get me and also my bicycle Johanna back to my hut. I remember as if it were yesterday the crowded dance floor, the blaring music, the blue, yellow, green, and white streamers lining the walls. I saw a pretty little WAAF[76] across the hall and said to the boys, "That's for Covert." I started across the floor but never made it, waking up next morning in my own bunk in time for breakfast. Two days later, the crew was sent to No. 6 Group Headquarters at Allerton Hall and told we would probably be sent home.

The month of April was quiet on the base – no duties – so I took off every moment I could. On the 8th a day at Middleham, then back to base the next day to take a summary of evidence.[77] On the 11th the skipper was posted to Warrington.[78] From the 14th to the 17th I had three days' leave. On the 18th, I returned to base to resume taking evidence, then on the 27th was given indefinite leave. Returning to base on 6 May I too was posted to Warrington, where Ted Hutton (bomb-aimer) and Don MacLean (gunner) already were. On the 8th came the official German surrender; the war in Europe was over. Two days later I travelled to Padgate and on the 13th to Gourock, in Scotland, where we boarded the *Ile de France* for New York. All the way home I played bridge, chess, and checkers; on the 22d we arrived in New York, to be greeted by tugs and fine seagoing vessels and all kinds of whistles and horns. That afternoon we boarded a train for Canada and at 5:00 am the following day arrived at Lachine. That was the end of my war. Looking back on it thirty-six years later and double the age I was then, I often wonder whether, if I had had any idea what I would have to go through, I would have had the guts to do it. I am sure I would not. Yet I am glad I did and would not want to have missed a minute of it.

CHAPTER SIX

The Forties

On 3 June 1945 we arrived in Halifax to be met by all the family. The next day it was over to the firm to see everyone in the office, except Roland Ritchie,[1] who had left the Stewart firm and joined the Daley firm.[2] I spent the 5th to the 7th visiting people; the 8th I went to Canning to see Mother. The federal election campaign was in progress, so I spoke on the 9th at Kentville with J.L. Ilsley, the local MP; two days later, the Liberals under Mackenzie King won another big victory. The 14th to the 19th I spent studying the statute law enacted over the previous five years, especially income tax. I had written Bill Kelley in Toronto, who sent me a list of twenty-seven books on income tax and told me that taxation and industrial relations were the two big new fields.

On 20 June H.P. MacKeen took me with him to assist the defence in a manslaughter trial in Yarmouth.[3] On the 22nd Stewart gave me the Zwicker and Company[4] reorganization. The following day I went with MacKeen to visit the scene of the crime (the RCAF officers' mess) and remained in Yarmouth for three days, while the case was adjourned for a week. On the 28th and 29th I was summoned back to Halifax to No. 1 RC (Release Centre), where I underwent blood tests and so on and my tiredness was diagnosed as operational fatigue.[5] Then with MacKeen back to Yarmouth, from where, on 5 July, while the judge[6] was giving his charge to the jury, I again had to leave for Halifax. The following morning I received a telegram on the train that the jury had brought in a verdict of not guilty.[7] Later the same day I went again to No. 1 RC for a medical, then the following day to the Navy Hospital for further tests; the doctors were worried enough by my blood tests that they brought me back again on the 10th for further tests. On 11 July 1945 I was discharged from the RCAF, after 1,017 days.

It was not until the middle of July 1945 that I really got down to business. On the 12th I addressed the Commercial Club of Halifax. On the 17th I got my own old office back and all seemed right with the world. Tired out as I was by about 4:00, the next day I went home a little after 5:00, lay down on the chesterfield and fell asleep – only to be awakened around 6:30 p.m. by a terrific explosion which shook the house. I heard dishes crash in the kitchen. Mollie and I ran outdoors and saw a big cloud rising northwards from the general direction of Bedford Basin, which grew higher and higher in the shape of a mushroom.[8] I could not imagine what it was. We turned on the radio and learned there was a fire in the Naval Magazine on the shores of Bedford Basin; everybody was warned to open all windows and leave them open. Perce Smith, who lived nearby, came over in his car and we started to drive around the city to see the damage. We got a few blocks along the way, before another explosion occurred and we saw store windows bend and crash. Perce drove us home, saying he was going to take his family to the country before panic set in. I decided to stay home. Small explosions occurred regularly until finally, at 1:40 am, the biggest; it drove our bed hard up against the wall. Fortunately no one was hurt or killed, but the damage was tremendous. The severe damage caused on VE day,[9] when there had been riots and looting, had just been repaired and now the storefront windows were smashed again.

On 20 July there was another company to incorporate. The following day Roy Jodrey, who had literally saved five years' work for me, summoned me to Hantsport and brought me up to date on all that had happened. I was there until the 28th, then back to work for Pitfields on a trust deed for Atlantic Fisheries.[10] From 7 to 10 August I was in Montreal with Perce Smith to work on the trust deed. On the 15th, I went with Frank Nightingale CA to New Germany, where we completed the reorganization of Zwicker and Company, which was being transferred from one generation to the next. The following day Atlantic Fisheries changed its name to National Sea Products. Between Jodrey and Smith, I was really getting back into the practice of law. On the 28th Stewart said that at the first of the year the firm name would be changed to include mine.[11]

On 2 September, having read twenty-three books on income tax, I decided to write a textbook of my own. I had drafted eight chapters, when a new Income Tax Act was passed.[12] So I abandoned the work – too lazy to start over again and, besides, I was getting busier. On the 9th I conceived and drafted a pooling agreement for Ralph Bell,[13] which enabled him to sell shares to his children but still retain control of National Sea.[14] He was very pleased and let me buy 2,000 shares at 36 cents a share; these grew greatly in value over the years. On the 23d I began to read all the Canadian cases reported during the five years I was away. A provincial election campaign was in progress, so I gave political speeches in Kentville and Canning and addressed factory workers on the final Victory Loan drive; on 23 October the Liberals scored a smashing victory – twenty-eight seats to two for the CCF. That same month I reorganized the Goodman companies, incorporated three new companies, and began work on the capital reorganization of Minas Basin Pulp & Power, as well as some refinancing for Manning's United Service Corporation. Jodrey got George Chase[15] to invite me to his home in Port Williams, so I began to work for him too – a relationship that lasted until he died.

The Minas Basin bond refinancing took me to Ottawa, where I was for three days and renewed a lot of acquaintances – Charles Gavsie, G.K. Sheils, F.H. Brown,[16] Martin, Boles, Jarvis and Fred Smye, Chevrier and Ilsley, Bill Bennett, and Senator Joe Bench[17] and, finally, C.D. Howe. It was a grand three days, except for a row with C.F. Elliott, deputy minister of national revenue (taxation). I had arranged an appointment over a week earlier, arrived on time, and was kept waiting an hour. Then Elliott called me in, started to put on his coat, hat, and scarf, and said he could give me three minutes. I said I could not even state the facts in three minutes; so he left. I went to see Gavsie, Gavsie talked to Howe, and Howe called Elliott's minister,[18] after I had talked to him. Elliott saw me the following morning, with very bad grace, and was very hostile. It took subsequent telephone calls to the minister, together with letters and telegrams, before Elliott finally came to his senses. Then we went ahead. On 28 December I appeared in chambers and completed the reduction of capital for Minas Basin Pulp and Power Company. Two weeks earlier, Mersey Paper had come back to my fold and I began working for them again. Most of my old clients were back to me, all except Nova Scotia Light and Power.[19] I felt as though the war years had not really hurt me but instead given me quite an education. I looked forward to the future with a great deal of confidence.

Unlike 1945, 1946 was to be a full year of law practice. The combination of Jodrey, Manning and Pitfields (through Perce Smith) really got me back into the swing and it was not long before my filing cabinets were full again. The aftermath of the war also played a part. In 1940 the Excess Profits Tax Act was passed in order to determine a fair base on which to assess corporate profits. The government set up a Board of Referees before which a company could appear by counsel and show why the company's profit base should be adjusted. I handled a lot of these cases for the Manning group of companies and for a subsidiary of Mersey – the Markland Shipping Company – among others. I had a brilliant young accountant, Harold J. Egan, as my chief witness. He was so brilliant that Stewart tried to get him to study law. We had great success on every case.

Another consequence of the war was the renegotiation of war contracts. The Department of Reconstruction and Supply Act (December 1945) provided that war contracts could be renegotiated, if it were found that profits had been excessive. One can imagine the consternation of businessmen when suddenly, long after they had completed their contracts, paid their income tax, and pocketed their profits, they received notices of renegotiation. I handled many such cases, which meant many trips to Ottawa, preparation of briefs, and long negotiations. I had great success with them and, as a result, attracted clients the firm had never had before.

Yet another consequence was the spirit of optimism fostered by C.D. Howe, minister of reconstruction and supply, as well as of trade and commerce. Business began to expand; this resulted in bond issues and financing, refinancing new companies, and reorganizing old ones – I had my share of them. There were trust deeds and supplemental trust deeds for Minas Basin Pulp & Power and Canadian Keyes Fibre (Jodrey) and trust deeds and supplemental trust deeds for Great Eastern Corporation (Manning). There were also bond issue opinions for Pitfields on Maritime Telegraph & Telephone and William Stairs Son and Morrow. Ralph Bell's sale of Pickford & Black to the employees meant a new company incorporation, a trust deed, etc. Mersey Paper completed the purchase of over 80,000 acres of timberland. National Sea Products had a refinancing and I worked on a reorganization of Eastern Securities and on the reorganization of International Patent Company, which included a scheme of arrangement.[20] I incorporated many new companies, which afterwards became clients. I also tried two abortive reorganizations, one for Stanfields Limited and one for Ashburn Golf Club. In both cases, when the first attempt failed, we tried another tack: for Stanfields it was a public stock issue, while for Ashburn a less satisfactory reorganization.

I studied income tax, company, and employment law, and commenced the practice of employment law in earnest.[21] There were at this time few, if any, lawyers in Nova Scotia who had made a study of industrial relations law, and the unions were beginning to organize as many workers as possible.[22] I read a great deal, started working on papers, and gave a few public speeches. I early adopted the viewpoint that trade unions, if properly run, properly understood, and properly treated, were beneficial because, during the term of the contract, there was industrial peace, with machinery provided for the final settlement of grievances. The collective agreement also ensured that all employees were treated fairly and equally, without discrimination. From the employer's point of view the main thing was to work hard preparing for the negotiations and not give way on principle for the sake of a settlement. Then once the contract was signed, it had to be fairly administered. I adopted the view that management should study the wage rates, working conditions, and fringe benefits, not only of its competitors, but also of businesses in the surrounding area. It should know what were the vacation schemes, holidays with pay, shift differentials, overtime rates – indeed all fringe benefits – what was the bottom, the top, and the average. So the real work had to be done before negotiations began. Once management had gathered all the data, I met with them, asked what they proposed and why, and eventually worked out with them what was the best they could, and would do.

Initially all my clients wanted to start low and work up. I argued very strongly against this on the grounds that no one would leave the bargaining table satisfied that they had done the best they could. So I persuaded my clients to let me first outline what the competition was doing and what was being done in the surrounding area; then what we were proposing to do on each and every one of our demands; and finally state that, unless the union could show we had made a mistake or were being unfair, the offer would be the highest we would go. Most of my clients were dubious at first and I met with a lot of opposition from union negotiators, who said that if we would not go up, we were not bargaining. It took awhile, but eventually every union negotiator knew that my first offer was my final one, unless he could show I was wrong. We often argued into the small hours of the morning, but over the years the changes made were almost nil. Up to the end of 1978 I successfully negotiated 440 contracts and had only five strikes; and each of those was settled at the original offer except one, where we added one cent per hour to the wage. The reason for my success was homework, resulting in a fair and reasonable offer. I was even called in to settle strikes where I had not negotiated the contract and succeeded on every occasion. I refused to negotiate for any new client unless he first agreed to tell me his top offer, and then undertook that he would *not* go above it on the threat of a strike or an actual strike. This was very important, because the employee must know that the employer is not holding back for a better bargain, but really feels that the offer is fair and just.

When Minas Basin Pulp & Power was being unionized,[23] Roy Jodrey called me and told me he was not going to let any union tell him how to run his business, and he wanted me to fight the certification. I told him that if they had a majority, the Labour Relations Board would certify the union, because it was the law of the land;[24] and, besides, unions were not bad. He hung up on me. I wrote him a letter telling him that he did not have to sign everything the union put before him and we could refuse to sign anything we did not think was fair. One day he telephoned to say the union was going before the Board, that I was to appear and consent, and then invite the labour representatives up to my office for a drink of scotch.[25] This was early in December 1946; on the 30th (after long sessions with the company, a couple of weeks earlier) I went to Hantsport and negotiated with the union a contract which they accepted. It was not many years later, when Jodrey had been operating under three contracts, that I was sitting with him at lunch at the Halifax Club with a group of Halifax businessmen who were complaining about unions and strikes. All of a sudden, out of the blue, Jodrey said, "I wouldn't do without a union in my plant." You could have cut the silence with a knife. Jodrey calmly continued, "It gives you industrial peace, you can plan ahead, and you treat everyone fairly." The shocked look on the men's faces was really worth seeing. Roy Jodrey learned extremely fast what some businessmen never learned in a lifetime.

I enjoyed negotiating collective agreements. Union negotiators were the salt of the earth and, of course, they were negotiating for their economic livelihood. And I always felt that an employer owed a duty to his employees; first, that he would run the plant so that it would continue to provide them with a fair living for the rest of their working lives, so that they could get married, raise a family, build a house, and live in the community; secondly, that the employer could pay fair wages and fringe benefits based on competitive rates and local conditions; thirdly, that in return he could expect good work from the employee. This was the theory I instilled in all my clients. When a contract was negotiated, I always felt that the economic livelihood of the number of employees multiplied by four had been determined for the year, or two or three years, depending on the term of the contract. It turned out to be the most rewarding part of my practice for years.

On 5 February 1946 I published in the Halifax *Chronicle* a letter to the editor entitled, "An Irresponsible Press."[26] Stewart saw it, laughed, and said, "Whenever you want to write for the press, put it away for a week and see if you still want to send it and, if it's controversial, try another week." It was sound advice. By the middle of March I suddenly woke up to the fact that Stewart was not giving me any work to do for him and that I had not even seen him for about three weeks.[27] This continued on and on and I wondered what was happening; then I saw some nice work going elsewhere[28] and I really was upset. Finally[29] I asked his secretary for an appointment on 15 November.[30] She told me he would see me on the 19th; he did not.[31] I waited over a month; then on 23 December Bill Kelley called from Toronto, and talked to me for over two hours, coaxing me to come join his firm[32] and offering what I could not hope to achieve in Halifax. I said no – I could not leave the firm. On the 29th I walked down to Stewart's house and was there for three hours. I outlined how long it had been – how I missed my hours with him and reminded him that in 1935 he told Mother I had given him a five-year vacation. Then I asked whether I had done something wrong or had he been told something wrong.[33] Tears came to his eyes and he said, "Don't ask me to tell you. Just let me say I'm sorry and I might have known." He extended his hand and we shook hands. From that moment we never looked back. There were times when curiosity made me try to guess, but I always said to myself to forget it; I never learned why. But it never mattered. I just missed him for nine months and everything else made up for it. On that occasion he told me that I had a great future, that one

blic at large is willing to
irresponsibility, inaccuracy
ty on the part of any sec-
this community, so long
ivic administration be im-
r of Halifax and the in-
ade to suffer.
f such a situation are ob-
he remedy. That remedy
anifest when more people
express themselves in the
ert has chosen to adopt.

ace Like Home!

luring Health Week give
to this old saying. During
, in a consistent series, one
fatal accidents in Canada
ne, and victims of nearly
fatal accidents have been
ears of age.
e falls, which caused 1,158
second place are fires, ac-
aths. Burns and suffoca-
and fourth places respec-

are careless people, or we
y proportion of plain bad

n The
Court Of Justice

Canadians must feel in the
ited Nations Assembly of
International Court of Jus-
with an especial sense of
city and province. For to
listinguished international
ed best as Dean of Dal-
while to members of the
he province and beyond, he
an who, through the most
ve years in the history of
, bore the heavy responsi-
associated with the role of
he Department of External

of such outstanding achieve-
d of jurisprudence should
ly considered for the high
the International Court of
rising. That such a Cana-
een found in the person of
self a graduate of Dalhousie
lty member, is in keeping
both of the province and of

Court of Justice may pro-
as the most august judicial
today. Before it will be
n matters affecting the very
The rights and responsibili-
be matters for adjudication
onfidence in the wisdom of
ons will be immeasurably
y in this country but among
generally in the knowledge
high qualities of character
s those possessed by John
its destinies.

The Mayor

H. W. Porter to the office of
e is a landmark of no mean
role of women in public af-
iay. That women should be
of equality with men in the
dministration and politics is
frequently, however, a quite
toward women taking their
has been sufficient to deter

The PEOPLE SPEAK

(The Halifax Chronicle will print
communications from readers as far as
space will permit. They must be free
of libel and short. The editor reserves
the right to shorten or summarize if
necessary. Letters must bear the name
of the writer for publication.)

AN IRRESPONSIBLE PRESS

The Editor, The Halifax Chronicle;

Sir:-On Saturday last you published a brilliant essay by Stuart J.
Shaw entitled "Freedom of The
Press." If it is examined carefully
and really analyzed it will teach
many of us a great lesson. Mr.
Shaw says:

1. An unfettered press is one of
   the essential bulwarks of a
   democratic world, and
2. The press is the principal
   agency by which the ordinary
   man receives the information
   he needs to judge the actions
   of his rulers and to make up
   his mind on public issues.

All will agree readily with the
two foregoing statements. Mr. Shaw
has pointed to the reason for this.
Nova Scotians are particularly interested in a free press because in
many respects one of the greatest
battles in newspaper history was
fought right in this city for that
same freedom by Joseph Howe.
Why do we have this freedom of
the press?

Why have legislators and judges
in our democracies legislated and
ruled time and again in favor of
that freedom?

Because, as Shaw says, it is one
of the bulwarks of democracy. No
other single factor can make democracy disappear as quickly as
the failure of a free press. Let
us never forget this one lesson!

Today in our country the press
is free—legal decisions guard it.
The press representatives are permitted to go everywhere, to report
proceedings and to comment fairly
thereon, and regardless of the truth
of the statements so reported are
free from fear of libel or damage
actions so long as their reports are
accurate, and made contemporane-
ously, and the comment is for and
in the public interest.

Why should this be? Why should
this freedom of the press be allowed wholly or partially to pre-
vail over the right of a citizen's
reputation?

The answer has been repeated
again and again in decisions of
every court of this land!

Because it is in the public interest!

That is lesson number one from
Mr. Shaw.

Mr. Shaw gives us another one,
however, that sometimes newspapers forget. It is just as important, however.

Whenever you get a privilege you
invariably owe a duty or obligation!
Take the example of the traffic
lights on the cross-roads of a busy
city. You get a green light — you
have the privilege of "going
through." You get this because if
it is a red light you must stop. The
system just would not work unless
you accept the duty with the privilege. Similarly you have property
rights respected by others because
you respect similar rights of those
others.

Mr. Shaw recognizes this because
he points out the duties of the
press:

1. It must be thorough, accurate
   and unbiased in its reporting.
2. It must be sincere and thoughtful in its editorials.
3. It must be cautious until it
   knows all the facts.
4. It must be bold when it is
   sure of the facts.
5. It must be truly free-resistant
   to all outside pressure.

"Such a press is worthy of the
privileges traditionally granted to
it!" says Mr. Shaw.

There is the point!

Conversely—if the press fails in

its duty it must follow that it loses
its privileges!

Surely if the press is the medium
through which the "little man" gets
his facts—he must be given accurate unbiased facts!

Surely the editorials must be sincere and thoughtful!

If not, the "little man" is deceived!

If not, the "little man" forms
wrong conclusions!

If not, the "little man" wrongfully blames his rulers!

Mr. Shaw says "the press claims
no right which should not belong
to any citizen." That may be true,
and is true if the press lives up to
Mr. Shaw's standards! But how
many citizens can reach the ear of
100,000 people or more? How many
citizens can wrongfully criticize
men in public office and then if
they find they are wrong save face
by publishing the other side of the
picture in an obscure place which
the readers of the first article may
never see? The damage is irre-
vocably done!

The fact is that the freedom of
the press is based on its proper
use. It must always be treated as
a privilege—a rare privilege! and
not as a license!

The press is a trustee of the
privilege—not for its own use but
for the "little man!" If it breaks
that trust, a new trustee should be
appointed!

Today in this city there is a feud
between the Mayor of Halifax and
a section of the so-called free press.
The writer holds no brief for either,
but recognizes that the Mayor was
rightfully angered by a press that
lacked accuracy in its reporting,
sincerity and thoughtfulness in its
editorials, displayed no caution
until it knew its facts, and the bold-
ness it assumes is in reality "brazen-
ness." The Mayor apparently assumed, and I think rightly so, that
that section of the press had lost
its privilege.

Maybe the Mayor moved too
quickly in his remedy. But why
should you then attack him? Why
not attack the real cause of the
trouble! One of your contempor-
aries is the root of the evil! Why
not blame it for the partial loss of
your privileges? Is not that your
duty? It is not a correct answer
for you to say "We should not suffer for the sins of our contempor-
ary." Every citizen pays taxes for
a police force because of the
wrongdoer. Every citizen loses certain privileges because others abuse
them and laws are passed to prevent such abuse, and strike equally
at the good citizen and the bad!

The real point that must be borne
in mind in this city and province
today is that gradually people are
either being driven from public
service or refuse to enter into it
because of the failure of the press
to carry out its duties while it
continually demands its privileges!

Let us have a press that is fair,
and we will have real men in public life. But if it reaches the stage
that the press cannot be "rapped
on the knuckles," then democracy
can fail because the courage demanded of a public man is too
great!

Ask yourself this question —
"Would you accept a position in
the government of this city today
with an irresponsible press sniping
at you all the time?"

F. M. COVERT.

Halifax, N.S.

Trial Of Totalitarian Peace-Criminals

ROOM

Missouria
Strategic

WASHINGTON.—N
has there been such
about the White Hou
of that long-ago
commando force m
Potomac and put the
President's dwelling,
crude, rough days.

Since that controve
House has had a fairl
ence until mid-Januar
dent Truman annour
going to spend $1,650,
the building enough t
seum and a conferenc
he could talk to 375
time.

Washington gape
sprang into action,
raised in angry prote:
passed resolutions. T
of Citizens Associa
objections and wrat
The Institute of An
tects formally prote:
dividual members s
mally but more vigo
it. The Association
habitants (it really e
their wheel chairs a
meeting to resolve
posed changes would
tion of a national s
ciety of Natives pas
motion. Why not a
or a dance pavilion?

Newspapers publis
slum conditions whi
could be cleaned u
money and individu:
viewed to say it wou
the housing situatio

Finally Congressi
political sophisticate:
joined the popular c
nounced they would
what some called "
However, the app
the job had gone t
ordinary December
the White House, go
noticed. Perhaps Con
too eager to get awa:
or failed to realize it
political ammunition
work was already

FROM C

THE SENSE OF TH

Canada's vigorous
the naval war agai
will have an endur
much importance: it
Canadian people as
deeply conscious of
relation of a free sea
The return to all pa:
try of the men who
ada's navy, should
communities the
they are part of a n

It is interesting at
call that Thomas D'.
seeking to unite the
of British North Am
on the coast, rejoi
union would make a
America a maritime
speech in 1884 there
passage:

"I rejoice, moreov
of insular origin a
cover one of our i
sense that compreh
that we are not nov
side into the chara
to all our antecede
mere inland people
the provinces resto
ocean takes us bac

day I would run the firm, and that I would become a director of
the Royal Bank, when he retired from it.

In January 1947 National Sea Products suddenly faced a strike
of deep-sea fishermen, whom the Supreme Court decided were not
employees of the company but joint venturers sharing in the profits
of the catch on each voyage.[34] The strike was led by H.C. (Bert)
Meade, secretary of the Canadian Fishermen and Fish Handlers
Union,[35] an avowed Communist with whom I had dealt when settling the strike at H.B. Nickerson and Sons Limited[36] in October-
November 1946. When I settled that strike, we had a memorandum
prepared and Meade said, "Sure, I'll sign it; if I don't like it, tomorrow I'll break it." I called in my secretary, repeated what he
had said, she typed it out, and he signed the paper – which I kept.
I did not realize how handy it would become.

The two sides in the strike began publishing advertisements in
the newspapers. I thought those by National Sea Products were not
good, so I drafted a set of eight short, snappy ads, which I thought
everybody would read, sent them to Ralph Bell, and criticized the
existing ad campaign.[37] He was very pleased with what he saw and
we worked together, which included spending some time with him
at his estate, Murder Point.[38] All through January and into February
we worked on it. I had meetings with the cabinet and also appeared
before the Legislature's committee on law amendments to answer
Meade, who was seeking to have fishermen included in the new
Trade Union Act.[39] When I rose to answer Meade, I opened with
the story behind Meade's "I'll break it" statement. Attorney General
MacQuarrie[40] stopped me and asked Meade whether that was his
signature; Meade admitted it was. From then on he was through,
his credibility gone. On 19 March the strike was ended. I prepared
and had published the joint statement. Three weeks earlier Bell had
had me appointed to the board of National Sea Products.

On 27 March I was elected member and chair of the board of
the Children's Hospital, for which I had been working a long time,
preparing a new set of by-laws and constitution. That October I
was to have a first-class row with the doctors on the staff of the
Children's Hospital. The administrator was a fine woman who had
run the Hospital for years.[41] One day she told me she was going to
quit and work for the Victoria General Hospital. I often wondered
whether she expected me to coax her to stay, but I simply said how
sorry I was, wished her luck in her new job, and asked her to let

me know the date she proposed to leave so that I could find a replacement. She let me know in two days, so I just moved in her assistant to take her place. All hell broke loose; the nurses signed a petition, in which they were joined by the doctors. I called the doctors together and suggested that this was a management problem and that it was a terrible thing for them to do to join the nurses in a petition. Most of the doctors saw immediately that they were wrong. One, however, had already spoken to the newspapers about the doctors resigning from the staff and he tried to lead a revolt at the meeting;[42] but the doctors gave me and the board a vote of confidence. The matter blew over. The Children's Hospital took up a great deal of my time; indeed I averaged about five days per month on hospital meetings and other work throughout the year.

On 31 March I was in Hantsport with Roy Jodrey attending eight company meetings and was elected a director of Canadian Keyes Fibre Company. The law firm had made a new division of the profits in my favour, which promised a good year. In the middle of April Fred C. Manning called from New York asking me to come down immediately. The next day I flew to Boston and took the train to New York, where I met Manning, Harold Egan, and R.W. (Dick) Harris[43] at the Roosevelt Hotel. Having outlined the situation, they then said they wanted me to take over command of the Venezuelan venture[44] for two years. The discussions lasted for three days. When I got back I went to see Stewart, who told me he had invested $150,000 in cash for shares in the venture and had also endorsed a $600,000 note; he stood to lose his entire life savings. He urged me to go. I said I would have a look at it and report, but the idea of being away for two years just did not appeal to me. During the next eighteen days I worked hard. There were conferences with the government about the Fishermen's Federation bill,[45] concerning which I addressed the law amendments committee of the Legislature. I completed the sale of Purdy Brothers Limited, had a Children's Hospital bill passed,[46] went to Canning to say goodbye to Mother, and finished working on the United Service Corporation capital reorganization draft. Then on 13 May I went to New York via Montreal and on the 14th flew by Constellation to Havana and thence to Caracas. My diary shows I thought 270 mph impressive.[47]

The day after arriving I had to be taken to the police station, where I was fingerprinted, photographed, and issued with a little book containing my picture, name and thumbprint; I was warned never to be without it. Of course, I had an interpreter with me; the attendant asked the question in Spanish, my interpreter then got the answer from me and returned it in Spanish. When I was filling out the forms – name, age, etc. – she asked, "Children?" "Two, ages eleven and one." There was a remark by the girl and all around me people laughed. I asked the interpreter to translate. The girl had said, "What was he doing between one and eleven?"

For about nine weeks I studied the operating company, which had plants in two areas. In Barcelona[48] there was a sawmill and oxygen plant, acetylene plant and machine shop, power plant, and ice-manufacturing plant; in Maracaibo,[49] an oxygen plant, acetylene plant, and machine shop. The oil companies welcomed plants that would take jobs like that off their hands and the prices paid for work were fabulous, until one began to check the costs. Something was always going wrong in all the plants. The sawmill steel girders fell during the course of construction and were a tangled mass of steel. The people who ran the oxygen and acetylene plants had failed to keep proper records of the containers, which were very expensive. Ninety per cent of the employees had to be Venezuelan; the company had brought in Canadians and Americans to fill the top jobs, but they were ineffective. Two of them, Waldrip and Campbell, who had been friends, fought and Campbell went back to Montreal.

All the non-native employees were living at the beach at Lecheria, driving over rough roads every morning and night to get to work and get home. To bring the staff in from Lecheria to Barcelona, the company had begun leasing homes, the prices of which were outrageous. Since we had a sawmill of our own, we built a long simple barracks-style house on our own land and cut out the house-leasing. The morale of the staff was low, production was low, and, generally speaking, tight management and control were completely lacking. There was no cash flow and the company was always in a crisis, requiring money, which Manning was borrowing and advancing. Calling on the oil companies next, I found out that the purported contracts we had for acetylene and oxygen were proposals by us – not contracts. I visited the power plant – it was incredible – held together by baling wire. We did get a capable engineer, who improved it. I worked out a labour contract and also worked on a contract the company had started for the building of a scow. With some help I rearranged the lumber yard, so that it was no longer a complete mess. I also rearranged the staff, firing some of them.

Through all of this I kept preparing a report on the whole organization and what I thought it required. One of the main problems was that the reports going to Manning from management were tainted with optimism and lies. As far as I could see, if one stayed long enough, one became a management toady and the truth was not in you.

I visited a lawyer in Caracas, having found we were lacking a deed in our chain of title to some property. I gave him the particulars. In Canada it would have taken ten minutes; he asked me to call next week. I called at the given time, but he had not returned from his siesta. When he did arrive, he presented me with a draft, which he read to me; I approved it, then was shocked to learn it was a week hence before it would be ready. I went to the consulate to have something certified and told the consular official the story. He said I would get used to it, that the Venezuelans have a saying, "Only Americans and burros work and even the burros take their time."

On 19 July management presented me with their two-part brief on cash requirements and plans, budgets, and hopes for the future. The next day I flew to New York via Barcelona, Maquetia, Ciudad Trujillo, San Juan. It was a rough flight; I was one of a very few who were not airsick. I finally got home via Boston, Greenwood,[50] and taxi to Halifax. On the 25th I reported first to Stewart, telling him that though the misrepresentations may have been innocent, they were serious and that he ought to ask at least to be released from his endorsement of the $600,000 note. With his permission I negotiated this. He insisted on my saying nothing about the $150,000 cash investment; he would take that medicine and say nothing. He was relieved and grateful. On the 26th I met Manning and Egan and reported fully. I advised Manning that the venture was a sinkhole, in which he would lose a great deal more money. First I advised him to be like a banker – take his licking now rather than a worse one later; secondly, to put someone in charge who would never vary the truth in his reports. Manning stuck with I&DCV until his death[51] and sank a great deal more money in it. (He afterwards told me that at that time he could not let it go, because it would take everything else with it.) I told him I really was not the man to run the operation and would not think of going back. He was disappointed, but very grateful to me for going down and reporting honestly to him; while I was there, on 12 June, he notified me that I had been elected a director of United Service Corporation.

Manning wanted me to write a report about the sawmill in Barcelona, so between 30 July and 3 August, Roy Jodrey, who had also put money into the venture, took me with him to Sayabec, Matane, and Mont Joli[52] to see sawmills in operation. I made notes and advised Manning that a lot of work had to be done to make the operation viable and that he must find a man who really knew the business. Later in August Manning and I went to Ottawa to see the Foreign Exchange Control Board about sending more money to Venezuela. Then to Montebello, where we spent three days at the Seigneury Club with all those interested in Venezuela. Then two days in Ottawa and Toronto, where Manning discussed the problems with E.P. Taylor and his partners, John A. (Bud) McDougald and Wallace McCutcheon.[53] They asked me what I had seen in Venezuela; I told them bluntly, but added that, with good management, something might be made of it. On the way back Manning and I stopped in Saint John to look at problems at New Brunswick Power relating to excess profits tax. It was the end of August before I got home. Throughout September a great deal more time was spent on Venezuela, including four or five days in Boston. To all intents and purposes I had spent five months on the Venezuelan venture and it seemed to me that the time could have been much better spent. In April 1949 Manning was to appoint me to the board of the Industrial and Development Corporation of Venezuela.

By November 1947 I was back in business in earnest. By the end of the year I had as clients the four leading industrialists in the province: Roy Jodrey, Fred C. Manning, Ralph P. Bell, and George A. Chase – every one of whom had once been with another firm of solicitors. In January 1948 I was called on to work out a charge on uncalled capital[54] for Annapolis Valley Canners. Solicitors for the company's bankers had been unable to work out a deal and give the bank a satisfactory opinion. I found some English authorities right on the point and worked out the deal; Jodrey was very pleased. I was retained by A.S. MacMillan, the former Liberal premier of Nova Scotia, to prepare a brief for the Board of Referees on a contract his company had carried out during the war.[55] I was appointed to a committee on labour legislation, debated the Trade Union Act at the Dalhousie Labour Institute,[56] and prepared a brief on the constitutional problem of delegation of powers.[57] In April I was retained to settle a three-union strike of seamen against Pickford & Black[58] and worked out an agreement. There were several appearances before the Legislature's committee on law amendments on the Trade Union Act and the Companies Act. I was elected a member of the Council of the Nova Scotia Barristers Society. In May I was elected a director of three more of Manning's companies – Super Service Stations, Super Service Stations (Eastern), and Superline Oils. Then in August Manning appointed me a director of Great Eastern Corporation,[59] of which, after his death, I became president and watched it increase in value a hundredfold.

On 3 December 1948 I went to Canning to deliver a speech in the by-election for Digby-Annapolis-Kings, made necessary by J.L. Ilsley's retirement from political life.[60] Then in April 1949 I was asked by the Liberals to run in Ilsley's old constituency in the federal election. On 8 May Angus L. Macdonald asked me to nominate him at the Halifax South Liberal convention the following night; I did so and made a fighting speech. A week later I was requested to come to Macdonald's house, where I met Louis St-Laurent, who had succeeded Mackenzie King as prime minister in November 1948. There was a whole group pressing me to run in Digby-Annapolis-Kings in the forthcoming federal election.[61] St-Laurent listened to them all and then asked me why I did not want to run. I told him I had been away five years during the war, had recently worked for seven months on a project in Venezuela, and now that I had a family of three I wanted to stay home. Without a moment's hesitation he turned to them all and said, "Leave the young man alone; he's entitled to say no." I was forever grateful.

A week after that, Ilsley told me confidentially that he was going to be made chief justice of Nova Scotia,[62] was therefore resigning his post as general counsel to the recently appointed Royal Commission on Transportation,[63] and that my appointment as his successor had been approved by all three Maritime premiers.[64] I went down to see J. McG. Stewart, who had been counsel, with St-Laurent, to the Royal Commission on Dominion-Provincial Relations and he told me I must accept; that it would make me known across Canada. So on the 23rd I accepted the post. On the 26th I went to Montreal,[65] where for four days Ilsley crammed me on freight rates, a subject about which I knew absolutely nothing. Then on to Ottawa and three days' more cramming while on the train from Ottawa to Winnipeg, where the hearings opened on 1 June. The commissioners were His Excellency W.F.A. Turgeon (chair)[66] and Professors Henry Forbes Angus and Harold Adams Innis, of the

University of British Columbia and University of Toronto, respectively. Turgeon was a remarkable man and had had a brilliant career. Born in New Brunswick, he went west in his youth, becoming at age thirty attorney-general of Saskatchewan and later chief justice. He was renowned as a royal commissioner and did more of that work than anyone else.[67] As a diplomat he held office as minister and ambassador to various countries[68] and was fluent in English, French, and Spanish. He was a magnificent raconteur and I spent many pleasant minutes with him after we ceased work.

When we were not at hearings we were reading briefs for the next venue, and I was studying night and day to learn freight rates. All our travelling was done by train, so we had a great place to study. I had as assistant counsel a French-Canadian lawyer, Gaston Desmarais, from Sherbrooke. The Commission hearings having begun in Winnipeg, we went from there to Regina to Calgary to Edmonton to Victoria and finally to Vancouver, where the hearings continued from 28 to 30 June. On the the 24th and 25th I was able to see two members of my aircrew, Hutton and MacLean, and met their parents and wives. Then on the night of the 29th I had an amazing experience. The whole group went to a Chinese restaurant in Vancouver. We occupied the whole room, except for a sailor alone at a table, whom we invited to join us; he sat next to me. I asked him where he was from. "Bergen," he said. I told him I had bombed Bergen and gave him the date. He said, "Let me show you something." He took off his coat, rolled up his sleeve and showed a deep scar over a foot long. He was in the house when the air raid took place and an andiron had flown out of the fireplace and torn his arm.[69]

En route back east we stopped for two hours in Winnipeg, where I saw Wib Pierce, our skipper. Then on 3 July there was a hearing in Fort William. From the 4th to the 9th I was studying under the tutelage of Leonard Knowles, a rate expert from the CNR, who was an excellent teacher.[70] Then we left for Halifax, where hearings took place 12 to 14 July. On the 15th we gave an outdoor party at Fraser Street for the entire staff of the Commission. Then on to Fredericton, Charlottetown, Quebec, Montreal, and Toronto. Then to Ottawa from 6 to 10 August and finally home to Halifax. After Labour Day I returned to Montreal, where for eighteen days Desmarais and I studied and worked over the evidence we had already taken in preparation for the final hearings. Then on 25 September we flew to

St. John's, Newfoundland, for three days of hearings, after which, on 1 October, we flew back to Ottawa, where the hearings opened on 1 November. The entire months of October and November and half of December I worked night and day preparing for the hearings. On the 17th I returned to Halifax. It had been an amazing year. I had seen Canada from St. John's to Victoria and had read the problems of the people in the many briefs submitted. It was a tough grind; it seemed to me I had been studying since 1945 and would never stop. I became very proud to be a Canadian and I had no doubts about the future. I did notice that there was no understanding of the French Canadian west of Manitoba.

I had no idea that 1949, much less 1950, would be almost entirely devoted to the Royal Commission. The hearings began again on 6 February. The CPR presented its brief and I cross-examined Jeffrey, their freight expert, for three days. The hearings went five days a week, but we worked Saturdays, Sundays, and every evening sifting through the evidence and preparing for the next hearings. On 31 March Innis invited me to spend the weekend with him and his family in Toronto, while I worked a bit. It was a very pleasant interlude. There was a two-week break in April, which I spent in Halifax. Due to my commitments, I advised the Children's Hospital that I would not reoffer as chair or member of the board of management.

On 17 April the hearings recommenced in Ottawa and lasted until 1 May. Again I worked day and night, Saturdays, and Sundays. On 1 May the last of the evidence was in. Now began the argument of government counsel of Manitoba, Saskatchewan, Alberta, British Columbia, Nova Scotia, New Brunswick, and Prince Edward Island. These lasted from 2 to 16 May and were followed by briefs on behalf of the CPR and CNR, which lasted until the 29th. The provinces had a right to reply, which prolonged the hearings to 31 May, when they finally ended. There were 138 days of hearings and 138 books of evidence. Now began work on the report; the chairman asked me to stay on. From 1 to 24 June we worked night and day on the report, sifting through the evidence and drafting judgments on specific items.

On the 24th I flew to Halifax. While on vacation I read the Beit lectures given by Harold Innis at Oxford University in 1948 and published as *Empire and Communications*.[71] He had said I would not read it. I read it, then read it again, and summarized it as I went along. Then I made a summary of the summary and memorized it. When

Innis asked me whether I had read it, I delivered the summary. He was properly surprised. Then I told him what I had done; he laughed.

For a month I practised law again. Then from 14 to 30 September I was day and night working on the report, trying desperately to get it finished. The professors on the staff, along with Commissioner Angus, had practically written a report of their own. Confidentially, the chairman called me to his room and showed me how full of generalities it was and that their recommendations could not be enacted into remedial legislation; he said, "I want it destroyed page by page, I want your opinions on each article." So we proceeded and at meetings with the full Commission we asked the draftsmen to give us a piece of legislation to carry out their draft reports. It was a shambles, so we started all over again. Turgeon was in complete control. We worked on the report for nearly two and one-half months, from 1 October to 12 December. On the 12th I flew home, following a meeting with the Prime Minister on the 8th, when he asked me to see it through to the end to add balance to the report.

On the 11th Innis had asked me to vet a small dissenting report for him; I gladly did so.[72] His premature death from cancer in November 1952 saddened me. We became great friends during the Commission hearings and when I learned he was not well I wrote him often. He had once told me that I was the first lawyer he had ever watched who made him think that "perhaps" the profession was entitled to some respect. He was a great friend of Angus L. Macdonald's;[73] when I told him Macdonald had wanted me to run in the 1949 provincial election and enter his cabinet, he said, "Covert, you might get elected once, but you'd never get re-elected. That's the difference between politicians and people like you and me – it's the ability to get re-elected – and we don't have it." I told him I was deeply flattered that he included me along with him. He looked at me with those clear, piercing blue eyes and said, "Covert, you really are a bastard."

In January 1951 I worked for five days going over draft reports of the Commission. Then in February I had word from the chairman that the report was finished and being printed and that he was returning to Ireland and would be in Halifax on 18 February. I picked him up at the railway station and he came to the house for dinner; later in the evening I drove him to the pier and we said our good-byes. He told me that I had been an ideal Royal Commission lawyer – impartial, kept it in hand, and had been of great help to the Commission, seeing to it that the report would not be open to criticism for mistakes. He said modestly that he felt it was a good report because it dealt in specifics and not broad generalities, which would make newspaper editorials but not bring about remedial legislation. On 15 March the report was tabled in the House of Commons. Turgeon was right in his predictions.[74]

I had been away from 1940 to 1950, so much that I was afraid my clients would begin to wonder when I would go away again. I decided then and there – never again, no matter what the inducements. My diary reads, "I've got to get back to the firm."

CHAPTER SEVEN

The Fifties

On board the great ship *Titanic*, when it sank in 1912, was a Halifax man, George Wright, who in his will left $20,000 to an organization that "would attract young people from the lure of the streets." As the years rolled by, the bequest grew through accumulated and compound interest. Numerous charities applied for it, but all proposals failed, including an early one by the YMCA. In 1950 I was retained by the Y, which was going to build a new headquarters on South Park Street in downtown Halifax. I read the applications that had failed and then proceeded to draft a case for the Y. I spent a great deal of time outlining the types of people who used the Y, amassed a great many statistics, finally prepared a brief, and persuaded the attorney general to bring a stated case before the Supreme Court in Banco.[1] Advertisement of the case was carried in the newspapers, resulting in other applicants, none of whom went about it in the right way. When the argument came on before the Court, none of the other applications equalled the Y's. The five justices sitting asked me why the Y was not precluded by the prior case[2] and I showed them that in 1925 it was a different Y. Then it did not fill the bill; now it did. The motion was heard in January 1951 and on 24 February I obtained a favourable decision and over $80,000 for the Y.[3]

Bill Kelley's father[4] recommended me to W.E. Clarke, the owner of Sydney Engineering & Dry Dock, as a result of which I reorganized its capital structure and disbursed tax-free the preferred shares. Clarke was pleased and later appointed me a director and also a co-executor of his will. After Clarke's death, I persuaded his family and the other executors to appoint his son-in-law, A. Bruce Rossetti, president and managing director of the company. I advised

Rossetti to buy up all the outstanding shares, because I was sure he could turn the company into something. But Rossetti had no money, so I further advised him to borrow from the bank. He asked me why I did not buy it myself. I told him I had learned a lesson: if the company was a success, the client began to think he was doing all the work, while the lawyer was making money doing nothing. However, I made a deal with Rossetti that, if at any time he wanted to sell, I would reimburse him with interest.

I learned from Roy Jodrey an investment policy for Canadian companies and persuaded Rossetti to adopt it; eventually Sydney Engineering had a fine portfolio and, for a long time, a substantial tax-free dividend income. Rossetti was a shy man, but a good operator and very far-sighted. When Rossetti died in April 1978, he owned nearly ninety per cent of Sydney Engineering. Two months later I assumed the presidency, to fill the vacancy created by Rossetti's death. I let the number two man go; Rossetti had not been happy with him and, fortunately, his five-year contract was due to expire. I promoted the office manager to general manager and then began to discuss with his other executors (I was one) the sale of the company. When we sold it, the estate received over $3 million, most of which went to educational institutions to set up scholarships in memory of Rossetti and his wife.

In the Supreme Court, before a jury, in April 1951 I defended George Wonnacott on a charge of attempting to bribe some members of the Halifax City Council. The defendant was guilty, but the crown was having difficulty identifying the accused. One witness to whom an envelope had been delivered was making trouble for the crown prosecutor, when suddenly the judge[5] took over and started to cross-examine the witness; despite my objection, he finally got her to say that the accused in the dock was the man who had delivered the envelope to her. In fact it was not the same man; the crown knew it and so did I. Justice Parker, satisfied that he had tied up a neat little package, gave a strong address to the jury and the man was convicted. I persuaded the crown prosecutor to come with me to the judge's chambers while the jury was out; we told His Honour that his cross-examination was so severe that he influenced a witness to identify the prisoner as having delivered an envelope when he had not; someone else had "delivered the mail." Just then the sheriff announced that the jury was coming in. If the jury had said not guilty, there would have been no problem, but the verdict was guilty. We persuaded His Honour to impose a fine of only $500. Justice was done; the accused had me apply for the money he used to do the bribing, which was put in as evidence.

While I was on a fishing trip to Ponhook Lake in May 1951, the Liberal government of Prince Edward Island retained me to oppose the abandonment of a railway line by the CNR. I agreed to take it on.[6] In the firm at that time was a young lawyer, Richey Love, who was ambitious and a prodigious worker.[7] I had him prepare the brief, then we went to Charlottetown, conferred with the government, and began to try to collect evidence to oppose the abandonment. It looked hopeless, but Love worked hard and we did produce some farmers who testified the abandonment would affect them adversely. Most of them did not stand up well under cross-examination. I called Premier Jones (at his request), but he did not endear himself to one of the commissioners, Howard B. Chase CBE, a former president of the Canadian Brotherhood of Railway Trainmen, by haranguing CNR employees. I enjoyed myself cross-examining the railway experts, but the case was hopeless. The chief commissioner of the Board of Transport Commissioners at the time was Justice Maynard Brown Archibald of the Exchequer Court of Canada, a former justice of the Supreme Court of Nova Scotia and law partner of J.L. Ilsley. Archibald apparently had some private conversations with CNR officials and the premier and gained some time, but in the long run the result was inevitable. Premier Jones was very pleased with my work, however, and told me so.

In July 1951 the firm received a call from the American consul in Halifax, Cabot Coville, asking whether we would act for the US Government in order to prevent the Russians obtaining some strategic material which was being salvaged from the *Kolkohznik* off Sambro Island.[8] H.P. MacKeen and I agreed to act. The *Kolkohznik* was a Russian ship torpedoed off the coast of Nova Scotia in 1942 while carrying a cargo of war materials from the US to Russia. By 1951, because of the Korean War, prices had gone up; the materials were very valuable and "strategic" in the eyes of the US Government. Furthermore, as the whole cargo had been on lend-lease from the US to the Soviet Union, the Americans were claiming that title had not passed. They wanted us to take possession of the goods, which were being salvaged and brought ashore by England's Besley Salvage Company. We had numerous trips to Washington, saw the original lend-lease correspondence between Roosevelt and Stalin, and came to the conclusion we had a good case. But we had to settle with the salvors and persuade the courts, if necessary, that the American claim was superior to that of the Russians. I went on to Washington for seven days on the *Kolkohznik* case. We succeeded and got the material for the US Government; it was worth far more in 1952 than when the vessel had been sunk.

On Halloween 1951 in Falmouth,[9] eight-year-old James Orland Lantz, wearing a mask, ran out into the road in the dark of night and was struck and killed by a car operated by Gerald Bent, whose wife was Roy Jodrey's secretary.[10] Grace Bent, terribly upset and worried, called me and I went to Windsor on 5 November for the inquest. I cross-examined, very gently, the children who gave evidence. They all had been wearing masks, and I elicited from one that she took off her mask when she crossed the road, because she could not "see sideways." I asked for a volunteer to put on the mask; a young boy came forward who claimed he was the same age and size as the deceased. I had him demonstrate the mask, showing that there were over one and a half inches between the eyes and the eyeholes in the mask and that unless one turned a full ninety degrees one could not see to the left or right. This boy had also worn a mask, but his was a cloth mask which left clear vision, while the mask worn by the deceased was papier mâché. I called Bent, who admitted to going about thirty mph, but "no more." The crown called one of the two RCMP officers who had left Windsor and arrived at the scene shortly afterwards. He thought it a very dark night and that 30 mph was too fast under the circumstances. I asked him what time the police received the call, what time they left, and what time they arrived at the scene. He had these recorded in his notebook to the minute. The next RCMP officer confirmed what the first had said. I asked him the distance he had driven from Windsor to the scene; he had a precise answer. I calculated the speed – at least sixty mph. I then asked why he had driven so fast and whether it was safe to drive so fast on such a dark night; was he not endangering lives? He finally admitted that he had not really felt there was any danger. The coroner found immediately that the cause of death was not the result of negligence on the part of Bent but the fault of the mask. The Bents were very grateful.

In 1952 Bill Kelley called me again and coaxed me to come to Toronto to join his firm. Though I thought the world of Bill and of Henry Borden, I could not leave the Stewart firm. In a big city like

Toronto one could never have business clients in such a personal way as Jodrey, Manning, Bell and Chase. Stewart told me that in Halifax a man could be a big frog in a small puddle and that, no matter what anybody said, it was a lot of fun. In November 1952 Stewart had a dinner party at his house for Ted Atkinson, general manager of the Royal Bank of Canada; he told Atkinson that, when the time came, I was the one to succeed him as a director of the bank. That was the sort of thing Stewart did frequently. Often he would introduce me to a client and say, "Frank knows more about this kind of thing than I do, but if you ever have any doubts, just call me." He weaned every one of his clients off to me that way. Now he was letting the bank know where to look when the time came.

There was a surprising amount of court work in 1952, culminating in November in a long and drawn-out case for Ralph Bell against Pickford & Black.[11] It was a bitter case and Bell was a difficult client. Eventually I had to write him that if he would not leave me alone and let me run it my way, I would have to retire so that he could retain someone else. He wrote me a fine letter of apology while I continued to work endlessly on preparation. At the conclusion of my opening he was pleased and at the conclusion of the argument, when I had summed up, he said, "Win, lose or draw, that's the finest presentation I've ever seen." I laughed, thanked him, and replied, "I wish you'd put that in writing." He looked at me quizzically and said nothing. Two days later he wrote me a letter reiterating his praise and adding to it.

I also worked many hours on a case with H.P. MacKeen involving a leading surgeon[12] who had left a sponge inside a patient, on account of which both he and the Halifax Infirmary were being sued; we were acting for the hospital. Given MacKeen's usual thoroughness, we had to go to the hospital and see the actual precautions which were taken. The doctor settled, so the case never came to trial and we took out an order dismissing (by consent) the case against the hospital. I felt I had wasted days and thought to myself, "This trial work is not for me."

In November 1952 I was elected secretary of the Nova Scotia Liberal Association, a position which I held until resigning in 1956.[13] In 1953 I drafted a new constitution and by-laws for the Association, and was re-elected secretary. Premier Angus L. Macdonald died in office on 13 April 1954. Macdonald, who had developed into a magnificent orator, won five provincial elections. When he died,

Harold Connolly, a senior minister in Macdonald's cabinet, became interim premier. A leadership convention was called for 10 September. There were many candidates but the two chief contenders were Connolly and Henry Hicks, who had been minister of education in Macdonald's cabinet. The elderly, retired premier, A.S. MacMillan, who was not well, asked me, as secretary of the Association, to read his speech for him. As I had not seen it before, I tried to read it as if I were delivering a speech. Stewart, who was listening to the radio, thought I was running as a candidate. There were a lot of party members who did not think that either Connolly or Hicks was the person to be premier and an attempt was made to draft me to run; I had not the slightest intention and no ambition for the job. Vote after vote was taken and Connolly held the lead until the final ballot between him and Hicks, who won. Connolly was very bitter and called it a religious vote. I believe that it may well have been just that; there were many Protestants who thought that after Macdonald's long reign the next leader should be a Protestant. And I expect the Catholics voted largely for Connolly. This religious schism, in my view, led to the Liberal defeat at the next election. Two weeks after the convention, a group of us tried to persuade Connolly to go to the World Series and make up a bridge team; he turned us down.

It was while I was secretary of the Liberal Party and Macdonald premier that I was visited by the party treasurer, Edmund Luther MacDonald,[14] who told me that though we had someone as party leader who appeared unbeatable, the party would inevitably lose sometime and that we ought to plan for that eventuality.[15] (At the time there was no salary for the leader of the opposition.) I drew up a trust instrument, under which we would deposit moneys with Canada Permanent[16] and use the income to provide a salary for the leader of the Liberal Party when leader of the opposition. I obtained a ruling from the Department of National Revenue that the trust fund was tax-free and the income only taxable in the hands of the recipient when paid. Not long after the fund was set up, Angus L. Macdonald died and Henry Hicks became party leader and premier; when he was defeated by Robert Stanfield in October 1956, we had the first use of the fund. I wrote the new premier stating that in most provinces it was recognized that the leader of the opposition, as an important part of governance, should be paid a salary. The reply was that Stanfield did not intend to help the man "whose sole object was to defeat me." But a year or so later, the leader of the opposition began to be paid a salary.[17] The trustees of the fund, Hawco, were Haw (for the man who brought in the money[18]) and co for me. Senator Hawkins died not long afterwards and I acquired two new trustees with me.[19] We invested the fund in Canadian common stock and saw its income grow nearly fivefold and the fund itself grow in value nearly fourfold. Since the fund was established we have paid three Liberal leaders of the opposition[20] and from 1970 to 1978 we paid the party leader when he was premier, because, based on our studies, the premier of Nova Scotia was not paid enough. The pay-outs were not large: the first, $4,000 a year; the second, $3,600 a year (because Earl Urquhart was paid a salary as leader of the opposition as well as his sessional indemnity). When Gerald Regan became party leader in 1965, he had neither a seat in the Legislature, nor a salary, because the official leader of the opposition was in the House of Assembly.[21] So we paid Regan $900 a month. When he was elected to the Legislature in 1967, we paid him the salary, which continued even though he was premier from 1970. When his government was defeated in 1978, the payments continued, only ceasing when he ran successfully in the federal election of February 1980 and became minister of labour in the second Trudeau government.

In March 1980 there was a suggestion in the media that Gerald Regan,[22] while leader of the Liberal Party, had been paid with tainted funds. On 20 March I was invited to appear on CTV's *Canada AM*. I was introduced by Craig Oliver, who described me as a "backroom Liberal," then asked four questions. I began by saying I did not know why he should have called me a backroom Liberal, as my politics were well-known; I had been secretary of the party. He had also begun a sentence with "I presume." I told him not to presume anything, but just to ask what he wanted to know. I then outlined the history of the fund and its operation.

He was so surprised by the facts that he said, "Thank you, Mr. Covert for throwing some light on the matter."

"What do you mean *some light*? If there is *anything* you want to know, just ask me."

"I'm sorry we've run out of time" – and he disappeared.

The local affiliated radio station asked me to do a tape for them, which I did. I had just returned to the office when the CBC called to ask whether I would give them an interview. They came with their equipment to the office and I answered every question. I never saw the telecast, but a lot of people did. I received letters of congratulation from Vancouver to Charlottetown; oddly enough, people were pleased with the way I had handled Craig Oliver. I had a very nice telephone call from Gerald Regan and dozens of letters and calls from friends all over the country.

Nobody but the trustees knew about the fund[23] and no premier ever saw its make-up or knew of its size or income. When the first trustee, Senator Hawkins, died,[24] the only person who might have known where the fund originated was no longer able to say so. The fund had no claim on anyone, not even the donors of it. Nor was one cent ever added to the fund since its inception. It just increased in value because it was invested in common stock. I was very proud of the fund and of the part I had played in its formation, growth, and administration. It ensured that the leader of the Liberal Party, whether as leader of the opposition or as premier, would always be free of any demands by anyone and guaranteed him financial independence.

In 1953 I was retained by a large law firm in New York, attorneys for Servel Refrigerator Company, who had contracted with Canadian Assemblies of Amherst to manufacture refrigerators under licence. The deal having worked out badly, Servel (Canada) wished to terminate the contract but were having trouble with lawyers on the other side. Servel had in the first instance retained a lawyer in Amherst, Alfred C. Milner KC,[25] but began to worry about the nature of the termination; so they retained me and in May Milner and I flew to New York. Finally, at about 10:30 Monday morning, we went to the law office; all the time we were there we never saw or heard a typewriter, never saw or heard a telephone – this impressed Milner tremendously. Moreover, the firm had four of its lawyers sit in on the conference. Milner was surprised how much the "youngsters" knew, and how little the seniors; I pointed out that the seniors after all made the decisions. We were there three days, in which I saw New York through a newcomer's eyes, and everything worked out to our client's satisfaction.

In June 1953 Ralph Bell sold his controlling interest in National Sea Products Limited to the Morrow, Smith and Connor interests.[26] He did so because the market for processed fish was decreasing, while the fishermen were still bringing in the fish, and inventories were reaching what Bell believed to be a dangerously high level. Bell proposed that the company refuse to buy any more fish. C.J. Morrow[27] disagreed violently, saying it just could not be done; the company would lose the fishermen forever; they would sell else-where. Bell insisted; Morrow said he would have to resign and that Bell should buy him out or, alternatively, he would buy Bell out. Bell asked at what price; Morrow told him to name it, saying they would both be bound either to buy or to sell at that price, and that it would be offered to all the shareholders. This meant, of course, that if Bell made the price of his shares too high, he would have to offer the same price to all the shareholders, so he had to select a price at which Morrow would buy. My recollection is that the price Bell came up with was $16 a share. Morrow brought W.W. Smith, R.G. Smith, and H.G. (Gary) Connor[28] together and they went to see Stewart, who got the Royal Bank to put up the money. (By this time I had 2,500 shares, for which I had paid $1,220. I was to get $40,000 for them.) Then Stewart called me in and we incorporated a holding company, Ocean Fisheries, which offered the shareholders of National Sea one common share and three five-dollar preferred shares of Ocean Fisheries for each share of National Sea Products common stock. I took this instead of cash. Then we did a bond issue and the preferred share issue for the new company. Best of all, there were profitable subsidiaries of National Sea Products, such as Lunenburg Fisheries, whose surpluses we were able to flush up tax-free into Ocean Fisheries and, consequently, buy National Sea without really putting out much cash.

I enjoyed working with Stewart on this deal, ended up with a nice holding in the new company, and became a director of Ocean Fish-eries. Bell made a lot of money out of National Sea, which made him a wealthy man after only eight years; but as soon as he saw how the Morrow group paid for National Sea out of the assets of the company he had sold, he told me selling out was the greatest mistake he had ever made. I suppose most of the shareholders other than Bell and his family accepted shares in the new company. Stewart was pleased that the Royal Bank had financed National Sea Products in 1945. However, when Bell became a director of the Bank of Nova Scotia,[29] he moved the account there. But Morrow[30] immediately brought it back to the Royal – of which Stewart was a vice-president.

In the summer of 1953 the great I.W. Killam decided he would like to revisit the scenes of his youth and renew old acquaintances; but after a day in Yarmouth he found little to amuse him, so he called Mersey Paper and they called White Point Beach Lodge, where Mollie and I were staying. There was no cabin for Killam.

The proprietor (Elliott) asked us whether we would mind moving into a room in the main lodge for a few days. Mollie disliked the idea but the Elliotts had been so nice to us over the years that we agreed. So Killam invited us to dinner along with the Mersey officials. He, of course, did not know about our dislocation. He spent the evening making his Mersey managers miserable by asking them questions to which they did not have the answers – which he mostly knew anyway. Everyone was glad when the evening was over. Killam was a brilliant man; he had the most deeply-set eyes and longest fingers I had ever seen. After dinner, as we headed to cabin 40, Killam walked on past it; I said, "This is it – Cabin 40." He asked me how I knew; I replied, "I knew you were in Cabin 40 and this is it." That was the first, last, and only time I met him.

In the winter of 1953 I held a watching brief for a good friend of mine, who came to see me about his divorce.[31] For nearly eight years he had been separated from his wife, having brought a divorce action on the grounds of cruelty some years before. The judge who heard the case[32] had seen the man play football and just did not believe that he could not handle such a situation. That his wife's parting words to him when he went overseas were, "I hope you don't get back," and that she had thrown his bedclothes and personal clothing out of the window one winter's night and then, when he went out to get them, locked the door after him and would not let him back in – made no impression on the trial judge. My friend the petitioner also lost the appeal, but did get a dissenting judgment.[33] In the meantime, and some years later, he had fallen in love. I told him he would have to make his wife so angry that she would bring an action. I advised him to take the other woman to Kentville,[34] stay at the Cornwallis Inn,[35] and commit adultery with her flagrantly. It was difficult persuading him to do it, but he finally did and I wrote his wife's lawyer about it. She brought the divorce action and was successful. My client married his new love and they lived very happily until he died.

In January 1954 I was retained by Alberta C. Pew, matriarch of a very wealthy family from Pennsylvania, to defend in the Judicial Committee of the Privy Council an appeal case that had been argued and won in the Supreme Court of Canada by William Pitt Potter.[36] The argument was extremely complicated[37] and Potter had briefed every case on the subject.[38] In 1953, however, Potter was made a justice of the Exchequer Court of Canada and he recommended me

to Mrs Pew. The action arose out of a mortgage on a small piece
of valuable land in Chester, fought over by two summering American families who had once been friends.[39] I studied the briefs,
retained counsel in England, and prepared the factum, which was
then beautifully edited and improved, especially as to language and
brevity, by my English junior. I was preparing for the trip when I
suddenly realized what a terrible thing it was to spend so much time
and money on a small piece of land. While I was on vacation I
wrote my client, suggesting the case should be settled out of court.
Mrs Pew's husband[40] telephoned me to ask whether I thought we
might lose and, if so, was that why I wanted to settle. I told him
no; that I was eager to defend the judgment because appeals to the
Privy Council had been abolished and this would be the last opportunity I would ever have.[41] I said, "But you used to be friends, this
case will ruin your neighbour and Chester is too small a village for
such a feud." He told me this had always worried him. Accordingly,
I proposed a friendly call by Mrs Pew on her neighbour, suggesting
that the lawyers settle the case on terms of no costs and compromise. Mrs Pew did so, while the lawyers did the legal work to end
the appeal.[42] Afterwards I received a letter from Mrs Pew saying
that she and her husband would like to meet me, that they had
never met a lawyer who wanted to settle a winning case, and that
everyone was very pleased with the result.

Gladys Porter was the Maritimes' first woman mayor,[43] but after
her second election as mayor of Kentville, Nova Scotia, in 1954 an
attempt was made to unseat her by having the election set aside on
the grounds of irregularities.[44] Mrs Porter was the sister of a great
friend of mine, Claude Richardson, a lawyer in Montreal, who was
very proud of his sister and afraid that the local lawyer, David J.C.
Waterbury, might lose the case. So in April 1954 I went to Kentville
and explained the situation to Waterbury, who was very gracious
and very helpful. We cross-examined the petitioner's witnesses and
made such a strong case that we did not even have to call Mrs.
Porter. In April 1954, a month to the day after the trial, the county
court judge handed down a favourable decision. In December 1954
I represented a union,[45] which, when unrepresented by counsel, had
lost before the Labour Relations Board; persuaded the Board to
give me a new hearing, then won the case for the union. One of
my corporate clients raised hell about my acting for a union. I told
him they deserved representation, that I was delighted to act for

them, and, furthermore, that they were among the most grateful clients I had ever had. I believe the unions began to think highly of me, because I had acted against a corporate employer. In February 1956 I was appointed a conciliator in the Dominion Coal Company wage dispute with UMWA Distict 26 and received a flattering editorial on my appointment.[46] In February 1957 I sat on another coal conciliation board, where we secured a unanimous decision.

In December 1954 I prepared the deed gifting James McGregor Stewart's Kipling collection to Dalhousie University. Stewart had been collecting Kipling since he was a young boy and ended up with what was reputed to be the second best Kipling collection in the world. Stewart wanted to be sure that his precious gift would be properly and safely housed and protected so that it could be made use of. Time and again I redrafted the deed; it took a great deal of courage for him finally to sign it. Eventually a special place, the Kipling Room, was built through the contributions of Stewart's friends, so that the collection is beautifully housed.

The year 1955 was really governed entirely by circumstances arising from the death of Stewart. The year started out with our working for Roy Jodrey on a deal to sell Bishop Asphalt;[47] together Stewart and I worked out all the problems. It was on 9 February that Stewart telephoned and asked whether I could come to his house; I was leaving in a few moments to go to Montreal for the Bishop Asphalt closing and asked whether I should try to postpone it; he said, "No, but come out as soon as you get back." It has been one of the great regrets in my life that I did not just cancel and go to him because he said it was "urgent." I have guessed that it was about his will; he probably wanted to appoint me co-executor[48] because of my knowledge of his affairs. So I went to Montreal, closed the sale of Bishop Asphalt, and got back after midnight on the 10th and, of course, could not go down at that hour. The next day Stewart was in a coma; he died at 9:00 pm,[49] without having regained consciousness. I suddenly felt low and depressed.

Stewart was undoubtedly the greatest man I had ever known. Working with him, talking with him, was a marvellous experience. All my friends used to laugh and call it "hero and hero worship," and many people, even twenty-five years after his death, would smile knowingly when I quoted the man I called "The Boss" or "J. McG." As close as we were, it was not until the last two years that, when we were alone, I stopped calling him Mr Stewart and called him

Jim. In 1953 and 1954, when he was unwell, I visited him at least once and sometimes twice a week. I never ceased to wonder at the breadth of his knowledge and his ability to solve any problem.

As a result of Stewart's death, many things happened to me much earlier than they otherwise would have done. I was elected a director of Eastern Telephone and Telegraph, Maritime Paper Products, Industrial Containers, and Mersey Paper, and advised I would be elected a director of the Royal Bank at the annual meeting in January 1956. Stewart had been on all of these boards. I was also elected to the board of governors of Dalhousie University to fill the vacancy caused by his death.[50] At the Royal Bank president's dinner on 12 January 1956, each newly elected director had to make a speech. It was a nerve-wracking task but one of the great moments of my life. This was followed in February by my election to the board of Montreal Trust.[51]

Fred Manning's United Service Corporation (USC) was the parent company for twenty-six subsidiary companies,[52] each run by managers handpicked and trained by Manning. He wanted to give them an incentive to buy stock in the corporation. So in February 1952 he called a dinner meeting and had me address the managers and explain the investment scheme. He let me buy a few shares. Oddly enough, most of the managers did not go for it. In 1955, when USC was sold to Canadian Petrofina, they saw the error of their ways.

Canadian Petrofina, controlled by Petrofina S.A. (Belgium), had been launched in Canada in 1953 by Pitfields; its president was Alfredo F.M. Campo. It would be fair to say that the petroleum industry did not believe that Petrofina could get off the ground against the competition of the great American oil companies operating in Canada.[53] They bargained without Campo – to whom my friend Percy Smith of Pitfields recommended me – and it was agreed between Manning and Campo that I would act for both parties. Having worked so long for Manning, I knew all twenty-six of USC's subsidiary companies in allied industries, service stations, bus companies, and automotive parts and sales.

I decided to draw a letter of agreement in narrative form, omitting legalese and giving each company the name by which it was commonly known. I worked hard and long on the letter and presented it for the first time to Manning, Campo, and Smith at a joint session. There was dead silence until they had all read it. Then Campo said to Manning, "Is that your understanding of the deal?" Manning said yes. Smith nodded agreement. It was signed then and there. Campo said, "Do we need a long legal agreement?" I said no; they agreed and that was that. Campo said it was the finest non-legal legal document he had ever seen. But Canadian Petrofina only wanted the service station companies,[54] so Campo began to sell off the rest of USC's subsidiaries. In two days in April 1955, Campo had me elected a director of all twenty-six companies and then we began to sell off the various companies to their employees; I was involved in all these sales. Manning was left with Great Eastern Corporation, North Star Oil in Winnipeg, the Industrial and Development Corporation of Venezuela – and cash from the sale of USC. He came to me to draw a new will.

I.W. Killam, who owned Mersey Paper Company, died in August 1955, and it was rumoured that Mersey was up for sale. When it was apparent that prospective buyers were looking at Mersey,[55] a group of us got together to see whether we could buy it – officers of Mersey Paper, Roy Jodrey, and others. We worked at it for a long time and then, in April 1956, Mrs. Killam announced that the English conglomerate Bowaters was going to buy it. Bowaters had retained John MacInnes of the Wickwire firm[56] to act for them; I thought to myself, losing a client of twenty-eight years. The officials at Mersey presented me with a beautiful gold watch – good-bye and thank you.

On 7 June the sale was agreed upon and on the 13th I had my last directors' meeting of old Mersey.[57] On the 17th work really started and it became apparent that the complete co-operation of our firm would be required. We knew all the inner workings, we had searched the titles, and so on. On the 19th and 20th I was called to New York and treated royally. On arriving I met the top brass in Bowaters, who asked whether there was a show I would like to see. I, still the country boy, said, "What about My Fair Lady?" A Mr Rye, who had come from England, said he would like that too. I also met and became friends with a famous lawyer, Archie Graustein,[58] who was acting for Bowaters.

There followed months and months of work. First, I was asked to prepare a trust deed for the $26 million bond issue, on which I was to collaborate with Blake, Cassels & Graydon. I immediately had a stroke of luck, for in June Blakes had, with Miller Thomson, drawn a trust deed; through Jack Miller I obtained a copy. Using this as a precedent, I drafted a trust deed and took it to Toronto –

very proud of my work. Here I met W.E.P. DeRoche and we started to work. He said he had looked up our firm and thought it too small to handle the whole deal. I replied that I intended doing it pretty well alone. Thus we started work on my draft. After half an hour DeRoche said, "This deed is no good; it's now outmoded;" he sent for a new precedent. While it was on its way, I told him the one we were using had been approved by his firm just three weeks earlier. That cut no ice. We worked for a week; on the last day he was rushed to hospital for a hernia operation. I finished the deed in *his* office using *his* precedent.

At the end of July I was back in New York to go over the trust deed with the New York lawyers for Morgan Stanley and the lawyers for the life insurance companies that were buying the bonds. DeRoche, of course, was unable to be present; to replace him Blakes sent David Guest. After we had worked on the draft for a while Guest said, "This deed is out of date. I don't know where it came from." I was thunderstruck; could not believe my ears. Then I saw red; was really angry. I spilled forth what had happened and said, "That's over three weeks' wasted work." Guest was very apologetic and very nice. We worked for three days, after which there was not a paragraph left untouched. Finally I said, "I'm going home. I cannot waste time like this. When you've finished, send it to me and I'll see if it complies with Nova Scotia law." I was beginning to learn how big law firms worked.[59] The six lawyers present at that session had a debate as to whether to use *shall* or *will* in a sentence. They split three to three, so Graustein asked my opinion: "You'd have to be born to the purple to know for sure. My opinion would therefore be a guess, but there's one way of being sure: ask your secretary." Graustein called in Miss Ewig. Guest dictated the clause using "shall." When Miss Ewig brought the clause back, Graustein asked whether she had any trouble with it. "No, except that I changed 'shall' to 'will.'" Graustein did not say a word, just looked at me and gave the slightest of winks.

There were many sessions in New York on the bond issue and sessions in Montreal on the preferred share issue, which was to be sold in Canada. I suppose we drew at least twenty drafts of the prospectus. We revised it, changing tons to long tons and back, again and again and again. After this had gone on for days I said, "Canadians will be buying these shares. They don't even know what a long ton is and, besides, it makes production look less than it will

be." Finally, the English agreed to tons.[60] As the prospectus developed we came to the question, who must sign. I said that Bowater
Paper Company of England would have to sign as promoter. Everybody was livid, especially the underwriters, and then the English
executives who were in Montreal. I continued, "I'm here to give an
opinion on Nova Scotia law. It's a Nova Scotia company, and Bowater
is the promoter." The Toronto lawyers and the Montreal lawyers
disagreed, so I suggested they cable their solicitors in England, Allen
& Overy, and refer to a page in Palmer which I gave them. We
received a reply the next morning: "Bowater's is a promoter." It
was only from then onwards that I was really asked for advice.
Eventually the task was completed, the bonds were taken up, the
preference share issue sold, and all the assets put into the new
company[61] – the selling price was $56 million.

We had to assign the newsprint contracts to the new company
with the consent of the newspaper proprietors. I was to draw the
instrument in Canada (Nova Scotia) form, Graustein the US, and
Allen & Overy the English. Mine was one and one-half pages long
when I sent it to Graustein, who sent me back his at about three-
quarters of a page. The English one came as a paragraph without a
single punctuation mark – it was beautiful. I sent it on to Graustein
saying only, "What do you think of the enclosure?" He answered,
"Dear Frank: I wish I had drafted it. Sincerely, Archie." Everyone
was so pleased with my work that they doubled my proposed fee and,
furthermore, advised the Wickwire firm that Stewart, Smith, MacKeen,
Covert and Rogers would be the solicitors for new Mersey.[62]

As if the Mersey deal were not enough, Moirs Limited, of which
the Stewart estate owned a large part, came up for sale. The manager, Roy Otto, told me Moirs could be bought, and should be, in
order to keep the industry in Nova Scotia; that, if outsiders bought
it, the plant would be closed and the manufacturing transferred to
central Canada. I spoke to Roy Jodrey, who was immediately sympathetic. We put together a group – Jodrey, J.H. Mowbray Jones,[63]
C.J. Morrow,[64] and S.C. Oland[65] – and then Jodrey said he would
buy control if I would run the company. I remonstrated that I had
never run anything in my life; his short answer was I could and it
was time I tried. I accepted the challenge and Jodrey acquired control through Argyle Securities, which controlled the common shares;
I invested about $25,000. On 14 September 1956, Jodrey purchased
Moirs and I was elected a director and then president. The first

thing I did was to have the head of each department write out what his department did. I visited at least twice a week, met with the executive committee and began to learn something about the business. When I became president, sales were just under $5 million; when we eventually sold out, sales were nearly $10 million. By installing new equipment, we not only reduced the number of employees from 1,230 to 625 but also began paying dividends. Despite the hours I spent on Moirs, I never took an increase in salary and only drew $4,000 a year. But it was an education; a company needs someone who knows nothing about the business in order to make the people who run it explain why they do things the way they do and whether some other way could be tried. Several times one of the executives suggested I would ruin the business. But reforms brought about great savings and did not adversely affect either sales or quality.

Lionel Forsyth, president of Dominion Steel and Coal Corporation (Dosco) died on New Year's Day 1957 and C.B. (Ben) Lang resigned as chairman to take over pending the appointment of a new president. I was approached to take on the job, but was not remotely interested. Forsyth had once asked me to become his executive assistant with a view to training me up for the job, but on another occasion told me that Dosco had no future in Cape Breton in the long run. The reasons for its being there – cheap coal and coke and cheap iron ore from Wabana (Newfoundland) – no longer applied, and continually increasing freight rates prevented its being competitive in the big upper Canadian markets which Stelco and Algoma had cornered.

Lang was a tired old man and, as a result, Dosco was ripe for the plucking. A.V. Roe Canada[66] was soon to make an offer of cash and shares in exchange for shares in Dosco. Roy Jodrey, who (through Minas Basin Pulp and Power) held a substantial number of Dosco shares, was not long coming to the conclusion that the offer was a "steal."[67] Jodrey was a patriotic Nova Scotian; he hated to see "foreigners take over Nova Scotian companies" – eventually they closed or moved them. Encouraged chiefly by J.H. Mowbray Jones,[68] he began a fight to prevent the takeover. He put up a remarkable resistance, but the odds against him were too heavy; A.V. Roe took over Dosco, called a special meeting of the shareholders and fired Jodrey from the board. Throughout, Jodrey sought my advice; I did the best I could but my heart was really not in it. Not only was I sure he could not win the fight, I feared losing it was going to hurt him. He was not a loser by nature and the fight was taking a heavy toll on him. All his friends encouraged him, but Jodrey was paying all the expenses, which were heavy, and that bothered him too. I vetted all the advertisements his side was publishing; I checked the letters he was writing; I advised him what he could and could not say. I wanted to do my best to ensure he did not provoke libel actions, and that he did not, in his anger, get into trouble. My last act in the Dosco fight was to advise Jodrey not to bring any lawsuits.

One of the bitterest pills to swallow came at the height of the fight, when Frank Sobey, a fellow member of the Dosco board who had originally sided with Jodrey, left the Jodrey camp and joined the foe.[69] We investigated the president and managing director of A.V. Roe, Crawford Gordon, of whom the magazines and newspapers wrote glowing articles. Close examination of his record showed he was a glib talker, had little business experience, and that his operations were cost-plus Government projects.[70] We sent an engineer through the A.V. Roe plants and they reported waste and extravagance. Jodrey was sure A.V. Roe would not do well with Dosco, and said so. Jodrey also had inside information that the Avro Arrow contract was going to be cancelled by Prime Minister Diefenbaker. All these things were denied. In 1959, however, Diefenbaker did cancel the Arrow contract. Though all of his prophecies came true, Jodrey was later invited to rejoin the Dosco board and also to join the A.V. Roe board; he did so. Jodrey maintained his holdings in Dosco and saw them go down, down, down.[71] I wanted him to sell, but he was very stubborn about it. Jodrey overcame his bitterness and he and Sobey became friends again. I was to observe over the years that Jodrey, though he would, like an elephant, never forget, did not bear a grudge.

The Dosco fight occupied much of 1957, but I spent as little time on it as possible. Ten years later Dosco announced it was closing the steel plant in Sydney, which resulted in the Nova Scotia government's purchasing it in November 1967. I wrote Premier G.I. Smith telling him that while I understood the immediate necessity to preserve jobs, the acquisition ought to have a definite limited time period, so that people would know there was a cut-off. I further stated that if the government did not do so, in the long run purchasing the Sydney steelworks would turn out to be one of the most expensive blunders in the history of the province. This has proved true.[72]

It was also in 1957 that the new Conservative premier, Robert Stanfield, told me he was going to form a company to help develop industry in Nova Scotia and asked whether I would take on the presidency. I met with the cabinet and discussed the plan and finally, after discussions with the head of the firm, H.P. MacKeen, advised the premier that I would set up the company for him and work with the board, but that I would not become president. MacKeen told me that Stanfield was asking me, a strong Liberal, to become president, so that the Liberals would not criticize the company. I incorporated Industrial Estates Limited (IEL)[73] and suggested a list of directors from various parts of Nova Scotia – all prominent businessmen.[74] When the company was incorporated and the board appointed, the board asked me to become president; again I refused, and Frank Sobey (a director) took on the presidency.[75] The first thing the IEL board did was pass resolutions appointing the solicitors and auditors and providing that they should not be chosen by the cabinet but by the board. Our firm was chosen as solicitors and I turned the file over to J. William E. Mingo, who over many years did extensive work for the company.

When IEL was set up I told the premier that the government should not interfere with it, but that whenever a plant was opened the president of IEL should officiate. In this way, if the plant was a success, the government would get the credit for setting up IEL. If the plant was a failure, then the IEL board would have to take the blame. I also advised that IEL should not help companies that needed money; ideally, companies such as General Motors or General Electric should found subsidiaries. IEL had many successes and some failures. At first, when plants were opened, the IEL president made the speech of the day. Later, I noticed the premier or a minister of the government became the man of the hour.[76] In the years to come there were two very important decisions to be made and the board showed me a brief they were presenting to the premier. I said the IEL board, not the premier, should be the one to make the decision; that was what they were there for. The board's excuse was that "there was so much money involved." I remonstrated that that was all the more reason why the board should make the decision. They let the premier make the decision and it was a political decision, not a business one; the result was disastrous in the long run.

Having done it once, the board did it again, and again the decision was political and again the results were costly and disastrous.[77] To me it is no secret why, as a rule, government-run business operations are unsuccessful. The reason is that a good politician gets re-elected and then makes political decisions which quite often are anything but good business decisions.

Fleming Blanchard McCurdy was wealthy by Nova Scotia standards.[78] Under his will Dalhousie University was one of the residuary legatees,[79] so in June 1958 the board appointed me watching counsel to attend the closing of the estate.[80] When I read through the accounts I was shocked at what I saw.[81] Eastern Trust Company (ETC), as co-executor of the estate of its late president, had sold properties to its own employees at less than inventory value; had been late filing succession duty returns; and had paid interest at six per cent, while investing estate funds in their own trustee certificates at three per cent and depositing several hundred thousand dollars in a current account carrying no interest at all. At the first day of hearings I cross-examined a witness for ETC, who frankly admitted these things and more. ETC had also, without approval of the court, already paid itself a substantial commission, which it included in its annual financial statements and on which it paid tax. The solicitor for the estate[82] secured an adjournment. A meeting of ETC's board was then held, at which I was severely criticized on the grounds that if a charity like Dalhousie was going to treat an executor in such a manner, then testators would not bequeath money to it. This criticism was carried to Dalhousie itself, where the matter was debated at a board meeting.[83] I pointed out, first, that the board included three directors of ETC, all of whom ought to declare their interest and perhaps refrain from voting; secondly, that I deemed it my duty to ensure that my client, Dalhousie University, received all that was coming to it; and, finally, that I had called no witnesses; the only evidence against ETC had been given by its own employees. Therefore, if ETC was right, the court would so hold; if wrong, the court would so find. I told the board that if Dalhousie did not want me to pursue the matter on that basis, they should retain another solicitor. The board asked me to continue.

The probate judge[84] cut ETC's fees by a large amount after argument. It was a great victory for me; despite that, when Roy Jodrey[85] first heard what had happened, he upbraided me publicly in the Halifax Club; of course, he had heard only one side of the story. I wrote him at length pointing out that that same trust company of which he was a director was an executor of *his* will, and asked whether he would want his estate managed in that manner.[86] It was the only argument Roy Jodrey and I ever had and he settled it one night at his house by just taking the letter I had written out of his pocket and shaking hands with me; neither of us said another word.

Mersey Paper Company's mill at Brooklyn in Queens County, Nova Scotia, was built in 1928–29. When Bowater bought it in 1956, a valuation of the mill was made by Stone & Webster Engineering Corporation and the results of the valuation became public property, by virtue of its inclusion in the prospectus for the sale of the preferred share issue. Thus it came to the knowledge of the tax assessor for the Municipality of the County of Queens, which had just built a new consolidated school.[87] In 1958 Mersey's property was reassessed so that it looked as if Mersey might pay for the County's new school in one year. The case was difficult to answer, for we were going to have to call the same expert and let him explain the difference between a valuation for pricing shares and a valuation for municipal assessment. The Municipality was firm and negotiations hopeless. The County Court judge[88] was less than sympathetic; our expert, though bright enough, just did not have the knack of explaining things in simple terms and gave incomplete answers under cross-examination. We had to appeal to the Supreme Court in Banco to get a favourable decision.[89] The point was that Mersey was a going concern: its product sold out every year, its order book was filled, its wood suppliers were in place, and there were hundreds of contracts, including one of the most advantageous power contracts in the country.[90] The total purchase price took goodwill into account, while the valuation of the properties by Stone & Webster was based on replacement cost less observed depreciation. I had Harry Rhude[91] with me and he really did all the trial and appeal work, while I sat by and watched. There were times when I despaired of success, but the work we put into it finally paid off. The Municipality was happy, because even the revised assessment caused a tremendous improvement in their finances. Over the years since, the two parties have realized the importance of one to the other and their relationship has been a good one.

In 1958 Arthur Stairs, who owned the shares from his late father's estate as well as those acquired from the Stewart estate, decided he would sell Maritime Paper Products,[92] a small corrugated cardboard box plant, which had a reputation for quality and service and which was the main customer of Jodrey's Minas Basin paperboard mill. There were two likely bidders: Canadian International Paper (CIP) and Bathurst Paper.[93] Jodrey eventually got together with Bathurst and they bid on and acquired Maritime Paper. We worked out a deal with Bathurst, whereby it would own one-third and Minas Basin two-thirds and each would supply one-half of the paperboard. Again Jodrey wanted to keep Maritime Paper from falling into foreign hands, so by persuading Bathurst to go in with him he was obtaining tremendous know-how as well as eliminating a prospective competitor from the bidding. Again Jodrey said he would go ahead if I would take on the presidency; I did and by 1980 had been president for 22 years.

In reality Maritime Paper Products was a holding company for the manufacturing company, Industrial Containers. When Minas Basin bought control, Maritime Paper had no surplus moved up, while Industrial Containers had years of accumulated surplus. There was no change in control, however, so the surplus of Industrial Containers was not designated. We acquired Maritime Paper in December 1958 and in January 1959 moved up the surplus from Industrial Containers, whereupon Maritime Paper declared tax-free dividends to Minas Basin and Bathurst, which then paid down the loans taken out to purchase control. The partnership between Bathurst and Minas Basin worked out well: Bathurst had a good customer in Maritime Paper, while Minas Basin obtained a partner who supplied all the plans for the new plant which Maritime Paper built in 1967[94] – a replica of one of Consolidated-Bathurst's own new plants. Maritime Paper Products completed, and had all the kinks ironed out of the operation of its new plant, so that, on 22 May 1968, we had the official opening with hundreds of invited guests. As president, I made a speech saying that I would not have dared; it was the Jodreys, Roy and his son John,[95] who had the courage and the foresight. More than anything I admired the courage of the Jodreys, for building the new plant meant years of losses and no dividends; but after many years it began to pay off. In the long run, had we not taken the risk, I suspect we would have died in our old location. I was even able to negotiate the sale of the old plant.

Maritime Paper and Bathurst competed for customers and occasionally there were differences; but Bathurst, from the very beginning, had a man at the top, Spike Irwin, who settled every difference with the wisdom of Solomon. As president of both Moirs and Maritime Paper Products, I put a team to work and, as soon as I found I had the right man for the job, gave the general manager complete freedom of action. The manager liked it that way and soon I had little or no work to do.[96]

In August 1958 I had my first strike, at Oland Breweries. In the thirteen years I had been negotiating collective agreements I had not met anyone with whom I could not negotiate – until Harold Martel, the union negotiator. Martel was stubborn, obstinate, unyielding, and dogmatic; he did not even know the meaning of the word compromise. For a time I wondered whether it was possible to meet anyone so unreasonable. He later negotiated for unions other than the Brewery and Soft Drink Workers Union;[97] everywhere he went he was the same, calling foolish and useless strikes. I could see the strike coming; we heard that Martel had advised his superiors a brewery could not stand a strike more than two weeks. I advised Olands that, with a man as stubborn as Martel, the strike would last for months, maybe even six months. The strike was a pathetic, useless one which went on for five months. When it was finally settled, on 14 January 1959, the union gained nothing; the contract was extended by the length of the strike. There was never a strike at Olands again.

During the early part of 1959 Fred Manning was working on the problems of I&DCV, had incorporated a company, Venezuelan Power,[98] to take over the power company, and was doing a public share issue for Venezuelan Power. In February he made me co-executor of his will and explained to me the tremendous value of North Star Oil. In May and June he spent a lot of time in Venezuela and in late June we went to Ottawa to discuss Venezuelan Power with the Secretary of State.[99] After we left Ottawa on 29 June Manning had gone on a fishing trip to New Brunswick. On 8 July I saw him at Michael Dwyer's cocktail party,[100] when I thought he looked a little less strained. I had to leave the party early to go to Dean Horace Read's house, where we were meeting to select the Dunn Scholarship winners.[101] When I arrived home I received the news, "Fred Manning is dead." He had died in his car at the top of Michael Dwyer's roadway. Two months later I succeeded Manning as president of Great Eastern Corporation.

Manning's corporate co-executor, Eastern Trust, wanted to call immediately for tenders on North Star Oil, on the grounds that the estate was losing interest on the moneys that would accrue from its sale. I wanted first to settle the succession duties as to its value. Eventually Roy Jodrey spoke to ETC and told them they were fools not to take my advice. Then came meetings with oil companies from all over: British American Oil, Canadian Petrofina, Shell Oil, Husky Oil, Royalite, Texaco, and many others I had never heard of. We refused to discuss price or terms, but assured each of them that when we sold, we would send out notice. In the meantime we learned all we could about North Star Oil and had meetings with the company management. Then in December I had a three-day session with the Department of National Revenue, at which we agreed on a price per share of $2 above the listed price on the day of Manning's death. We signed an agreement to the effect that, regardless of the eventual sale price, the agreed price was binding on both parties and there would be no appeal. It saved the estate millions. On 6 January 1960 tenders for the sale of North Star Oil were opened; the three top bidders were Shell Oil, British American Oil, and Canadian Petrofina. Shell was five cents per share above B/A and B/A five cents above Petrofina; and they were all more than double the market price per share. What Manning had told me proved correct; everybody wanted to buy North Star Oil. The Manning estate was happy; the only unhappy tenderers were B/A Oil and Canadian Petrofina, both of whom would have gladly bid ten cents or fifteen cents per share more. They had all bid higher than the figure they thought North Star Oil would bring – just to make sure of getting it. Shell Oil became a client after the sale.

The North Star Oil sale meant many things. To begin with, we had to consult with a recalcitrant management that was not anxious to become part of the Shell organization and did everything to try to block our progress. Then the underwriter of Shell stock had sold two classes: voting, which Shell paid handsomely for, and non-voting, for which the offer was much less; of course, Shell wanted to acquire not the share control that the Manning estate held but 100 per cent of the shares. Shell asked me to work with them, which I did, in Montreal, Toronto, and Winnipeg. Eventually everything was settled and the Manning estate had the money to invest.

In March and April 1960 we invested $600,000 (in one day) for Great Eastern Corporation and $625,000 for the Manning estate. I had to go to Montreal and Ottawa on the valuation, for succession duty purposes, of Great Eastern. The Department of National Revenue had engaged Royal Securities Corporation, while I retained Pitfields. It was a ding-dong battle, because the Department was upset over the North Star Oil valuation. We also set up all the charities in perpetuity for the Manning Estate Charitable Fund; in March 1961 I had retroactive legislation enacted to prevent duties being exacted on the charities.[102]

These were strenuous days; again Eastern Trust wanted all the estate's money invested in bonds, which were paying $6\frac{1}{4}$ or $6\frac{1}{2}$ per cent, "the like of which" they said, we shall never see again. I bitterly opposed this and, finally, with Jodrey's help, persuaded ETC to back down. The Charitable Fund saw the bonds drop at least 20 per cent in value and the stocks double, so that the eventual yield on the stocks was double that of the bonds. I lost all faith in the Eastern Trust Company. Fortunately, the moneys that came into Great Eastern were invested entirely in Canadian common stocks, which grew beautifully. We never let ETC have any say in the operations of Great Eastern, though, year in and year out, they wanted to.

POSTSCRIPT

On 18 November 1959 I dined with Lester Pearson, who had succeeded Louis St-Laurent as leader of the Liberal Party.[103] Two days later, he telephoned asking me to become treasurer of the party – said to be a sure road to a senatorship. The answer was no; I was not the man for the job.[104]

CHAPTER EIGHT

The Sixties

In 1960 I was retained twice by the Canadian Manufacturers Association to prepare and present briefs on trade union matters – once before the Legislature's law amendments committee to oppose the unions' request for legislation making union shops compulsory.[1] This led directly to the appointment in July 1960 of A.H. McKinnon[2] as a "fact-finding body" to study the Trade Union Act and labour legislation generally; the Nova Scotia branch of the CMA retained me to present a brief. In February 1962 Judge McKinnon filed his report, in which he suggested that labour and management should consult together and work out their differences rather than going unilaterally to the government for legislation. The McKinnon Report resulted in the establishment, in May 1962, of the Nova Scotia Joint Labour-Management Study Committee, at the invitation of Dalhousie University's Institute of Public Affairs.[3] Originally a group of businessmen and labour leaders meeting in secret, we began to get a better understanding of each other's problems; after months of meetings, we agreed on certain points for submission to a seminar composed of labour and business representatives.[4] Over the years, the Joint Study Committee (JSC) became influential; governments of the day consulted it and never introduced legislation relating to the Trade Union Act without the prior approval of the JSC. By 1963 the Committee was in full swing; we met every month for at least four or five hours, had meetings with cabinet, the premier, and the minister of labour, and appeared on local radio to explain to the general public what was happening.

The committee continued until 1979, when it collapsed because the management members would not condemn legislation introduced by the new Conservative government of John Buchanan.[5] The labour members, led by a trade unionist with less wisdom than mouth, retired from the committee and thus helped kill an organization that had fostered labour management relations that were perhaps the best in Canada. I spent many hours working on the committee and was one of the few old originals left when it fell apart. Twice before, when the labour representatives threatened to quit over differences with the management representatives, I almost single-handedly convinced them they had a great deal to gain and nothing to lose by staying in and fighting on. Unfortunately, I was away during the crucial session in 1979,[6] but I doubt whether even I could have deterred Gerald Yetman.[7]

Early in 1960, I was retained by Metropolitan Life to act as their Nova Scotia counsel in the Nova Scotia Pulp[8] bond issue. We had received advance information and questions from New York counsel, Willkie Farr, so on 24 February, Bill Mingo and I went to New York expecting to be one, two, or three days; we were there for twelve. We left Nova Scotia in the dead of winter (there had been a thirty-inch snowfall early in February), so Bill and I were wearing overcoats, scarves, and overshoes. When we arrived at the offices of Shearman & Sterling & Wright[9] – note the two ampersands – we looked in through the glass doors and saw a deep-piled white carpet; so we took off our overshoes, walked up to the reception desk with briefcases in one hand and overshoes in the other, gave our names, and were told we were expected. The receptionist pointed to a door at the end of the hall where we were to go. As we left, I noticed another woman come up to the reception desk and heard her say, "There's a couple of kids from the country if I ever saw any." When we entered the conference room there were eight lawyers around the table. After being introduced and welcomed, I told the "country kids" story. Our host, rather than seeing the humour of it, was quite upset. I thought to myself, "This is going to be difficult." We worked day after day and most evenings; it was the old story of ten lawyers each wanting to have a hand in, and improve the draftsmanship of the others – a terrible waste of time.

In the autumn of 1966 the president and general manager of Nova Scotia Pulp, Karl A. Clauson, had a dispute with Stora Kopparbergs, in which Shearman & Sterling & Wright sided with Stora. Clauson came to us for advice and Mingo and I worked on his claim; under the terms of the contract, an arbitrator was appointed in New York, so we engaged a small firm there to make the presentation. I have found again and again that a lot of the corporation law firms in New York are very weak on litigation; our small firm won the case completely.

James Muir, chairman and president of the Royal Bank, died on 10 April 1960, and at his funeral on the 14th I saw the infighting already starting. Because the board could not agree on the man who was the logical successor, K.M. Sedgewick,[10] late in May we elected Madison (Matt) Walter,[11] who died a little over six months later. We met again in December to elect W. Earle McLaughlin, who held the position for nearly twenty years. It was my first opportunity really to see the executive suite in action – Sedgewick blew it.[12]

On 31 December 1960 C.D. Howe died; an American by birth, he had become perhaps Canada's greatest Canadian. This country owed its war contribution in large measure to his organizational genius; Canada's becoming an industrial giant was due to his foresight during the war and his work as minister of reconstruction after it. We had become close friends and I spent some wonderful hours with him after the war. I once asked why he stayed in politics and stood the criticism that he received. He grinned broadly and said, "I often wonder myself." Then he added, "However, every once in awhile something happens that makes it worthwhile;" and told me of his hours alone with Churchill, the other prime ministers of England after the war, and the leaders of India – "something," he said, "which would never happen to me in the business world."

In January 1961 Lord Thomson had me try to buy the Halifax *Chronicle-Herald*. I met with Gordon McLaren Daley (the proprietor's lawyer) and Graham Dennis (the proprietor), whose answer was that no matter how good or how attractive the offer, there would be no sale. Dennis said they regarded the ownership of the newspaper as a trust for Nova Scotians. Years later, in the 1970s, I was to try again for John A. Tory, president of the Thomson Corporation; the answer was the same.[13]

Early in July 1961 a group of farmers, headed by Harold F. Curry and J. Watson Maxner, came to see me about forming a co-op to buy Farmers Limited and Maple Leaf Dairy. They said it was time the farmers made the money instead of people not in the business, but that they had no money. Though they had been referred to me, Curry said he was afraid someone of my reputation would not think much of co-ops. I told them that, when I was a young man, my father, a country doctor, had brought a co-op man all the way from California to try to convince the apple growers to form a co-op, but they turned him down. My father always said that, as a result, the farmers never made the money; it was made by the speculators. I said to Curry, "I'm with you, but you couldn't sell a public issue on a co-op." I asked how many farmers would go into the deal and whether, if the bank advanced the money, the co-op would submit to a check-off to reduce the loan. We met many times and I brought in the bank, which agreed to advance the money on the basis of an assignment of the check-off funds. Then we negotiated with the owner of Maple Leaf Dairy,[14] who also controlled Farmers. I had the farmers themselves act as salesmen and gather up all the outside shares of Farmers in exchange for new co-op shares and/or cash. It worked so well that Curry always referred to me as the midwife at the birth of Twin City Co-op, which became a very large and successful organization owned by the farmers.[15] I was put on the board but, a few years later, sensing that the farmers wanted all farmers on the board, I sent in my resignation. They let me keep my share, so I continued to receive the annual report and an invitation to the annual meeting. I have always been very proud of the part I played in the formation of the co-op and regard it as one of the best things I have done in the practice of law.

Ben's Limited, the leading bakery in Halifax, was owned by Ben Moir,[16] whose father and namesake started it in competition with Moirs Limited. Unable to use the name Moirs, Ben Moir Sr called his company Ben's. During the war, his son wisely refrained from bidding on war contracts for the army and navy. While Moirs took these on for the fast buck, Ben's continued to expand their routes and, after the war, ended up with the bigger volume, which Moirs could never get back. Moirs Limited bread bakery was second fiddle, even in its own organization, where candy and chocolates were king. In the autumn of 1961, hearing that Ben's Limited was for sale, I wrote Ben Moir, who came to my office with his accountant, Harvey Crowell. Moir named his price, which was about $600,000 too high. I pointed out that if he got the extra $600,000, over one-half of it would go on succession duties, so he should get used to the idea that he was really talking about $300,000. Furthermore – and the same went for income on the investment – only about thirty per cent could be retained, as Moir was in the top tax bracket. I told him that as he had stripped the surplus, it would take us a long time to pay off the purchase loan; he would not sell assets, only shares, so as not to have any tax problems (there was no capital gains tax at the time). I think Crowell saw I was making progress, for he told Moir there was "no deal here" and that they had better go.

As Moir got up to leave I said, "If you change your mind, we want you to stay as a director and join the Moirs board." He had not been gone ten minutes when he came back to say: "If I sell for $2,400,000, when can you have the money?" It was then 30 October. I said, "If we sign in two days, I'll have it for you before the middle of November." We shook hands, saying, "It's a deal."

Now I had to win over Roy Jodrey, whom I telephoned and told what had happened. He said that John[17] said the price was high. I explained I could have the interest on the loan allowed for and that we could turn over the Moirs bakery to Ben's.

"You really want it, don't you?"

"Yes."

"Then go ahead."

It took less than ten minutes on the phone. On 2 November we signed a short purchase agreement, on the 14th we took over Ben's Limited, and on the 15th I was elected a director and president – the firm had a new client. Under the tax laws, if a company borrowed to buy shares in another Canadian company, the interest was not deductible as an expense, because the dividend from the purchased company flowed up tax-free to the purchasing one. Therefore, when Moirs borrowed to buy shares in Ben's Limited, the interest on the loan was a non-deductible expense. However, Moirs stopped paying its bills, the Christmas trade money came in, and when we had accumulated $2.6 million we paid off the loan; less than two months' interest was lost. Moirs then borrowed from the bank for working capital. I had no trouble negotiating with the Department of National Revenue. Ben's took over Moirs' bakery, amalgamated it with its own, and operated profitably afterwards.

In 1962[18] I was elected to four more boards: Canadian Petrofina, Bowater Mersey Paper, General Mortgage Service Corporation (a new company with head office in Toronto), and Nova Scotia Light and Power (NSL&P).[19] Election to the board of NSL&P was a dream come true. In the days before the war I had done a great deal of work for NSL&P, which was a major company with a board where one could learn a lot. It was the only client that did not come back to me after the war. When a vacancy did occur,[20] the board split equally on the candidates and neither of the two proposed was elected.[21] Finally, thanks to Roy Jodrey, supported by Gordon B. Isnor,[22] I was elected to the board on the next vacancy.[23]

In June 1963 I prepared a power brief for NSL&P and in September a group of us presented it to the new Liberal minister of finance – Walter Gordon. Our group had presented a similar brief to George Nowlan when he was minister of finance.[24] The two interviews were an object lesson in politics. Nowlan said he was familiar with the brief and the problem and would like very much to hear us and to take as much time as we needed; at the end everybody was happy, because he expressed his agreement with our brief. He never did anything about it. Yet everyone left the room saying what a fine minister he was; I said nothing because I knew Nowlan. Gordon, on the other hand, told us he had read the brief, asked a few questions, said he did not need to hear any more, and that he doubted much could be done. Everybody felt angry, frustrated and disappointed; called him conceited, not a good minister. Yet Gordon secured passage of the amendment to the Income Tax Act, which we had asked for.[25] Walter Gordon was anything but a politician; George Nowlan was a past master of the game.

In February 1963 H.P. MacKeen, with whom I had worked for thirty-three years, was appointed lieutenant-governor of Nova Scotia.[26] One of nature's noblemen, MacKeen may have been the greatest trial lawyer ever to grace the bar of Nova Scotia. It is doubtful whether anyone had a success equal to his. Preparation was the key to his developing into a true forensic orator. Though a slow starter – most of the trial work was done by C.B. Smith – after the war MacKeen began to come into his own. He and his wife, Alice (Al), brought a new dimension to Government House, where MacKeen did many things to bring importance to the office. His speeches were gems, which I begged him to save and have collected in a book. He polished and shined his speeches, as he did his pleadings and jury addresses.

By the time MacKeen died, in April 1971, we had been associated for over forty years. The only disagreement we ever had was in 1955, when I took on the presidency of Moirs Limited without consulting him and he read about it in the newspaper. The whole matter was supposed to be very confidential; his younger brother

Jack was one of the parties involved and Harry had not heard about it from either of us. Looking back, I realize I should have told him; after all he was the head of the firm. He soon got over it, however, and our friendship continued to his death. Though asked to be a pallbearer at his funeral, I felt so badly about his death I doubted whether I could attend without breaking down; and my hypoglycaemia was at its worst. The family were very understanding. With MacKeen dead, all the partners who were there when I went to work for the firm were gone; I felt a great sense of emptiness.

In February 1964 I was asked to join the board of Sun Life Assurance Company of Canada, but not until a vacancy occurred in February 1966 – they spoke for you early. I accepted, of course, and in 1965 resigned as a director of Acadia Life. It was a very prestigious board, Sun Life being the largest life insurance company in Canada, with substantial business in the UK and USA and an excellent reputation. The members of the board were leading industrialists from all across Canada. Sun Life had a huge common stock portfolio, which it maintained through thick and thin, bearing out my theory that, in the long run, common stocks are the best investment. It was Sun Life, incidentally, which, thirty years earlier, had turned down my application for a $5,300 mortgage on our first house.

By 1967 Sun Life was worried about keeping its head office in Montreal, where the FLQ had been particularly active; there were indications it was losing business because of the situation in Quebec. The Parizeau Committee[27] did not report until June 1969, but it was apparent as early as 1965 that the government of Quebec might place restrictions on Sun Life's operations. As a result, senior management at Sun Life wanted a brief prepared on how to move its head office out of Quebec – what this would mean, the advantages and disadvantages, and whether or not it could be prevented from doing so. In December 1967 I was retained to prepare the brief and I worked on it through March 1968, together with Richard Hurlburt[28] and a very famous attorney brought in from Washington to assist us.[29] We produced a brief nearly two inches thick, including exhibits, a draft document, and case summaries.[30]

In April 1968, I was asked to, and did present the brief to the executive committee and afterwards to the full board. At the time there were four men on the Sun Life board who would hardly have dared vote in favour of the move because of their positions in business in Montreal.[31] Indeed they might have had to resign from the board, which would have been disastrous. Not only would the head office move require a unanimous (or nearly unanimous) vote of the board; it was equally important it not become known that the move was contemplated until everything was in place. There were constitutional problems involved, not to mention a host of legal niceties. But above all it required the exercise of careful judgement. In sum and substance I pointed out how the move could be done and the care that would have to be taken. I warned that it would be an earth-shaking event in Canada, but that the longer it was delayed the more difficult it would become. The executive committee were of the opinion that there were members of the board who would undoubtedly feel they had to resign if the move were made. So it was postponed. Little did anyone think that ten years later[32] the move would be made and would cause much trouble.

Ben's Limited did their own labour negotiations, just keeping me advised as to progress and what the offer was. Suddenly, on 2 August 1964, they called to say their employees[33] had gone on strike and asked me to see whether I could settle it. A strike in a bakery usually has disastrous results: the customers quickly buy another brand, the competition prospers greatly, and it takes time to win back lost customers. I worked at it very hard, until finally the International representative[34] came down from Toronto after a telephone call to me. When he arrived, I asked him to bring along the union negotiator who had called the strike.[35] I then outlined point by point the demands, the offer, and the differences. By way of comparison I also outlined the competitors' contract. I asked the negotiator to deny or admit point by point and he admitted every one I raised. The International representative asked him what the hell he had called a strike for, then sent him out of the room, and asked me whether there was anything we could do to save face for the union. I told him I would prepare and sign a joint statement showing nothing but gains that the union had made; this would help them publicly. Ben's management disapproved, because they had offered the very same things before the strike. I argued it did not matter at all – we knew, the union knew, and the employees knew. I also told them that a short strike did nobody any good; it took at least a seven- or eight-week strike to teach both sides a lesson and I presumed they did not want that. I also pointed out that their methods of bargaining were conducive to strike action. Finally I told the International representative that I was leaving on vacation the night of the 8th and would not be back until 7 September, so he had better settle the strike. He asked for one little change to a fringe benefit, so that he could go back to the union and say they did gain something. I granted it and the strike was settled. I did not count the strike at Ben's as one of mine because I had not negotiated the contract; I still had a record of one strike in 19 years,[36] of which I was very proud. The strike had lasted seven days; it took months to get all the customers back.

In January 1965 I was elected to the board of Trizec Corporation Limited,[37] a real estate company with shopping centres, offices, and apartment buildings. It had an aggressive, youthful management that provided excellent information to the directors so that board meetings were fascinating. Their jewel in the crown was Montreal's cruciform Place Ville Marie, head office of the Royal Bank. By 1976 the Bronfmans had gained control under an arrangement with the English co-owners, so that the company would not be classed as foreign under the Foreign Investment Review Act. One morning early in June, I had a call from their lawyer on the board,[38] who asked me when next I would be in Montreal, as he wanted to see me. I had nothing to take me there for two weeks; he seemed disappointed, so I asked him what he wanted to see me about. He told me that the Bronfmans wanted their own men on the board – assured me I was not the only one being called.

I said, "You want me to resign?"

"Yes."

I asked when; he said, "As soon as possible."

"You have it now."

I confirmed it in writing. Later I found out that several others had met the same fate; afterwards several, including the chairman and president, resigned as well. I missed the meetings; Trizec was a very aggressive company and a great acquisitionist.[39] It had all been extremely interesting.[40]

I had worked for many clients setting up private investment holding companies in order to provide for themselves and their families. One day in 1965 I told Bill Mingo it was time I did so for myself but could not seem to find the time. He said he would do it for me if I would give him the instructions. And so in May 1965 we incorporated a company, Canning Investment Corporation (CIC) named after my hometown. We retained Pitfields to sell a public issue of preferred irredeemable and preferred voting shares and prepare the prospectus; I sold most of my securities at market value to CIC and bought most of the common stock, selling lots of 100 shares each to my friends who would be directors: Percy Smith, Sheldon Fountain,[41] John Jodrey, and Bill Mingo. These four, with me, made up the board; Percy Smith became president and Mingo secretary. As the preferred shares had as many votes as the common, some of which did not belong to me, I did *not* control the company; hence, dividends would accrue tax-free. The company grew and prospered and the board invested wisely. Unfortunately, in later years, the law was changed so that unless its shares were listed on a stock exchange the company was subject to tax. Nevertheless, CIC has done well. Though control no longer mattered, I gradually bought up the preferred shares, so that by 1980 Mollie and I controlled the company. From an original income of $22,000 per annum, its dividend multiplied at least six times in fifteen years and its value grew over three times.

In 1965 I tried unsuccessfully to negotiate the sale of Moirs to Standard Brands Limited.[42] Though retail sales were increasing, volumes were constant and in some lines falling off. Salaries and wages were low, though they had increased greatly since my taking over ten years earlier. The multi-storey plant and inside transportation were very expensive to operate. I foresaw vulnerability for the boxed chocolate business, the more so in that we had been unable to develop the chocolate bar business, where the real profit lay. I prepared a brief on the subject, while management wrote a counterbrief, a large part of which I could demolish and which eventually turned out to be badly skewed. Though the plant lay on valuable land in the heart of downtown Halifax, management could not think of anything but asset values, which are not much good if one cannot earn a fair yield on the investment. We could sell Moirs' assets and business, while keeping Ben's Limited assets and business and the timber limits[43] in Bedford. J.H. Mowbray Jones,[44] who was on the board, opposed the scheme on the grounds that we should get more. (Mobe always wanted more for anything he owned.) Anyway, led by him, the board rejected the offer, so we carried on.

I foresaw great problems ahead. Moirs needed something to go with it or it was doomed to die. Throughout 1967 I lobbied a big drug company, Warner Lambert; but, when they saw the earnings and the low wages paid, they were not interested. Finally, on 21 September

1967, I got the board to agree that I should again approach Standard Brands, which had remained interested. On 20 and 21 October I worked out the terms of sale and, with the board's approval, on the 24th announced the sale first to our employees and then to the press. On 13 and 14 November we concluded a formal agreement with Standard Brands. This was followed by special shareholders meetings, which approved the sale finally on 12 December; the closing took place on the 28th and 29th. Moirs' name was changed to Ben's Holdings Limited, sole owner of Ben's Limited, a successful bakery which made more money than Moirs did. Ben's owned timber limits in Bedford, which we sold and invested the proceeds in Canadian common stocks. By 1968 I had the pleasure of helping invest over $1 million for Ben's Holdings – I wanted to invest it all in Canadian stocks, while the investment advisers wanted it in American stocks. (John Jodrey said there was no point engaging experts if one did not take their advice. So we did buy some American stocks.) Events had proved Moirs management wrong. Though we sold at the same price and on the same terms, we really lost money by the delay because, when we did sell, we invested in stocks at a higher price. However, it worked out alright: the securities tripled in value and Ben's Holdings did well. Had Jodrey kept Moirs, it would have been bankrupt.

Standard Brands operated the Moirs' plant, but even with enhancements could not do so successfully. In 1972 they decided to close it down; I knew they would have to do this eventually. I pointed out that they would be closing two little plants before long, so ought to consider building a small plant in Dartmouth, which could produce something other than chocolates if necessary, and persuaded them to approach the government. We had an initial conference with Premier Regan and, so says my diary, "Things are going to work out alright." They did. With the help of IEL, Standard Brands built a new and modern plant in Dartmouth (Woodside). I also negotiated for Standard Brands concerning the proposed new plant and attended the sod-turning, on 8 November 1973.[45] Standard Brands operated the new and modern plant in Dartmouth with less than one-quarter the number of employees. Then in 1974 there was a dispute with the Sobeys, who said they had a verbal commitment of first refusal on the old Moirs' property on Argyle Street. They threatened and got my back up. I had Trizec look at the property and they made a good bid on it; then Standard Brands gave Sobeys first refusal, which they met. Though the sale did not take place until August 1975, Standard Brands was very pleased. Sobeys had the site purchased for Scotia Square.[46] When the property was later expropriated, our firm acted for Halifax Developments and got a good award – so everybody made money. The City of Halifax had the Metro Centre on prime real estate rather than the old, multi-storey, ugly Moirs factory.[47]

Mollie and I were in France during the Canadian federal election of November 1965 and had a difficult time obtaining information about it. The election changed the party standings hardly at all – it really was abortive. We were dining at the Tour d'Argent in Paris; among the guests were two young Canadians whom I asked whether Robert Winters[48] had been elected. They did not know, but asked me whether Pierre Elliot Trudeau had been elected. When I replied I had never heard of him, they were both shocked and told me how he had fought Maurice Duplessis almost single-handedly in the pages of *Cité Libre*. I made a note and, when I got back to Canada, looked into the matter and followed Trudeau's career, read his speeches on the Limitation of Capital Punishment bill[49] and on the new Divorce Act, and watched him at the federal-provincial conferences. I wrote Trudeau a letter saying that he should try for the leadership of the Liberal Party when Pearson stepped down. He waited until Pearson announced his retirement and then wrote me.[50]

On 30 March, five days before the leadership convention began, I had a private meeting with Trudeau – one of the nine candidates. I had never met anyone who listened so intently and answered so fully, so directly and with no evasion whatsoever. I did not believe a politician could last long who did. On the the night of 5 April, while the leadership convention was in progress, J.C. MacKeen had a party at his house; among those present was Robert Stanfield, who had gone through his party's convention the previous autumn to become leader of the opposition. He was holding court and I heard him express the view that the Liberal Party would not accept Trudeau. I said, "Bob, the wish is father to the thought; they will select Trudeau because it's the turn of a French Canadian and, furthermore, he's the only man who could beat you." On 6 April, Trudeau became leader of the Liberal Party and prime minister. Shortly afterwards he dissolved Parliament, called an election, and on 25 June was elected by a sweeping majority. I almost felt sorry for Stanfield – until Trudeau came along he had the prime ministership in his grasp. Re-elected by

a thin minority in 1972, in 1974 Trudeau won a majority. That was
the end of Robert Stanfield's leadership of the Progressive Conservative Party. They always kill their leaders if they do not win.

In August 1966 Gordon Cowan was appointed to the Supreme
Court of Nova Scotia.[51] A Newfoundland native, Cowan was a
Rhodes Scholar and had had a brilliant career in teaching and at
the bar. He joined our firm after I went to Munitions and Supply
and into the RCAF. In those five years, he ended up with all my
clients and it must have been difficult for him to see them gradually
return to me; I appreciated this because I saw how long it took for
some of them *to* return to me. So for awhile there was some tension
between us. Cowan was one of the most brilliant legal minds our
firm ever had and he soon developed a large clientele and a great
reputation. No other lawyer in the firm ever reached the degree of
efficiency that Gordon attained. No one ever had such a neat and
tidy desk; no one thinned, completed, and closed files as he did. He
had an unlimited capacity for work, did it quickly and well, and
was capable in any field he entered. I was surprised that he went
on the bench and asked him what made him do it. It was about
6:30 one afternoon and he said, "You and I are the only two who
haven't gone home to dinner. It will be like this always. I want to
take it easier."

Cowan's years on the Supreme Court were outstanding. In 1967
he became chief justice of the Trial Division. He drafted new Civil
Procedure Rules[52] and whipped his associates into line, so that his
court had a reputation unequalled in Canada. At one time in 1979
there was not an undecided case. Again and again Cowan handed
down oral judgments at the conclusion of the trial. His addresses
to lawyers on their call to the bar were masterpieces of advice. He
did not permit sloppiness or non-compliance with the rules of court.
It is doubtful whether there has ever been his equal in the Supreme
Court of Nova Scotia. His elder son, James, joined our firm after
his father went on the bench;[53] his second son, Hugh, was also with
us for a short time – only to be lured away by the Royal Bank and
thence by Gowling, Strathy & Henderson (Ottawa).

In August 1966 Bell Telephone made an offer to the shareholders
of Maritime Telegraph & Telephone Company (MT&T) that was so
attractive it was bound to succeed.[54] The officers of MT&T did not
want to be taken over and went to see Premier Stanfield, who too
hastily said he would not permit it.[55] He did not want control of

the utility to go out of Nova Scotia. The question was how to stop it. I was on vacation when Bill Mingo called me to ask whether I could find out what the stock exchanges might think of legislation[56] limiting the number of votes any shareholder could have, regardless of the number of shares held. I knew Charles B. Neapole, president of the Montreal Stock Exchange well because he had previously been general manager of the Royal Bank. All Canada knew of Stanfield's statement, so when I called Neapole and asked the question I prefaced it by saying, "This is, at least, not as bad as an expropriation." I got grudging agreement from Neapole, who sounded out Toronto for me, and reported back to Mingo, who drafted the necessary legislation; though opposed by Bell Telephone, it passed.[57] So Bell ended up buying the shares but did not have a controlling interest. MT&T permitted two Bell directors on the board and relations were good, but MT&T executives remained in complete control.

In 1966 Minas Basin Pulp & Power sold the greater part of its timber limits to Scott Paper. For many years Roy Jodrey had been acquiring timberlands, patiently adding to his holdings in order to ensure pulp for his groundwood mill and also the lumber trade with England. When Scott no longer required groundwood pulp and Jodrey only needed a supply for CKF, the question became the cost of carrying the timber limits. Taxes were increasing annually along with the cash needs of municipalities, there was always the danger of forest fires, and the time was coming when expensive silviculture would be required. The debate at the board meeting was not one-sided, and the issue took a long time to resolve. I was in favour of selling and argued that we could invest the proceeds in common stocks earning tax-free income. Eventually we sold for over $9 million and invested the proceeds in common stocks, which have greatly increased in value. Those who were opposed can easily argue that, had we waited a few years, we could have done much better. Scott might have paid the enhanced price for the timber limits, but we would have paid an enhanced price for the stocks.

The death of Charles Gavsie, on 6 July 1967, was a great tragedy – he was just 60. When I was at Munitions and Supply during the early part of the war and the legal branch was looking for lawyers, I recommended Gavsie, who came to Ottawa and I got to know him even better. We travelled to Washington and worked on some big contracts together. When I joined the RCAF, I told C.D. Howe that Gavsie would do my job better than I. Howe told many people that Gavsie was one of the best men he had ever known to get things done the way one wanted them done, and quietly – without fuss or feathers. Gavsie stayed on after the war as general counsel of Reconstruction and Supply and when V.W. Scully[58] was asked to take on the job of deputy minister of National Revenue, he insisted that Gavsie accompany him. When Scully went on to become comptroller (later president) of Stelco,[59] Gavsie succeeded him as deputy minister. Never before had the Department of National Revenue had such a low profile. Then in 1957 Howe needed someone to take Lionel Chevrier's place as president of the St. Lawrence Seaway Authority, and chose Gavsie. On the change of government, Gavsie resigned and joined Montreal's Common, Howard, Cate, Ogilvy, Bishop & Cope (Ogilvy, Renault), soon becoming recognized as one of the leading tax lawyers in Canada. Gavsie was one of my dearest and greatest friends. In his quiet, serene way he gave solid advice and readily solved most problems just on the basis of sheer common sense.

In the spring of 1967 there was a new entry in the labour field in Nova Scotia, Edward James (Ted) Gravefell, who began by calling two strikes, one at Jodrey's CKF plant in Hantsport.[60] A provincial election campaign was in progress[61] and politicians were getting into the act, so the government quickly appointed Judge Nathan Green an industrial inquiry commission to mediate. We met at the courthouse in Windsor, where Gravefell opened by saying the union would strike until Mr Covert came on bended knee, begging to accept the union's demands. Judge Green said he doubted that would happen and suggested we cool off and meet again. I advised Jodrey that, in my view, the strike would have to last seven or eight weeks to teach both sides what a strike meant. As the strike wore on, the strikers became restless, while the people of Hantsport knew that the other two plants[62] were working to acceptable contracts. After about five weeks, I had a telephone call from an anonymous union member asking how the strike could be settled. I advised that the union should offer to accept the company's proposal plus half a cent per hour increase to save face. On the forty-third day (six weeks) we settled the strike on those terms. In later years, Gravefell became a pretty stable labour leader.[63] The important thing was that unions knew the company could stand a strike and that they meant what they said.

In 1968 Nova Scotia's Conservative minister of labour,[64] pressed by the unions to grant collective bargaining rights and the right to strike to policemen, summoned me to his office. I gave him excerpts from Calvin Coolidge's famous speech on this subject[65] and advised against conceding. A year later, with an election coming and his being from Cape Breton – the stronghold of trade unionism – he granted the right and legislation was passed.[66] I told him he would see the first police strike in his own city of Sydney.[67] It is extraordinary what happens even in a small community when the police go on strike; it is really blackmail bargaining.

CHAPTER NINE

The Seventies

In January 1970 Archbishop James Hayes of Halifax, chair of the Roman Catholic Episcopal Corporation (RCEC), consulted me about problems at Saint Mary's University, which was owned and really run by the archdiocese.[1] It seemed there was a desire on the part of the students and faculty not to be run by the archdiocese; not to be a religious institution but to be masters of their own destiny. The corporation was going to have to pay off a bond issue and, of course, the property[2] was very valuable. Every parish in the archdiocese had contributed towards the building of the university and these properties had been mortgaged to provide the money. Most of the more recent buildings on the campus were built with government assistance secured by self-liquidating mortgages.[3] So the RCEC could sell the campus and buildings at a bargain and come out square. This was the basis on which I consented to the Corporation's selling the University to its board – on generous terms as to interest and long-term payment, the latter secured by a mortgage the rate of which was to be linked to the prime (less a point or two). This involved getting through the Legislature a new Saint Mary's University Act amending the university's charter.[4] The negotiations were lengthy and Archbishop Hayes more than generous – I think he might have given the university away had I not had the help of two of his very able assistants, especially Monsignor Campbell.[5] During all the negotiations I was deeply impressed by the wealth of talent in the Church available to assist me. We completed the negotiations, agreements, deeds, and mortgage to the satisfaction of all; the University was freed from control of the Archdiocese and became independent and secular.

In February 1970 Premier G.I. (Ike) Smith asked me to come see him and told me the province had entered into agreements with Dr Jerome S. Spevack,[6] inventor of the standard process for extracting heavy water.[7] Spevack was the former president of Deuterium of Canada Limited, which was building a heavy-water production plant at Glace Bay – probably the greatest disaster any government had suffered in the province's history.[8] Given Spevack's contract,[9] no one could be persuaded to take over the plant for fear they would be sued for stealing Spevack's invention. Nor would any scientist really study the process – afraid that if he later did anything involving the commercial manufacture of heavy water for someone else, he might be sued. Spevack knew the province's predicament and would not grant a release.

After I was retained[10] and had done some study, I telephoned Spevack to say I wanted to talk to him about a release, so that the plant could be appraised and taken over.[11] He said he would not see me or even discuss it until he received all the payments set out in the contract and payable over a period of time. He was so violent and abusive over the phone that finally I said, "Well Mr Spevack, I thought we could at least get together to discuss it, but if we can't I'm afraid I'll have to advise the Government to introduce legislation cancelling your contract without payment." He told me that was impossible; I replied, "You engage an independent Nova Scotia lawyer and ask him if that can be done and when you find out it can be, call me back. I'll give you four days." He went into a long tirade and again said he would not do anything until he got paid. "Mr. Spevack, you have four days and if you have nothing to say other than these tirades, I propose to hang up; but I'll give you the first chance to hang up so it can't be said I was rude." When Spevack did not hang up, I knew I had him. He talked for one and a half hours, but agreed to see me. I had David Chipman[12] work on the release[13] and then afterwards, because of complicated problems involving technology and patents, I consulted Thomas Montgomery,[14] who eventually came with me for the negotiations in White Plains, New York. Forty days after our first telephone call[15] Montgomery and I went to see Spevack in his office at White Plains. Spevack's wife, Ruth, a very clever woman, was present during the negotiations.[16] We finally settled the terms of the release, subject to approval by Spevack's attorney. All the while Spevack kept insisting he would not sign the release until the agreed amount was paid. Whenever he spoke in that vein I would say, "I guess I may as well go home and get the legislation passed." Finally Mrs Spevack drove us to the airport. A few days later Spevack and his wife came to see me in Halifax; Spevack started all over again. I asked Mrs Spevack whether she would like a cup of tea or coffee; she replied yes, and that her husband would too. So Spevack continued the attack until the tea arrived. After the tea in my cup was half gone, I said to him, "Mr. Spevack, I have half a cup of tea left. It will take not more than five sips and when I have finished, the interview is over. There will be no second chance; so you have very little time left." At the end of one sip I said, "four more," then "three more," and finally "two more." Mrs Spevack then said, "Darling, you'd better sign." He signed and I delivered the notes payable over a period of years. I sent the release agreement to the Premier with a covering letter and received a letter of thanks from him.[17] This enabled Atomic Energy of Canada Limited (AECL) to take over the plant and "rebuild it."[18]

In April 1970 a CBC newscaster stated that I had used my position as a member of the board of governors of Dalhousie University to secure a contract for a company of which I was the agent. I was out of town,[19] but someone told me about it, so on my return I went over to the station and had the tape played back. The statement was so far from the truth it was almost laughable. First, I had never done any work for that particular "client;" I was merely acting as the "recognized agent"[20] under the Companies Act – the one on whom writs or notices against the company are served. (The annual fee was then $25 a year.) Secondly, when the contract came up for discussion at the Dalhousie board meeting, I was absent. Finally, though the company did bid on the contract, it was not successful. Nevertheless, I was telephoned again and again and asked whether I was going to sue and told that if I did not people would assume the allegation was correct. I phoned Kennedy[21] at his office and he said he would look into it; one can imagine my amazement when the statement was repeated on air. By now very angry, I called Kennedy at his house. His first reaction was that he did not discuss business at home. I told him this was now serious and he answered he would give me "free time to reply." I told him I would not waste my time replying; that I wanted an apology broadcast at least four times a day for two days and that he had better call head office in Ottawa that night because I would not wait; and that I wanted to hear from him immediately after he had made the call. I pointed out that before such trash was broadcast the facts could have been checked and that the CBC was negligent. That night from Ottawa the CBC read the draft apology – to which I made them add that they had checked the records and found the statement to be false – and they stated the true facts. The CBC did proceed as I requested, yet long afterwards I ran into friends of mine who had heard the original statement but not the retraction.

On H.P. MacKeen's retirement in February 1963 I became head of the firm and immediately began to take Bill Mingo and Harry Rhude[22] into every decision I made. Seven years later the firm reorganized its management structure. Until 1970 there was no partnership agreement; the head of the firm[23] made all the decisions. As I had got into the habit of discussing all decisions with Mingo and Rhude things were working reasonably well, but the firm was growing very rapidly;[24] there were rumblings that the partners had no say, were not really being consulted but merely presented with decisions as faits accomplis. As a result, in June 1970, we drew up a constitution (not a partnership agreement) according to which

1 No one was admitted to partnership or taken into the firm without the unanimous approval of all partners
2 No major change in policy was made without unanimous approval
3 The firm would be run by a five-member Executive Committee elected annually by the partners and consisting of three senior partners (ten years), one intermediate partner (six to nine years) and one junior partner (two to five years)

The whole constitution was worked out carefully and met with unanimous approval, even though decisions of the executive committee were final. It was like Parliament: the cabinet made the decisions. The only remedy was to elect a new cabinet next year. Once the constitution was agreed to, we adopted it and then had our first election. I refused to run and never did so. There was not a single year when I would have changed the chosen committee even if I had been able to.[25] My friends in the big firms in Toronto and Montreal told me it would not work, but it did. Over the years, some members of the committee tried their decisions on me for size before announcing them. However flattering that was to me, I was very proud of the way they handled things. There were times when I thought they were being extravagant with offices and furnishings; once, when they wanted to give everybody the proper priority in choosing new offices, it meant that almost all were changed. I realized then how far they were prepared to go to keep everybody happy. I doubt whether there was a happier, a finer, or an abler group anywhere in the country. I made the proud boast that if they went about it the proper way, they could divide the firm into three and still have the three best firms in the province.[26]

In 1971 Nova Scotia's new Liberal government decided to take over Nova Scotia Light and Power and unite it with the Nova Scotia Power Commission.[27] The secrecy was magnificent and the takeover cleverly executed. Shareholders were offered a price above market and it was pointed out that, if the offer were accepted before 24 January 1972, the sale would not be affected by the new capital gains tax which was to come into force that month. The NSL&P board met on many occasions and at first thought of opposing the takeover, which was hopeless. The only real grounds for opposition could be that the price offered was too low; so the directors waged a contest and were successful in getting a majority of the shareholders to lodge their shares with the board. But we could not hold them beyond the offering date and risk the shareholders' forfeiting the offer. It was an empty victory, because the government could hold the shares turned in and just wait for the rest to follow. On 5 January 1972 I was sent, along with the president of NSL&P,[28] to interview the premier, the attorney general, and the minister of finance in an effort to convince them that they should set up an arbitration panel to determine a fair price. Though the board held proxies on a majority of the shares and thought arbitration might work, I had warned the board it was a hopeless proposal, which became evident five minutes after the meeting started. The cabinet was not interested in negotiating or in having the share price arbitrated. Their failure to have a majority of the shares turned in really did not matter, though they were a little upset that the takeover had not been well received. Of course they knew that the board would not dare take responsibility for withholding the shares turned in and letting the acceptance date pass. On 6 and 7 January, the board held further meetings and on the 7th the president and I called on Premier Regan. When we told him we had capitulated, he was stunned; the look of shock and surprise on his face was something to behold. Apparently, it was our waiting until the last minute that had worried him. We arranged for a pension for the president and for dates of the takeover. On 19 January the old board held its final meeting – it was long and bitter. On the 27th we met with the board of the Nova Scotia Power Commission, resigning one by one as the vacancies were filled with the government's nominees. Later by legislation NSL&P and the Commission were amalgamated;[29] those who had not turned in their shares were given a limited time in which to apply for reimbursement.

As it turned out, in years to come NSL&P would have been in desperate straits, thanks to the increased price of oil. Furthermore, NSL&P had a very advantageous contract with Imperial Oil, if NSL&P's interpretation of the contract and the facts was correct. The case eventually came to trial and our firm was retained. We won through all the courts, including the Supreme Court of Canada; it cost Imperial Oil over $100 million.[30] I doubt whether NSL&P, as a private company, could have survived through the 1970s, with low power rates. So, from the shareholders' point of view, it was a good thing the government took it over. Yet the increase in power rates brought about by the increased price of oil was the major factor in Gerald Regan's defeat in 1978. On 3 July I spent five hours with him at Mersey Lodge. He told me he was going to call an election that year; I told him he could not win, given rising power and inflation rates and the string of Tory victories in federal by-elections. He called his election for 19 September and lost to the Tories thirty-one seats to seventeen.

In January 1973 a good friend of ours who was assistant general manager of Eastern Telephone & Telegraph[31] (of which I was a director) resigned after having stolen $500,000 from the company very cleverly and over a period of years.[32] He dragged down with him a much younger man with a young family. We had to attach moneys in banks in England, Montreal, New York, and Nova Scotia. Later both men pleaded guilty; for the younger man I was able to obtain a job in a telephone company in British Columbia – he got off very lightly and afterwards did well. I did not see my friend again;[33] he cooperated with the company, which got back a lot of the money and so, with insurance, he was alright. ET&T continued to pay his pension. He was a fine man and an able manager and so trusted that it was easy for him to do what he did.

On 2 January 1974 Angus L. Macdonald[34] came into my office to tell me he had been appointed to the Nova Scotia Supreme Court (Appeal Division).[35] He wanted to thank me for all I had done for him. He said that if it had not been for me, he would never have received the appointment and that it would be "another gem in your crown." I was delighted that he had been appointed a judge, which I felt would relieve him of a lot of pressure. He had become a great criminal trial lawyer, perhaps by long odds the most successful criminal lawyer in the province. He was a close student of the law and had a very pleasant manner in court, showing deference to the judge but always getting his point across. Though not an orator, he was one to whom the jury listened very attentively, because he was so sensible, factual, and straightforward.

In February, March, May, and October 1974, I worked for the Sisters of Charity on negotiations to try to sell Mount St. Vincent University.[36] My diary says, the "present board of the College has no guts or leadership – it won't come to pass under that board." And it did not. By 1980 the Sisters still had not sold it.[37]

In February 1976 the management of Industrial Acceptance Corporation Limited, of which I had been a director since 1960, advised the board that IAC should become a bank.[38] They outlined the reasons and the directors voted in favour of it. The change was to take about three years to complete; first, legislation had to pass Parliament.[39] Those of us who were directors of banks or trust companies[40] were asked not to resign immediately. Afterwards I wrote the chairman[41] that though the proposed act would permit the directors' staying on and however much I would miss IAC board meetings, I suspected there would be criticism in Parliament. There was; the New Democratic Party filibustered the act. I told IAC they could have my resignation any time they needed it and I advised them on a successor.[42]

In 1976, when I was trying to cut down rather than add to my activities, the government asked me to become chair of the board of Nova Scotia Technical College (NSTC).[43] On 19 November I was invited to lunch with the ministers of finance and education and the deputy minister of education, who presented me with some of the facts and then asked whether I would take on the job for two years.[44] The minister of finance showed me a draft order in council, which read two years to the day;[45] in a weak moment I replied, "Yes, for two years and you are not even to ask me for one day extra." They agreed, the deputy minister handing over a file that he had brought with him. It was the beginning of two years' concentrated work. NSTC had had a rough five years, which began in

1970 with an internal row between the faculty of engineering and the president,[46] his resignation, and the appointment of a temporary president,[47] who, because of circumstances, remained acting for five years. During that time Dalhousie University and NSTC worked on an amalgamation agreement, which was approved by the boards of both, only to be defeated in the Legislature because of opposition from those universities in Atlantic Canada that sent their pre-engineering students to NSTC for degrees in engineering.[48] So the five-year hopes of the faculty that NSTC would become part of Dalhousie University were dashed.

It was my job to find a new president, rebuild morale, get NSTC back on a smooth cooperating basis with the associated universities, and regain board control of the administration. My first thought was to reorganize the governing structure of the college, whose board included representatives of other universities in Atlantic Canada – Acadia, St. Francis Xavier, Dalhousie, Mount Allison, Memorial University of Newfoundland, and the University of Prince Edward Island. Though there was obviously a conflict of interest, it would be delicate asking for resignations, so I conceived the idea of an advisory board to represent the interests of the associated universities. My next task was to secure an effective board of governors that would provide spark and let the world know NSTC meant business. Then I had to convince administration and faculty that NSTC would "do its own thing" free from control of the associated universities. And, in order to allay their suspicions of Dalhousie, I had to convince the associated universities that NSTC would give up forever any thought of union with Dalhousie.[49] I had to procure legislation; I had to obtain the cooperation of the government, I had to recruit people to serve on the board; and, first of all, NSTC had to select a new president. The position had already been advertised and the applicants short-listed; on 12 December 1976 we interviewed the first candidate.

In 1977 NSTC generated a great deal of work and consumed a great deal of time. We found a new president, Clair Callaghan,[50] who was not only the best candidate but also the person most needed for the job. We had the NSTC Act amended as requested[51] and appointed a new board of governors. But there were difficulties – I had to meet the alumni. I had an amazing five-hour session one evening with the professors; it was demanding, but they gave me a standing ovation when I was through. I set up the advisory board, and, despite strong representations made over our heads to the government, had the representatives of the associated universities removed from the board of governors. I also set up various board committees, including executive and finance (a very strong one), and appointed effective people to them in order to divide up the work and ensure an active board. I met with the Association of Professional Engineers.[52] I appointed a woman to the board, Mary Moore (formerly Sister Mary Moore, treasurer general of the Sisters of Charity). NSTC now had a rudder – a proper board to assist the new president – and a sense of a future. My second year at NSTC, 1977–78, was a busy one. There were many executive and board meetings. I found President Callaghan decisive and good to work with, and the whole administrative staff cooperative, able, and devoted to the college. I was satisfied with the contribution of the board of governors and its committees. The final step – I got the process underway – was choosing a new name: *Technical University of Nova Scotia*.[53] There is so much in a name that it was difficult to please everybody.

When my term expired in November 1978, I tendered my resignation as chair of the board.[54] The president coaxed me not to go and I did feel guilty leaving him after such a short time. But I was seventy years old and the job had added many more hours to already crowded days. I was pleased when one of the governors whom I had recruited was appointed to the board and then elected chair in my place.[55] On 22 January 1980 I was informed that the senate of NSTC had unanimously resolved to invite me to accept an honorary Doctor of Engineering degree at convocation in May; I naturally accepted. The irony was that, in my youth, I wanted to be an engineer; Father had planned that I should go to his alma mater, McGill, whose faculty of engineering had a great reputation.

In September 1976 I appeared for only the second time before the Canadian Transport Commission,[56] again on an application by Canadian National Railways to discontinue local rail service. Bowater Mersey Paper asked me to act for one of its woodchip suppliers.[57] I prepared a brief and went to the hearing at Caledonia to oppose the application.[58] I observed that CN's main witness[59] was meticulously following notes; so pat were his answers that I suddenly realized they had been prepared for him. Taking a shot in the dark, I asked whether he had received all of his advice and instructions from CN's regional head office in Moncton; on being pressed, he admitted as much. I tried two more questions: "Did you consult at all with the local customers, or was that done in Moncton?"

"In Moncton."

"As a matter of fact, of all of the evidence you have given, none was of your own personal knowledge?"

He admitted it. Their whole case destroyed, CNR sought an adjournment of one-half hour (to get instructions from Moncton, no doubt).[60] The application was dismissed.

By 1977 there were many companies that had entered into special power contracts with the Nova Scotia Power Commission, as an incentive for locating in Nova Scotia. Under new legislation,[61] however, the legality of such agreements came into question and a case was stated for the appeal court.[62] I advised my clients, Bowater Mersey Paper, CKF, and Minas Basin Pulp and Power, not to enter the action; in the event, the contracts were held to be illegal. Then came the rate hearing. For months my clients prepared their cases, my strategy being to present briefs and not witnesses, unless the Board required them. In the Bowater Mersey brief I argued that Mersey Paper had paid cost and depreciation since the very beginning, the power plant had been built for Mersey, and the terms of the contract were unique,[63] and that the company and the Nova Scotia Power Commission were in effect partners in the venture. During the hearing, I summarized the case in so short a time that the Board heard all three of my briefs in less than half an hour; my cases gained headlines in the press the following day.[64] Bowater Mersey's contract was the only one not struck down.

For several years, due to unsettled conditions in Quebec – terrorist bombings, FLQ (Front de Libération du Québec) kidnappings, and the rise of the separatist Parti Québécois – the management of Sun Life Assurance Company had been considering a head office move from Montreal to Toronto and had prepared for it in case of need. Finally, in 1977, the Quebec legislature passed Bill 101,[65] which, to say the least, would have made it difficult for the head office of an international company to remain in Montreal. This was but the last straw; the real reason was that Sun Life was beginning to lose international business as well as business in the rest of Canada. Insurance is a matter of confidence. Internationally, the situation was not only promoting a lack of confidence in Quebec, but also, because of the possible secession of Quebec and the effect that would have on Canada, it was hurting Canada. After a great deal of thought and study by management and the executive committee, the matter came before the full board on 2 January 1978. After debate and discussion a vote was taken which was overwhelmingly in favour of moving to Toronto. (There was one abstention.[66])

Under the Insurance Act, notice of such a change had to be published in newspapers all across Canada, so it became a very public matter. The Parti Québécois government was angry, the minister of finance, Jacques Parizeau, making some very foolish statements.[67] But it was the press which, with little or no research, wrote article after article missing the point entirely. Day in, day out the subject was front page news, everybody expressing opinions that generally showed a complete lack of knowledge both of facts and of law. On 12 January, in the early morning, the executive committee had a two-hour meeting, adjourned it, and then met again in the afternoon for two and a half hours more. Under the law, an insurance company like Sun Life which is mutualized[68] – no shareholders, just policyholders – may execute proxies for three years; the reason being the cost of preparing and mailing the documents to as many as 900,000 policyholders all over the world. The cost of postage alone would have been over $100,000, not to mention the cost of printing, etc. It would have taken about three months to get the proxies out and back, and by that time there would have been thousands of new policyholders. The question was whether it was fair to use proxies for such a purpose, even though it was legal. But was it fair to change head office without a specific proxy for that purpose? The board decided unanimously to cancel the meeting which had been called for 27 January and to call a new one for late April. It was gratifying to see how fully the board understood every aspect of the problem and exercised their judgment in the interests of the company – regardless of the effect it might have on their businesses or indeed on themselves. My diary for 14 January reads, "The full Board of Sun Life met and confirmed unanimously the views of the Executive Committee." Due to a snowstorm I missed the meeting on 27 January, when the situation was explained and the meeting rescheduled for 25 April in Toronto. All the time in between, the media kept it on stage. The meeting on the 25th lasted more than three hours, but the vote was over five to one (an eighty-four per cent majority) in favour of the move.

The board generally was amazed at the very proper attitude that Prime Minister Trudeau[69] took with the chairman (Alistair Campbell) and the president (Thomas Galt).[70] I always had great faith in Trudeau so was not surprised. He apparently showed flashes of brilliance as well. He made it clear he would not apply pressure, nor would he attempt to prevent the move by legislation. He was the first to realize that insurance is a matter of confidence. The board then decided to make public what it had already told its staff, that the move would be spread over two years. Campbell and Galt were extremely good, especially Campbell, who was a very strong man.[71] In 1980 the move was still being talked about; it proved to be sound. The Parti Québécois government really had no idea what they had lost by the move of Sun Life's head office and head office personnel and what went with them. The growth of Sun Life's business since then has been phenomenal, especially in England, Western Canada, and the United States. In Quebec itself, however, the drop in business was sharp; other companies poached Sun Life's agents and the Quebec government cancelled large group policies. But gradually the Quebec business began to come back; we recruited new agents while some of our old agents returned.

In February 1979 Harry Rhude, one of the firm's senior members, became full-time chair and chief executive officer of Central & Eastern Trust.[72] He had been with us for twenty-eight years and was one of the most brilliant members of the Nova Scotia bar. There was no area of the law that he could not do well. I persuaded him not to resign the partnership but from then onwards he gave the trust company his full time. He had had a brilliant start as a navigator in Bomber Command, became a Pathfinder,[73] won the DFC, and finished three tours and started on a fourth. He soon convinced his clients there was no one quite like him and reached the stage where the Sobeys and the Nickersons[74] and Central Trust demanded so much of his time that he could not handle them all. Even after he left the firm, the Nickersons asked him to stay on as chair of National Sea Products, which he did briefly.[75]

"A Colossus in the Profession"

In 1981 Louis Dubinsky, a supernumerary justice of the Supreme Court of Nova Scotia, Trial Division, published in book form a selection of legal anecdotes which had appeared as a weekly series in the Halifax *Chronicle-Herald* in 1977–78.[1] He concluded the work with a moving tribute to Frank Covert, a "giant in the profession of law."[2]

Though nominally retired as of 1978 Covert continued to practise, giving up, very reluctantly, only those directorships, such as Molson's and Royal Bank, from which age compelled him to retire. In February 1980 the jubilee of his call to the bar was lavishly celebrated by the grand old firm where he had spent his entire career; Covert was the first member of Stewart MacKeen & Covert ever to have reached that milestone. In May 1980 Nova Scotia Technical College conferred on the former chair of its board of governors an honorary doctorate in engineering – Covert's chosen but unrealized profession. Ironically, what Covert had set out but failed to do and was still a matter of regret to him was soon accomplished; within days the institution's name was changed to *Technical University of Nova Scotia*. In 1982 Covert was appointed an Officer of the Order of Canada. In 1983 Peter Newman described him as "still the central authority of who does what in the province."[3] In 1984 Covert served as chair of the committee attempting to restructure National Sea Products in order to save it from nationalization or bankruptcy.[4] In 1985 the library of Dalhousie Law School was destroyed in a disastrous fire; Covert individually made a substantial contribution towards its rebuilding, which he did not live to see. In 1986 he completed a documentary history of Bowater Mersey Paper Company, of which he had remained an active director.[5] When he died of leukaemia on 1 November 1987, he was chair of three company boards and a member of several others. "Endowed with a strong intellect and a high energy level," declared the Nova Scotia Barristers' Society in its resolution in Covert's memory, "he developed the discipline, and the clientele, that permitted him, at the height of his practice, to become the acknowledged leader in the province in the fields of corporate, income tax and labour law. He was the architect of one of the largest law firms in eastern Canada."[6] Moreover, as a forward-looking, outside-the-box thinker, he laid the groundwork for the creation of the largest of them, which came into existence less than three years after his death. Though Stewart McKelvey Stirling Scales does not bear Covert's name, it bears his indelible stamp. Frank Covert helped ensure that the legal profession in early twenty-first century Canada is built around large law firms, large law firms around corporate lawyers, and corporate lawyers around big business clients.

Notes

EDITOR'S FOREWORD

1 Edward L. Greenspan [with George Jonas], *Greenspan: The Case for the Defence* (Toronto: Macmillan, 1987); Clarence Day Shepard, *My Personal Parade: The Life of a Canadian Prairie Boy from 1914 through 1987* (Elgin, Ont.: C.D. Shepard, 1987); David James Walker, *Fun along the Way: Memoirs of Dave Walker* (Toronto: Robertson Press, 1989); Ian Scott, *To Make a Difference: A Memoir* (Toronto: Stoddart, 2001); and R.A. Kanigsberg Q.C., *Trials and Tribulations of a Bluenose Barrister* (Halifax: Petheric Press, 1977).

2 See, for example, Charles Pullen, *The Life and Times of Arthur Maloney, the Last of the Tribunes* (Toronto: The Osgoode Society for Canadian Legal History, 1994); Barry Cahill, *The Thousandth Man: A Biography of James McGregor Stewart* (Toronto: The Osgoode Society for Canadian Legal History, 2000); Laurel Sefton MacDowell, *Renegade Lawyer: The Life of J.L. Cohen* (Toronto: The Osgoode Society for Canadian Legal History, 2001); and, most recently, George D. Finlayson, *John J. Robinette, Peerless Mentor* (Toronto: The Osgoode Society for Canadian Legal History, 2003). Maloney was an eminent criminal defence counsel, Stewart a corporate lawyer, Cohen a lawyer for labour, and Robinette an all-round advocate and general counsel.

3 David Ricardo Williams, *Just Lawyers: Seven Portraits* (Toronto: The Osgoode Society for Canadian Legal History, 1995), xiv, [3]. The six others were Eugene Lafleur (Quebec), William Norman Tilley (Ontario), Aimé Geoffrion (Quebec), Isaac Pitblado (Manitoba), John Wallace de B. Farris (British Columbia), and

Gordon Henderson (Ontario). Tilley and Geoffrion were corporate lawyers, though, unlike Covert, they were also celebrated counsel. On the difference and relationship between the two see Williams, *Just Lawyers*, 176.

4 On this subject see, most recently, Gregory P. Marchildon, "Corporate Lawyers and the Second Industrial Revolution in Canada," *Saskatchewan Law Review* 64, no. 1 (2001): 99–112. See generally David Smith and Lorne Tepperman, "Changes in the Canadian Business and Legal Elites, 1870–1970," *Canadian Review of Sociology and Anthropology* 11, no. 2 (1974): 100.

5 For the dimensions of the Jodrey-Covert legacy, see *Minas Basin: Proudly celebrating 75 years* [newspaper supplement, August 2002].

6 Among the companies of which Covert was a director were Acadia Life, Acadian Lines, Argyle Securities, Atlantic Seaboard Agencies, Atlantic Traders, Ben's Holdings, Ben's Limited, Best Yeast Limited, Bowater Mersey Paper, Cameron Contracting, Canada Southern Petroleum, Canadian Keyes Fibre, Canadian Petrofina, Canning Investment Corporation, Coastal Enterprises, Consolidated Investments, Consolidated Supply, Eastern Telephone and Telegraph, General Mortgage Service Corporation, Great Eastern Corporation, Hants Investments, Haylock Enterprises, Holman's, Home Care Properties, IAC Limited, Industrial and Development Corporation of Venezuela, Industrial Containers, Lindwood Holdings, Maritime Accessories, Maritime Containers, Maritime Paper Products, Maritime Steel & Foundries, Minas Basin Pulp & Power, Moirs Limited, Molson Companies, Montreal Trust, National Sea Products, North Eastern Corporation, Nova Scotia Light & Power, Ocean Fisheries, Phoenix Assurance, Piercey's Supplies, Royal Bank, Scotia Investments, Standard Brands, Standard Woodworkers, Sun Life Assurance, Sydney Engineering & Dry Dock, Trizec Corporation, United Canso Oil and Gas, United Service Corporation, Wood Brothers, and York Securities.

7 Harry Bruce, "Nova Scotia's Mr Lawyer," *Commercial News* (October 1984): 56–60.

8 Brian Flemming, "More than a lawyer: Meet Frank Manning Covert and other men who suffered the Curse of Multiple Talents," Halifax *Daily News*: 27 September 1995.

9 He was named for his father's younger brother, Frank Manning Covert (1872–1924), a salesman in New York.

10 See Elizabeth M. Clarke, *The Way It Really Was: The Clarkes of Kings, Ancestors and Descendants* (Berwick, Nova Scotia: n.p. 1998), 40–3.

11 His paternal great-uncle, lawyer Daniel Lionel Hanington (1835–1909), was briefly Conservative premier of New Brunswick in the 1880s; Hanington went on to become a justice of the Supreme Court of New Brunswick.

12 Kings County's long-time Liberal MP, Sir Frederick William Borden, was also a small–town doctor. A powerful minister in the Laurier cabinet, Borden was a Canning resident whose two wives were sisters and Frank's maternal great-aunts. See generally Carman Miller, "Borden, Sir Frederick William," *Dictionary of Canadian Biography* XIV 1911–1920 (Toronto: University of Toronto Press, 1998): 97–100.

13 Covert's paternal grandfather, Walter Scott Covert, was an Anglican priest.

14 Concerning the Stewart-Covert relationship see Cahill, *Thousandth Man*, 152–7.

15 Frank M. Covert, "Atlantic provinces cannot afford Accord," Halifax *Chronicle-Herald*: 6 October 1987; "This may be the worst thing that has ever happened to Canada."

16 There is a world of difference between a lawyer acting for organized labour and a corporate lawyer like Covert specializing in labour-management relations in the interests of business capital corporations.

17 Harry Bruce, *Corporate Navigator: The Life of Frank Manning Covert* (Toronto: McClelland & Stewart, 1995).

18 Adapted from "Autobiography" (typescript), 486–7.

19 Robert Covert and the late David Covert, who became a member of Covert's law firm.

AUTHOR'S PREFACE

1 Until 1989–90; now Stewart McKelvey Stirling Scales – the largest law firm in Atlantic Canada.

2 Not published.

CHAPTER ONE

1 See generally Margaret Ells, "Canning in the Seventies," *Nova Scotia Historical Review* 8, no. 2 (1988): 113–24; Eric Niemi, "Canning Then and Now," *Atlantic Advocate* 74, no. 11 (July 1984): 38–40. The site of Canning formed part of the old New England planter township of Cornwallis, established in 1759.

See also Arthur Wentworth Hamilton Eaton, *The History of Kings County, Nova Scotia, Heart of the Acadian Land* (Belleville, Ont.: Mika, 1972 [repr. of 1910 ed.]), 151–4.

2 Julia (Mrs Lewis Clarke), Harold, Frank, and Madeline (Mrs T.H. Coffin).

3 Home of Acadia University.

4 Run by Covert's father, Dr A.M. Covert, and afterwards by his widow.

5 Roy MacLaren, "Borden, Harold Lathrop," *Dictionary of Canadian Biography* XIV 1891–1900 (Toronto: University of Toronto Press, 1990), 114–5.

6 A. Marie Bickerton, comp., *Old Timers: Canning and Habitant* [Canning, Nova Scotia: n.p., 1981], 16.

7 A reference to the Kerr Evaporating Company of Canning; Bickerton, *Old Timers*, 13.

8 Softwood shavings used for stuffing, packing, etc.

9 The projecting rims at the end of a cask.

10 "A Brief History of Hockey In Canning," Kentville *Advertiser*: 21 November 1974.

11 A disease of poultry, etc.

CHAPTER TWO

1 Dr Covert was a captain in the Canadian Army Medical Corps.

2 Lincoln's Gettysburg Address.

3 Doubtless a reference to the provincial election of 1920, in which the Farmer-Labour coalition took eleven of the forty-three seats and the Conservatives only three.

4 Dr Covert lived to see the United Farmers of Alberta form a government in 1921.

5 The Reverend Walter Scott Covert (1833–1902).

6 The South African War.

7 The failure of the Home Rule Bill (a Liberal initiative) in 1914, the Easter Rising of 1916, and the Irish War of Independence (1919–21).

8 The American War of Independence, which made the Covert family political refugees.

9 In 1867–71 and 1884–87; see generally J. Murray Beck, *Politics of Nova Scotia, Volume One: Nicholson-Fielding, 1710–1896* (Tantallon, Nova Scotia: Four East, 1985).

10 Dr Covert's older brother, Walter Harold, was a prominent Conservative who was lieutenant governor of Nova Scotia when his daughter and his nephew married in 1934.

11 The pre-1928 diaries, excepting only 1923, are not now extant. It is not known what became of them.

12 Dr Covert graduated MD, CM in 1898.

13 On this subject generally see Stanley Brice Frost, *McGill University: For the Advancement of Learning*. Volume II, 1895–1971 (Kingston & Montreal: McGill-Queen's University Press, 1984), 478, Index, s.v. "Engineering, Faculty of (Applied Science). Law, no less than engineering, appealed strongly to Covert's practical, problem-solving cast of mind.

14 Clara Pearl, who was with the Covert family for nearly sixty years until her death in 1964.

15 Dr Covert was a registered pharmacist.

16 So called from 1917; affiliated with Dalhousie in 1912; incorporated into the university in 1961; see P.B. Waite, *The Lives of Dalhousie University*. Volume Two, 1925–1980: *The Old College Transformed* (Montreal & Kingston: McGill-Queen's University Press, 1998), 273.

17 Lewis Harper Clarke.

18 Minnie Covert died 4 April 1965.

19 They were All Canadian-American Investments, Atlantic Traders, Canadian Keyes Fibre, Eastern Telephone and Telegraph, Great Eastern Corporation, Halliday Craftsmen, Mersey Paper, Minas Basin Pulp and Power, Minas Shipping, Moirs Limited, Montreal Trust Company, National Sea Products, North Eastern Corporation, Ocean Fisheries, Royal Bank of Canada, Standard Woodworkers, Super Service Stations, Superline Oils, Sydney Engineering and Dry Dock, United Service Corporation, and Wood Brothers.

20 Newman contributed a foreword to Bruce, *Corporate Navigator*.

21 "Canada's biggest big businessmen," *Maclean's* (12 October 1957): 13. Covert stood 55th on the list of directors of companies with "assets directed" in the millions of dollars, in his case $3,669 millions.

22 Covert became a director of the Royal Bank of Canada in 1956 and remained one until reaching the mandatory retirement age of 75 in 1983. By 1972 Covert, with twenty-nine directorships, was eleventh on Newman's list of "Canada's Top One Hundred Bank Directors and Their Corporate Connections": Peter C. Newman, *The Canadian Establishment*, Volume One (Toronto: McClelland and Stewart, 1975), 106.

23 Newman's definitive statement on Covert appears in *Canadian
   Establishment*, 203 ("No matter where they originate or where they
   eventually end up, the lines of established business power in Nova
   Scotia lead to Frank Manning Covert"). This is an accurate
   assessment of Covert's "corporate power" at its zenith in the 1960s.

24 The reference is to senior matriculation, which reduced the undergraduate degree course from four years to three.

25 The newspaper in which these advertisements appeared would have
   been the Kentville *Advertiser*, which does not survive from the mid-
   1920s.

26 Mrs Covert had resided with her brother-in-law while taking the
   pharmacy course at Dalhousie in 1922: Clarke, *The Way It Really
   Was*, 41.

27 Covert, Pearson and Rutledge; now Cox Hanson O'Reilly
   Matheson.

28 In 1926 W.H. Covert became president of N.S. Tramways & Power
   Co (now Emera Energy).

29 W.F. Page Clothier, Furnisher and Hatter was a gentleman's tailor,
   not a haberdasher.

30 Murray Macneill, professor of mathematics. On Dalhousie when
   Covert was a freshman see P.B. Waite, *The Lives of Dalhousie
   University, Volume One, 1818–1925: Lord Dalhousie's College*
   (Montreal & Kingston: McGill-Queen's University Press, 1994),
   258 et seq.

31 According to law faculty regulations, any Dalhousie BA graduate
   who, during the arts course, had taken as electives the first-year law
   classes, could complete the LL B course in two years. Covert
   graduated BA in 1927 and LL B in 1929.

32 Analytic geometry.

33 Quoted by Waite, *Old College Transformed*, 14 apparently from
   Bruce, *Corporate Navigator*, 30.

34 "Le corbeau et le renard," *Fables* I,ii.

35 Murray was also dean (vice-president) of the university and chair of
   the provincial Advisory Board of Education.

36 That is, the Roman alphabet according to Latin received
   pronunciation.

37 "He won fame in his first year at college when he held the floor in
   Professor Murray's room for the record time of 46 ... minutes. This
   record, though since surpassed, must stand as Mr Covert's greatest

contribution to Dalhousie": *Pharos* (Halifax: Dalhousie Student Union, 1927), 33.

38 Uranium fission was discovered in 1938; "Jack" Johnstone taught physics at Dalhousie from 1914 to 1960.

39 Inaugural holder of the Eric Dennis Memorial Chair of Government and Political Science, 1921–26.

40 A theme was an essay on a given subject.

41 This essay, now lost, probably forms the basis of chapter 1 of the present work.

42 During the 1910s through the 1940s, the Hackmatack Inn was a fashionable watering place on Nova Scotia's touristy South Shore.

43 This section is based in part on Covert's contribution to "In my day at Dalhousie Law School," *Ansul* (13 January 1976): 40–3.

44 Probably in 1941, when Read was placed in charge of the department's legal division.

45 That is, 1930. It is not strictly true that Covert was a "late" lawyer. Articled clerkship was for three years, provided the clerk was engaged in full-time law studies; the term could not be foreshortened.

46 See generally Karen Smith, *Vessels of Light: A Guide to Special Collections in the Killam Library, Dalhousie University Libraries* (Halifax: Dalhousie University Press, 1996), 16–19.

47 Predecessor of the Nova Scotia Court of Appeal.

48 It was unusual for the client to appear at the appeal. In the manner of an English barrister, appellate counsel would be briefed by the client's solicitor and would have little or no contact with the appellant, unless the trial and appeal lawyers were one and the same, which was often, though not invariably, the case.

49 [1897] A.C. 22.

50 John Willis, *A History of Dalhousie Law School* (Toronto: University of Toronto Press, 1979), 98; "the unusually distinguished corporation lawyer in Halifax" was, of course, Covert.

51 Covert, Gavsie, and MacLellan with high honours; Gavsie went on to graduate LL M from Harvard in 1930.

52 Thomas H. Coffin (1907–1992) was married to Covert's younger sister Madeline.

53 In 1942, when Covert joined the RCAF, Gavsie replaced him as assistant general counsel in Munitions & Supply.

54 See below chapter 8.

55 Feaver also graduated LL M from Harvard in 1930.
56 Afterwards president of both the University of Manitoba and the University of Toronto and briefly minister of external affairs under Diefenbaker.
57 A point of contract law, the substance of which is not known. See generally "Covert and MacLellan Win Smith Shield," Halifax *Dalhousie Gazette*: 1 March 1929.
58 Covert, Hugh Hatheway Turnbull (afterwards a corporate lawyer in Montreal), Duncan MacLellan, and John Thomas MacQuarrie (afterwards briefly an assistant professor in Dalhousie Law School).
59 All three of them graduates of Dalhousie Law School.

CHAPTER THREE

1 More a pre-campaign, in that the legislature was not dissolved until September 1928. The government of the day was Conservative and all the seniors in the firm were Conservatives. Thanks to Covert, over the years the political complexion of the firm would change so much that it became identified more with the Liberal Party than with the Conservative.
2 Now Bowater Mersey Paper Company Limited.
3 W.A. Henry (1864–1927), son and namesake of the founder of the firm, was head from 1915 until his death in December 1927. He was a noted admiralty lawyer and his firm was the leader in maritime law.
4 Dower was the widow's common-law right to one-third of her deceased husband's real property; curtesy was the widower's common-law right to all of his deceased wife's real property. Matrimonial property legislation has rendered this inequitable division of assets nugatory in Canadian jurisdictions.
5 "Describes shares which have no nominal value but represent some portion of a company's net assets": Daphne A. Dukelow and Betsy Nuse, eds., *Dictionary of Canadian Law*, 2nd ed. (Toronto: Carswell 1995), 808, s.v., "no par value."
6 Carl Burton Robbins, *No-Par Stock: Legal, Financial, Economic and Accounting Aspects* (New York: Ronald Press, 1927).
7 Elizabeth Wilson, Stewart's fiancée and future wife.
8 Wilson, as secretary to the head of the firm, acted as solicitor's clerk and paralegal.

9 Alfred F. Topham and Alfred R. Taylour, eds., *Palmer's Company Precedents ... Thirteenth Edition* (London: Stevens, 1927).

10 Mersey was incorporated on 31 July 1928; Covert's 21st birthday was 13 January 1929.

11 Probably *Re Laxon & Co (No. 2)*, [1892] 3 Ch. 555.

12 McCleave, aged 36 and a returned veteran, was the first winner of the university medal in law. He died in June 1926, one of several victims of cerebrospinal meningitis (or typhus), contracted while attending the General Assembly of The Presbyterian Church in Canada in Montreal.

13 Until 1949 the court of last resort for Canada; the Supreme Court of Canada was not supreme, not even in Canada, for appeals could be carried direct from provincial courts of appeal to the Judicial Committee of the Privy Council.

14 Kaningsberg, *Trials and Tribulations*, 72.

15 Mr Justice Tecumseh Sherman Rogers, a former senior member of the firm, died in 1928.

16 In 1954, the final year of his life, Rogers joined Stewart and Smith as counsel to the firm.

17 In Nova Scotia the Liberals took ten seats, the Conservatives two and the CCF one. (At that time, federal public servants were not permitted to stand for Parliament.)

18 From about 1908.

19 Now 1657 Barrington Street in downtown Halifax and still an office block.

20 In 1980 thirty-two members (partners) and associates (juniors).

21 Also the stipendiary magistrate.

22 *Glesby v. Mitchell.*

23 Now Provincial Court.

24 Possibly George Farquhar, an ex-United Church minister turned lawyer turned journalist. He graduated from Dalhousie law school in 1927, two years ahead of Covert.

25 Incorporated federally in 1917 and registered in Nova Scotia in 1921, ET&T was acquired by AT&T, in order to provide facilities in Canada that would interconnect with the transatlantic telephone cable system under construction in the late 1920s.

26 S.N.S., 1930, c. 139.

27 Marzo, a civil engineer by training, was solicitor for ET&T, of which he ultimately became vice-president.

28 A mere ten days after Stewart's death on 11 February 1955 Covert was invited to replace him as director.

29 The occasion was the retirement from active business and political life of the company's president, Frank Stanfield, who in December 1930 became lieutenant-governor of Nova Scotia.

30 New Stanfields was incorporated 29 November 1930.

31 More likely cousin; a reference to Patrick Kerwin, chief justice of Canada, 1954–63.

32 O'Hearn was judge of the County Court of District Number One (Halifax County) from 1928 to 1933.

33 Dr Kirwan was found dead in his bed on 17 August 1931.

34 A civil engineer by profession. Phil H. Moore (1879–1961) was better known as a sportsman and writer than as a company promoter.

35 Situated on the eastern side of Port Mouton Harbour (Queens County, NS); it still flourishes.

36 Nova Scotia Trust Company.

37 *In re White Point Beach Company Limited*, (1931) 13 C.B.R. 277 (N.S.S.C.).

38 A director of the company and surety for one of its notes; MacDougall was also vice-president of Maritime Life Assurance.

39 The first two operations were successful, while the third proved fatal.

40 The company was incorporated by Stewart's law firm in November 1920 and capitalized at $200,000.

41 Almost certainly Royal Securities Corporation, another client of Stewart's law firm.

42 Now Workers' Compensation Board.

43 [1933] 2 D.L.R. 97.

44 *Doyle v. Mersey Paper Company*, [1934] 2 D.L.R. 296.

45 Shire town of Cape Breton County (now Cape Breton Regional Municipality).

46 It was exceptional for an associate to become a member (partner) after two years; Stewart himself was such an exception – from associate to member in seven months – but then only because a partner had retired from the firm.

47 Born 1913, the youngest child of Walter Harold Covert, Frank's father's older brother.

48 Of which Stewart was vice-president and Covert eventually president.

49 Now Burchell Hayman Parish.
50 A pair of proverbial cats in Ireland who fought each other until only their tails remained.
51 Frederick Carl Manning (1891–1959).
52 Minas Basin Pulp and Paper Mills Limited (Minas Basin Pulp and Power Company Limited), of which Manning was a director.
53 See Harry Bruce, *RA: The Story of R.A. Jodrey, Entrepreneur* (Toronto: McClelland and Stewart, 1979), 158–62.
54 CKF Inc. now produces foam and pulp products.
55 *Whelpley v. Auto Parts Company Limited.*
56 [Harry Flemming], *McInnes Cooper & Robertson – A Century Plus* [Halifax: n.p., 1989], 47–8.
57 And of which Stewart was a director, afterwards chairman.
58 George Russell Ramey, afterwards crown prosecutor.
59 Lead counsel for the defendant company.
60 This appeal case was not reported. The plaintiff-respondent was a machinery-equipper suing for alleged nonpayment of debt.
61 Lovett was 62, Covert 27.
62 Bill 91, An Act to amend Chapter 15, Acts of 1932, "The Nova Scotia Architects Act," was given the three-month hoist in April 1935.
63 In relation to Mrs Covert's entitlement to the military pension of her late husband.
64 Halifax County wills, No. 13722 (9 April 1935); Newberry had been executive accountant of Acadia Sugar Refining Company Limited, of which Stewart was president.
65 Not until the passage in 1964 of the Human Tissue Gift Act was it legal in Nova Scotia to "leave one's body to science."
66 Then a suburb, afterwards a district of the former City of Halifax; the Reverend gave his name to Dentith Road.
67 The parish, which Dentith had served for over twenty-five years, seems to have been in dire financial straits.
68 Stewart, Smith, MacKeen, Rogers, and Connolly.
69 *Saunders v. Goodwin*, [1937] 1 D.L.R. 621. "A verdict cannot stand where the negligence returned by the jury was not alleged in plaintiff's particulars."
70 A committee of the board of governors of Dalhousie University, of which both Covert and MacCulloch were members.
71 Charles E. MacCulloch died suddenly in October 1979.
72 Mrs Arthur Moreira.

73 "Eleven Hurt as Yacht Explodes," Halifax *Chronicle*: 27 August
   1936.
74 Areas of forested land where the company has the right to fell and
   remove timber.
75 Respectively president and secretary-treasurer of the McLeod Pulp
   and Paper Company Limited.
76 Concerning Jones see Thomas H. Raddall, *In My Time: A Memoir*
   (Toronto: McClelland and Stewart, 1976), 155.
77 NSL&P (of which Stewart was vice-president) was both a holding
   and an operating company. It was controlled by I.W. Killam through
   Royal Securities Corporation.
78 Small rural communities in the constituency of Halifax East, which
   returned the Liberal incumbent.
79 *Cox v. Warne*; see below.
80 Now merged in RBC Dominion Securities.
81 *Instalment Payment Contracts Act*: S.N.S. 1938 c. 8.
82 [1939] 1 D.L.R. 719.
83 *Corporations Tax Act, 1939*: S.N.S. 1939 c. 2.
84 In the spring and summer of 1939 an attempt to consolidate the
   entire Canadian sugar refining industry, masterminded by Stewart
   and financed by Lord Beaverbrook, was underway. Only the
   outbreak of the Second World War seems to have prevented its
   going forward.
85 S.N.S. 1939 c. 34. This anti-discrimination act was passed on
   15 April 1939 but not proclaimed. It was repealed and re-enacted
   by R.S.N.S. 1954 c. 288 and afterwards became law.
86 In order to consult with Lord Beaverbrook on the proposed
   consolidation of the sugar refining industry; see note 84 above.
87 Meaning, of course, it would not work to Famous Players'
   advantage. It would have imposed a $250 licensing fee on each film
   distributed.
88 Nathan L. Nathanson and Thomas J. Bragg were, respectively,
   president and secretary-treasurer of Famous Players Canadian
   Corporation Limited.
89 The elderly Lieutenant-Colonel John Alexander Cooper LL B (born
   1868) was not in fact a lawyer but president of the Canadian
   Motion Picture Distributors Association.
90 Durbin (born 1921) was a major Hollywood star of the 1930s and
   1940s; she received a special Oscar in 1938.

91 *Pygmalion*, the first important cinematic adaptation of a Bernard
   Shaw play, was made into a film in Britain in 1938. It was the basis
   of the musical *My Fair Lady*.
92 Tom Mix was a star of the early silent westerns.
93 Section 91(2) of the Constitution Act, 1867.
94 In Nova Scotia the Liberals took ten seats, the National Government
   (Conservative) two and the CCF one. Nationally, the Liberals took
   184 of 245 Commons seats, the largest majority up to that time.
95 F.B. McCurdy (1875–1952), a stockbroker by profession, was the
   most powerful and feared financier in eastern Canada. Proprietor of
   the Halifax *Chronicle*, he was a former MP and minister in the first
   Meighen government. It would appear that McCurdy, a director of
   Canadian General Electric, was aiming at a consolidation of light,
   heat, and power companies in the Maritimes – an eastern Canadian
   equivalent of Sir Herbert Holt's Montreal Light, Heat & Power
   Company Limited. McCurdy's Eastern Utilities Limited never got off
   the ground.

CHAPTER FOUR

1 The act creating the new department was proclaimed in force in
   April 1940.
2 Canadian National Railway intercity train.
3 Concerning the work of the legal branch, see John de N. Kennedy,
   *History of the Department of Munitions and Supply: Canada in the
   Second World War*, 2 vols. (Ottawa: King's Printer, 1950), 2:332–44.
4 Boles, Lemay, Turnbull and Fraser were all solicitors in the legal
   branch; all except Lemay joined the armed forces. Fraser, like
   Covert, enlisted in the RCAF and was awarded the Distinguished
   Flying Cross.
5 Long a highly charged political issue; see Robert Bothwell and
   William Kilbourn, *C.D. Howe: A Biography* (Toronto: McClelland
   and Stewart, 1979), 121–2.
6 Of the firm now known as Ogilvy Renault.
7 Sir John George Hay, chairman and director of many rubber and
   palm oil companies, was a member of the International Rubber
   Regulation Committee.
8 Kennedy, *Munitions and Supply*, 1:98.
9 Regrettably none of these letters survives.

10 Howe returned to Ottawa 27 January 1941 after a two-month absence in England.

11 Howe was appointed professor of engineering at Dalhousie University in 1908.

12 The nature of the problem is unknown.

13 December 1940-January 1941.

14 Apparently a reference to Order in Council PC 932 (7 February 1941), relating to a contract with Canadian Westinghouse for the production of mobile anti-aircraft guns, etc.

15 Minister of national defence for naval services and member of the Cabinet War Committee.

16 Kennedy, *Munitions and Supply*, 1:318–22. APEL was a crown corporation set up to finance the extension of the Atlas Steels Limited plant.

17 A reference to the Hyde Park Declaration of April 1941 and to the Canada-United States Joint Defence Production Committee established in November 1941 as a result of it. The chair of the Canadian Committee was Deputy Minister Sheils.

18 "Order in Council authorizing uniformity in method of refund of taxes and duties on supplies and munitions of war," PC 8255 (24 October 1941). On this subject generally, see Kennedy, *Munitions and Supply*, 2:302–3.

19 A wholly-owned subsidiary of General Motors Corporation of Detroit.

20 Some 3,700 auto parts workers went on strike, 11–27 September 1941, for higher wages. While the strike was in progress an Order in Council was passed restricting the right to strike: PC 7307 (16 September 1941).

21 Under the *War Measures Act*; "Order in Council authorizing active militia to be called out to suppress riots, etc. on request of Minister of Munitions and Supply," PC 5830 (29 July 1941).

22 The post of solicitor-general was in abeyance from 1935 to 1945.

23 Then vice-president of Sorel Industries Limited.

24 The British prime minister was referring to a prediction made by Maréchal Pétain, after the fall of France in June 1940, that in three weeks England would have its neck wrung like a chicken. On Churchill's Ottawa visit, see J.W. Pickersgill, *The Mackenzie King Record*, Volume 1, 1939–1944 (Toronto: University of Toronto Press, 1960), 325–32.

25 Probably a victim of sudden infant death syndrome.

26 Chevrier, who was afterwards appointed parliamentary assistant to C.D. Howe, became minister of transport in 1945. See generally Bothwell and Kilbourn, *C.D. Howe*, 174–6.

27 "Electric Shock Kills Two Halifax Officers," Halifax *Chronicle*: 11 August 1942; Robert L.B. Covert was born in 1911, the year in which his father's political associate, Robert Borden, became prime minister.

28 The chronology is mistaken; Howe and Ralston did not depart for England until after 26 September.

29 "Aircrew candidates had to be fit males between eighteen and twenty-eight years of age": W.A.B. Douglas, *The Creation of a National Air Force – The Official History of the Royal Canadian Air Force*, Volume II (Toronto: University of Toronto Press, 1986), 278.

30 Chief of the air staff.

31 Member of the air staff for training.

32 Gavsie joined the legal branch of Munitions and Supply as solicitor in May 1941.

33 At the same time Henry Borden also left the legal branch, becoming chair of the Wartime Industries Control Board.

CHAPTER FIVE

1 No 1 Training Command Headquarters, Toronto. On Air crew training flow 1942–45, see Douglas, *Creation of a National Air Force*, 264; on the British Commonwealth Air Training Plan – Pilot training facilities and Air crew (other than pilot) training facilities, 1940–45, see colour maps between 236 and 237. The Manning Depot, known in peacetime as the Coliseum, was the home of the annual Royal Winter Fair. See also John D. Harvie, *Missing in Action: An RCAF Navigator's Story* (Montreal & Kingston: McGill-Queen's University Press, 1995), 3–16.

2 Spencer Dunmore, *Wings for Victory: The Remarkable Story of the British Commonwealth Air Training Plan in Canada* (Toronto: McClelland and Stewart, 1994), 72.

3 Cf. Douglas, *Creation of a National Air Force*, 278.

4 "The Link trainer was a crucial test of a recruit's suitability for pilot training": Douglas, *Creation of a National Air Force*, 162.

5 Flying the aircraft at a speed too low to permit effective operation of the controls.

6 "Circle an aircraft vertically in the air."

7 "In the early days of the British Commonwealth Air Training Plan, the Avro Anson, a low-winged, twin-engined, very stable mono-plane, was selected as the standard aeroplane for advanced training of pilots, navigators, wireless operators and bomb aimers": Kennedy, *Munitions and Supply*, 1:351.

8 Quoted in Dunmore, *Wings for Victory*, 178.

9 Under date 6 August 1943; Covert's wartime RCAF private diaries, all of which survive, are a superb documentary source meriting publication in their own right.

10 Borden was created Companion of the Order of St Michael and St George in June 1943.

11 William A.G. Kelley, formerly of Sydney, Nova Scotia, was a senior member of Borden's law firm and a director of Atlas Plant Extension Limited. Kelley's brother was to be killed while on active service with the RCAF.

12 RMS *Mauretania*, the second Cunard liner of that name, was launched in 1939.

13 The RCAF reception centre was at Bournemouth.

14 After the outbreak of war in 1939 Lady Frances Ryder CBE established the Dominion and Allied Services Hospitality Scheme.

15 Informal military usage for anti-aircraft guns.

16 Air Force derogatory slang for nonflying administrative staff officers; the officer concerned would have have been a Colonel in the British Army's Royal Air Force Regiment.

17 At 2,034 feet Snaefell is the culmination of the central mountain mass on the Isle of Man.

18 Order in Council, 29 February 1944.

19 A raincoat made of "a smooth, durable twill-woven worsted or cotton cloth" (*Concise Oxford Dictionary*).

20 For Wib Pierce's version of this meeting, see Williams, *Just Lawyers*, 195. "Frank's memory of this is different [from] mine ... I just wanted the sharpest navigator I could find!" (Pierce to editor, 20 April 2000).

21 A reference to the Grevenbroich raid (op no 30), 13–4 January 1945, for which both Covert and Pierce were awarded the Distinguished Flying Cross; see below.

22 RCAF Squadron No. 405. Pathfinders were aircraft or pilots sent ahead of bombing aircraft to locate and mark out the target for

attack, and to continue to mark it, if necessary from overclouding, as the raid progressed.

23 A flight consisted of ten aircraft, a squadron of twenty.

24 On Hutton's view of Covert, see Williams, *Just Lawyers*, 196–7.

25 "A device, typically conical or funnel-shaped, towed behind a boat, aircraft, etc., especially to reduce speed or improve stability" (*Concise Oxford Dictionary*), and, in this case, for gunnery practice, towed many yards behind the towplane.

26 Covert's account, as revised and expanded by Wib Pierce: letter to editor, 20 April 2000.

27 Ordered to stand down.

28 No. 433.

29 A reference to Gee; see below.

30 w/o A.T. Smith.

31 The term gen crew meant top-notch or ace. It signified a crew (or individual) that was regarded as fully informed and completely capable.

32 Gee (from G for Grid) was an electronic navigation system.

33 "A defence against hostile aircraft consisting of a connected system of balloons carrying wire cables reaching to the ground" (*Oxford English Dictionary*).

34 The Miles Magister was a very small, low-winged monoplane for two passengers, with open cockpits.

35 Allied invasion of western Europe.

36 Perfect result.

37 RCAF bases No. 61 and No. 76.

38 Flight Lieutenant George H. Pierce (1905–1972) joined the RCAF in 1941; when Covert met him he was Education Officer serving various stations in No. 6 Group.

39 A British coin worth five shillings, or 25 pence.

40 No. 433 Squadron was the fourteenth and last RCAF bomber squadron formed overseas (25 September 1943). See generally Brereton Greenhous, Stephen J. Harris and William G.P. Rawling, *The Crucible of War, 1939–1945: The Official History of The Royal Canadian Air Force*, Volume III (Toronto: University of Toronto Press, 1994), and Allan D. English, *The Cream of the Crop: Canadian Aircrew, 1939–1945* (Montreal & Kingston: McGill-Queen's University Press, 1996). The only scholarly monograph dealing with No. 6 Group, Bomber Command is William S. Carter,

*Anglo-Canadian Wartime Relations, 1939–1945: RAF Bomber
Command and No. 6 (Canadian) Group* (New York & London:
Garland, 1991). Carter co-wrote with Spencer Dunmore, *Reap the
Whirlwind: The Untold Story of 6 Group, Canada's Bomber Force
of World War II* (Toronto: McClelland & Stewart, 1991). See also
[Historical Section of the RCAF, comp.], *The R.C.A.F. Overseas: The
Sixth Year* (Toronto: Oxford University Press, 1949), which covers
the period September 1944 onwards.

41 RCAF Skipton-on-Swale opened as a satellite to Leeming in August
1942, becoming No. 63 Base substation in May 1944.

42 Covert and Hutton, absent for five days, thus missed the costly raid
on Hamburg (28 July), vividly recollected by Wib Pierce in
Dunmore, *Reap the Whirlwind*, 303–4. H₂S was used mainly as a
navigation aid but was also to define the target if it was necessary
to bomb above the clouds. Even then it was standard practice for
Pathfinders to mark and re-mark the target with coloured markers
on parachutes above the clouds, to serve as aiming point.

43 "One such operation, against the V-1 storage site at St-Leu-D'Esserent
on 5 August, saw No 6 Group deliver 1193 tons of bombs, the
most it dropped on any one raid during the whole war": Greenhous,
Crucible of War, 811. See generally "No. 6 Group Bombing Targets,
1943–1945" [map], between 840 and 841.

44 Wib Pierce writes, "We were a few minutes short of the target when
we suddenly lost all oil pressure on our port outer engine. The same
reservoir served to lubricate and operate the hydraulics on the propeller, so it could not be feathered [shut down]. As it windmilled,
the bearings burned out and the vibration was severe. I shook the
aircraft and broke the propeller off; it just missed the mid-upper
turret and the tail. The vibration broke a gasline, [so that] when
Fred [Haynes: flight engineer] switched tanks we lost power to
another engine; he switched to another tank. The abandon a/c
[aircraft] was cancelled and we headed back with two good engines
and one more overheating": letter to editor, 20 April 2000.

45 An Australian station at Church Broughton, a hamlet due west of
Derby.

46 "Edible paper made from the pith of an oriental tree and used for
painting and in cookery" (*Concise Oxford Dictionary*).

47 A joint army-air force operation.

48 That is, four hours fifty minutes from departure to return.

49 This was not the raid on which Canadian aircraft bombed Canadian troops near Falaise – a mishap blamed on poor navigation: Greenhous, *Crucible of War*, 816–20.

50 The aircraft's codename.

51 Covert's diary refers to marshalling yards east and south of Paris.

52 In the Pas de Calais (north Picardy); flying-bomb site.

53 The raid against Dortmund, on 6/7 October 1944, was the maximum effort by No. 6 (RCAF) Group, Bomber Command, involving 293 Lancasters and Halifaxes; see Greenhous, *Crucible of War*, 832–4.

54 This meant target time less four minutes, to help the Pathfinders by being flak bait. Wib Pierce writes, "The first Pathfinders over a target, with no other a/c around, were easy 'marks' and sitting ducks for the guns below. There may only [have been] two or three of them before the raid started. To provide more a/c over the target, [the Pathfinders] asked for perhaps one a/c from ten squadrons to go in with them, to be, as we called it, 'flak bait':" letter to editor, 20 April 2000. On the 'double' raid on Duisberg (14 October 1944), see Greenhous. *Crucible of War*, 835–8.

55 The station commander, Group Captain H.H.C. Rutledge.

56 Harry Joseph Kelley, son and namesake of the vice-president and managing director of Dosco, was killed in a plane crash in Scotland in January 1942 while serving with the RCAF.

57 Greenhous, *Crucible of War*, 843.

58 It was during this raid that the bombers were attacked by Messerschmitt 163 rocket fighters: Greenhous, *Crucible of War*, 849.

59 Each engine had two magnetos (electrical generators).

60 i.e. 400 miles.

61 "*Brit., informal, dated* an aircraft" (*Concise Oxford Dictionary*).

62 On 26 December 1944 63 No. 6 Group bombers joined over 200 aircraft from other RAF bomber groups to attack St-Vith in support of U.S. army troops fighting the Battle of the Bulge.

63 "*Military slang* a push-button, especially one used to fire a gun or release a bomb" (*Concise Oxford Dictionary*).

64 Northwest of St. Andrews.

65 Flight commanders were restricted to three trips per month, so they could serve four or five months as commander.

66 *Brit. informal* be ruined, destroyed or killed … Second World War (originally RAF slang) perhaps referring to Burton ale, from Burton-upon-Trent (after *Concise Oxford Dictionary*).

67 F.T. Smye was then assistant general manager of Federal Aircraft Limited, a crown corporation.

68 "Nos. 424, 427, 429 and 433 Squadrons received Lancaster I/IIIs between January and March 1945 once Lancaster Xs had become available": Greenhous, *Crucible of War*, 604 note.

69 Halifax III Y-Yokum M2910 flew 32 missions with 433 Squadron and was transferred to another squadron when No. 433 converted to Lancasters in January-February 1945. Piloted by F/O Keeper of Vancouver, it was shot down returning from a raid on Witten in the Ruhr Valley in March 1945.

70 Russell Manning was a good friend of Covert, with whom he played hours of bridge.

71 One of No. 6 Group's "four bad raids" in February-March 1945; "five of 182 Canadian crews went missing at Dessau and Hemmingstedt": Greenhous, *Crucible of War*, 858.

72 Afterwards director of air staff at RCAF overseas headquarters.

73 Due south of Brussels.

74 Covert's diary says seven. The incident was suppressed and remains officially unacknowledged to this day. Wib Pierce writes, "Our last trip – HAGEN – was shaken up by the Army's (Allied) opening up on us and 6 or 7 bombers went down. We were down at a lower level so the small-calibre guns could reach us [with] light flak. We always had a Very pistol [light] through which you could fire 'the colours of the day' (colour-coded and changed every few hours), e.g., red-green-red from 6 to 10 pm; yellow-blue-red 10 to 2:00 am. This was fired to identify you as 'friend'. My engineer [Haynes] wanted to fire it and I said 'No, you'd just give them a visual on us'. So he didn't. Moments later one a/c did fire it, on our right, and seconds later they exploded – a direct hit ... I put the nose down, put 350 mph on the clock and got away" (letter to editor, 8 March 2000).

75 "The Rows" are 16th- and 17th-century double tier shops.

76 A member of the Women's Auxiliary Air Force (UK), 1939–48.

77 Clearly a court martial was in progress. It was understandable that Covert, a barrister and KC, should have been ordered to participate.

78 Equidistant from Manchester and Liverpool; the assembly point for aircrew returning to Canada. Wib Pierce writes, "The posting came a week before, and, unbeknownst to Frank I went to RCAF Headquarters to see if I could have my posting switched to Frank. As [he was] a married man with family ... this made great sense to me.

This was refused and, as it turned out, my draft consisted entirely of senior [and 'A' Class medical] officers" (letter to editor, 24 February 2000).

CHAPTER SIX

1 Afterwards Mr Justice Ritchie of the Supreme Court of Canada.
2 Now merged in Patterson Palmer. Covert wrote that Ritchie, who had articled with J.McG. Stewart, "on his return accepted an offer to join Gordon Daley's firm. I think had I been home this would not have happened and I was shocked when I came home to find him gone! He had been best man at my wedding in 1934 and we had been close friends. His bent was trial work and he worked very closely with Harry MacKeen in the 6 years [1934–40] he was with us": Frank Covert, "Stewart, MacKeen & Covert: Firm History" (unpubl. ms., 1980), xi–2. Ironically, A. William Moreira QC, a senior member of Daley Black & Moreira and H.P. MacKeen's grandson, joined Covert's firm in 2003, when his former one was absorbed by Patterson Palmer.
3 The accused, an RCAF officer, John David Mill (afterwards managing editor of the Montreal *Star*), was involved in a fatal altercation with another RCAF officer.
4 A venerable family firm of fish-merchants and West Indies traders, founded in Lunenburg, Nova Scotia, in 1789.
5 Formerly known as shell shock.
6 Mr Justice W.L. Hall.
7 The proceeding was exceptional in that the coroner's jury had brought in a verdict of accidental death; the crown prosecuted nevertheless.
8 On the Magazine disaster, see Thomas H. Raddall, *Halifax: Warden of the North*, rev. ed. (Toronto: McClelland and Stewart, 1971), 306–10.
9 8 May 1945.
10 The shell company for navigating the merger afterwards known as National Sea Products Limited (now High Liner Foods Inc.).
11 It remained so until 1989.
12 S.C., 1948, c. 52.
13 Promoter and president of National Sea Products Limited.
14 Bell sold his controlling interest in 1953.
15 George A. Chase was a director of Minas Basin Pulp & Power.

16 Frank Herbert Brown was financial adviser to the minister of munitions and supply.

17 John Joseph Bench KC (1905–1947), a director of St Catharines Steel Products Limited, was a failed Liberal candidate appointed to the Senate in 1942.

18 James Joseph McCann.

19 NSL&P work was being done by Gordon Cowan, whom Stewart had hired after Covert joined Munitions and Supply.

20 Company creditor arrangements.

21 The tradition which Covert inaugurated continues to this day. Stewart McKelvey Stirling Scales has a Labour and Employment practice group, which, among many other things, negotiates and administers collective agreements on behalf of employers. In 2000 the firm absorbed Petrie Goss, "one of New Brunswick's leading employment, labour and administrative law practices."

22 Nova Scotia's first Trade Union Act was passed in 1937.

23 In 1946, by the International Brotherhood of Pulp, Sulphite and Paper Mill Workers.

24 Wartime Labour Relations Regulations, Order in Council PC 1003 (17 February 1944); the provinces yielded their control over industrial relations to Ottawa for the duration of the war.

25 The application for certification was approved by the Nova Scotia Wartime Labour Relations Board.

26 The letter had less to do with the freedom and responsibility of the press than with municipal politics. The then Conservative mayor of Halifax, Allan MacDougall Butler, was attempting to staunch the unrestricted flow of politically damaging information from city hall to the Liberal newspapers, the *Chronicle* and the *Daily Star*. A press campaign against the mayor's action seems to have been orchestrated by his chief opponent, the Liberal deputy mayor, John Edward ("Gee") Ahern, a newspaperman who went on to defeat the Conservative candidate for mayor in the civic election in April 1946. Stewart, a highly partisan Conservative, was not amused.

27 "4 big things in office which I might reasonably have expected to be given to me were not": Covert diary, 15 March 1946.

28 To Gordon Cowan, Covert's chief rival. The files concerned included Nova Scotia Light & Power, the Sobeys Stores flotation, and the William Stairs, Son & Morrow reorganization, on the latter of which Covert had done considerable preparatory work. "Bitter Blow to-day – found I'm not to do the Stairs Reorganization. But spent

all evening looking over G.S.C. [Gordon Stewart Cowan] draft of T[rust] Deed": Covert diary, 6 September 1946.

29 Covert was careful to attend the funeral of Stewart's last-surviving spinster aunt, Elizabeth Helen Stewart: Covert diary, 3 September 1946.

30 "Waiting to see Mr Stewart – didn't": Covert diary, 2 October 1946 [a Saturday]; "finally after 5 wks. trying got an interview with Mr Stewart & he agreed to see me about personal matter on Tuesday night": Covert diary, 15 November 1946.

31 No record in Covert diary; "Home all evening – waiting for Boss [Stewart] to phone re appointment. – He didn't": Covert diary, 21 November 1946.

32 The initiative almost certainly came from Borden himself. In February 1946, having been offered and having accepted the reversion of the presidency of Brazilian Traction, Borden became a director; in June he became president. As the co–founder and head of his firm, Borden had the privilege of nominating his own successor. Stewart would have been highly displeased by Borden's trying to poach his number–one protégé.

33 Emphasis added. This is the crux of the matter: Stewart had obviously been given to understand that Covert had been recruited to fill the vacancy created by the departure of Henry Borden. Given the friendship and excellent working relationship between him and Borden, Covert would have been the logical choice.

34 The reference is to the *Zwicker* decision, [1947] 3 D.L.R. 195, which effectively decertified the union; see generally the sources cited in Cahill, *Thousandth Man*, 207 n. 114. The only scholarly account of the strike against National Sea Products is L. Gene Barrett, "Development and Underdevelopment, and the Rise of Trade Unionism in the Fishing Industry of Nova Scotia, 1900–1950" (MA thesis, Dalhousie University, 1976), 194–207; cf. C. Keith Reyes, "Some of the Problems of Collective Bargaining for Nova Scotia Offshore Fishermen" (MA thesis, Dalhousie University, 1971). The Trade Union Act, passed four months after the Supreme Court in Banco handed down its unanimous judgment in *Zwicker*, entirely took away the court's power to review any decsion of the Labour Relations Board established to administer the act: S.N.S., 1947, c. 3, s. 58.

35 "The Canadian Fishermen's Union ... flourished for eight years in Nova Scotia and endured two tremendous strikes: one in 1939, and

another in 1947. It was organized through the efforts of the
Communist Party of Canada and the Canadian Seamen's Union and
represented a very militant trade union unifying all workers in the
fishing industry": L. Gene Barrett, "Underdevelopment and Social
Movements in the Nova Scotia Fishing Industry to 1938," in Robert
J. Brym and R. James Sacouman, eds., *Underdevelopment and Social
Movements in Atlantic Canada* (Toronto: New Hogtown Press,
1979), 160 n. 200.

36 Fish-processing company of North Sydney, Nova Scotia; the union
concerned was the Canadian Fish Handlers Union. Covert's reward
was a directorship in Nickerson's.

37 "Throughout February and March [1947], Bell ran huge one-page
advertisements which clouded and ignored the issues and were meant
solely to incite anti-Communist hysteria among the public toward
the union": Barrett, "Development and Underdevelopment," 199.

38 Martins Point, Lunenburg County.

39 On 24 April 1947, a month after the strike at National Sea
Products was settled, Russell Cunningham, one of the two CCF
members making up the official opposition in Nova Scotia's legislature, presented a petition asking that the new omnibus Trade Union
Act be amended so as to bring deep-sea fishermen within its
purview. No action was taken on the petition.

40 Two months after the Trade Union Act was proclaimed, J.H.
MacQuarrie was appointed to the Supreme Court. His successor as
attorney general was the minister of labour, L.D. Currie, who had
drafted the act.

41 Marjorie Jenkins RN.

42 Probably Dr Gordon B. Wiswell, attending physician, who in 1948
became physician-in-chief of the Children's Hospital.

43 Richard William Harris was vice-president of Manning's United
Service Corporation.

44 A reference to the Industrial & Development Corporation of
Venezuela. Manning's attempt at indirect investment in the burgeon-
ing petroleum industry of a developing country like Venezuela was
through a holding company providing infrastructural support to the
industry. The I&DCV, incorporated under the Canadian Companies
Act in 1946, had its headquarters in Halifax; Manning was
promoter, chair, and president.

45 The Act to Amend and Consolidate the Fishermen's Federation Act
(S.N.S. 1947 c. 4) was aimed at containing the worst effects of the

Zwicker decision by granting a semblance of collective bargaining rights to offshore fishers. The Fishermen's Federation Act was not repealed until 1971, in the wake of a protracted and bitter strike in the deep-sea fishery; S.N.S. 1970–71 c. 40.

46 S.N.S. 1947 c. 116.

47 The Lockheed Constellation (1943) was a four-engined airliner carrying up to 65 passengers at 260 to 300 mph for 2,000 to 3,000 miles.

48 A city and port on the west bank of the Neveri river; capital of the state of Anzoategui. The development of petroleum in Anzoategui brought some measure of prosperity to Barcelona.

49 Capital of the state of Zulia, Maracaibo is Venezuela's second-largest city, most important seaport and oil metropolis. It is one of the leading petroleum-exporting centres in the world.

50 RCAF base in Kings County, Nova Scotia. Until construction of Halifax International Airport in the early 1960s Greenwood was the routine terminus for flights unable to land in Halifax because of fog.

51 In 1959.

52 All in Quebec.

53 The principals in Argus Corporation.

54 The part of the nominal value of shares issued which does not yet need to be paid.

55 MacMillan, a building contractor by profession, was president of Fundy Construction; the work concerned naval facilities at Dalhousie University during the war, when MacMillan was premier and his predecessor (and successor) Angus L. Macdonald, minister of national defence for naval services.

56 Inaugurated in the spring of 1944 by Dalhousie's radical president, Carleton Stanley, the DLI was the first of its kind in Canada. Its purpose was to train trade unionists in industrial relations.

57 This was in relation to the leading constitutional case, *Nova Scotia Interdelegation*, a provincial reference which reached the Supreme Court of Canada in 1950: [1951] S.C.R. 31. See *Re Bill 136 in the Nova Scotia Legislature, 1947, re Delegation of Legislative Jurisdiction*, [1948] 4 D.L.R. 1 (NSSC in Banco). Covert's role was probably limited to preparing a brief on behalf of his senior, C.B. Smith KC, counsel for the intervenant Lord Nelson Hotel Company Limited, of which Smith was president. On the other hand, Covert may have prepared a brief for the attorney-general of Nova Scotia, who led the government's defence of the constitutionality of the bill.

58 A venerable mercantile and shipping firm in Halifax.

59 An investment company formed in 1941, the Great Eastern Corporation Limited now has assets in excess of $100 million. The basis of the Fountain family philanthropic fortune, its current president is Halifax lawyer Frederick S. Fountain, Manning's grandson.

60 Ilsley resigned from the government in June and from Parliament in October. The by-election, on 13 December, returned the Conservative, George Nowlan, in the seat which Ilsley had held for twenty-two years.

61 Nova Scotia's provincial election took place on 9 June; Canada's federal election on 27 June. The Liberals won both handily. In Digby-Annapolis-King's the Conservative incumbent was defeated by four votes, but the result was overturned and a new election held in which Nowlan was victorious.

62 That is, after the death of the eighty-six-year-old incumbent, Sir Joseph Chisholm, which occurred in 1950. Ilsley was appointed a puisne judge of the Supreme Court in May 1949, it being customary to appoint the chief justice from among the judges of the court.

63 Order in Council PC 6033 (29 December 1948); see *Report of the Royal Commission on Transportation* (Ottawa: King's Printer, 1951). The inquiry's chief concern was the financial position of the railways, which had suffered as a result of the immediate post-war decline in rail traffic, leading to drastic increases in freight rates. Though none of its recommendations was implemented, the report was the first attempt at developing a national transportation policy.

64 All three of them Liberals.

65 Where Ilsley had been practising law with James Layton Ralston, another former federal cabinet minister, since leaving the cabinet in June 1948. In May 1949 Ralston died and Ilsley went looking for work.

66 Turgeon, a former chief justice of Saskatchewan, was on leave from his post as Canadian high commissioner to the then Commonwealth of Ireland.

67 Grain trade, 1925; transfer of natural resources of Manitoba, 1928–9 (chair); textile industry, 1936 (sole commissioner); grain inquiry, 1936 (sole commissioner); and agreed charges, 1954 (sole commissioner).

68 Argentina and Chile, Mexico, Belgium, and Ireland.

69 The raid on Bergen by no. 6 Group, Bomber Command took place on 4 October 1944. A city and seaport in western Norway, it was occupied by the Germans between 1940 and 1945.

70 L.J. Knowles was traffic adviser to the Commission.
71 Oxford: Clarendon Press, 1950; Innis's final, most difficult and most seminal work.
72 It seems unlikely that Innis's Memorandum on Transportation (*Report...*, 294–307) was "dissenting": "This memorandum is intended as an elaboration of the basic argument behind the conclusions of the Report" (p. 294 note). (It was H.F. Angus, not Innis, who dissented.) Covert's correspondence with Innis, September–October 1950, is among the records of the Royal Commission; RG 33/27 vol. 61 file 2150–3, NA.
73 The friendship went back to 1934, when Macdonald appointed Innis a member of the provincial Royal Commission of Economic Inquiry. I am grateful to Stephen Henderson for drawing this to my attention.
74 Nothing was done; the outcome of the Royal Commission on Transportation was another Royal Commission on Transportation, appointed eight years later by the new Conservative government and chaired by another former attorney-general of Saskatchewan and expatriate Maritimer, Murdoch Alexander MacPherson. Commission counsel was the Halifax Conservative corporate lawyer, A. Gordon Cooper. See generally Jerry Fast, "Economic Efficiency and National Transportation Policy: A Study of the Turgeon and MacPherson Royal Commissions" (MA thesis, University of Manitoba, 1972), 66–113.

CHAPTER SEVEN

1 *Re Wright*, [1951] 2 D.L.R. 429.
2 *Re Wright*, 56 N.S.R. 364.
3 *Re Wright*, [1951] 2 D.L.R. 429; Chief Justice Ilsley did not sit for this in banco (appellate) proceeding.
4 H.J. Kelley, senior vice-president and managing director of Dosco.
5 Eugene Troop Parker; appointed 1948.
6 *Province of Prince Edward Island et al. v. C.N.R.*, (1951) 68 C.R.T.C. 113.
7 Richey Bryce Love QC (died 1995) was for many years a prominent corporation and tax lawyer with McLeod Dixon in Calgary.
8 Just beyond the western reaches of Halifax Harbour.
9 A dispersed rural community west of Windsor, NS.
10 "Falmouth Boy Succumbs To Injuries," Windsor *Hants Journal*: 7 November 1951.

11 *Picbell Limited v. Pickford & Black Limited.* Judgment for the plaintiff was rendered in November 1953; the action was for breach of contract.

12 The doctor concerned, who is named elsewhere in these memoirs, was head of surgery in the faculty of medicine at Dalhousie University.

13 The Liberal Party was defeated in the provincial election of October 1956, after twenty-three continuous years in office.

14 E.L. MacDonald (1882–1957), a millionaire capitalist, was president of S. Cunard & Co. Ltd.

15 On this subject generally see Stephen Kimber, *"Not Guilty": The Trial of Gerald Regan* (Toronto: Stoddart, 1999), 71.

16 Of which E.L. MacDonald was a director; now Canada Trust.

17 An allowance was being paid the leader of the opposition before the Conservatives came to power in October 1956; afterwards, it was doubled.

18 Senator Charles G. Hawkins (1887–1958), sometime president of the Nova Scotia Liberal Association.

19 Irvine Barrow (afterwards Senator) and Charles MacFadden.

20 Henry Hicks (1956–62), Earl Urquhart (1962–65), and Gerald Regan (1965–70).

21 Peter M. Nicholson, afterwards minister of finance in the Regan government.

22 The former Liberal premier was then MP for Halifax and minister of labour in the second Trudeau government.

23 Ironically, the whistle-blower was to be Senator Hawkins's son, George, a lawyer and perennial Liberal insider, whose revelations in 1991 helped to bring down the then Liberal leader of the opposition, Vincent J. MacLean. See Kimber, *"Not Guilty,"* 70–2.

24 In 1958.

25 Milner (died 1990) was Amherst's town solicitor.

26 See generally Stephen Kimber, *Net Profits: The Story of National Sea* (Halifax: Nimbus, 1989), 117ff.

27 Vice-president of National Sea Products.

28 Among the original directorate of National Sea Products.

29 In 1952; Bell subsequently became a vice-president of the Bank of Nova Scotia.

30 C.J. Morrow replaced Bell as president of National Sea Products.

31 Dr Charles MacLean Jones (died 1968); Covert and the second Mrs Jones were co-executors of his estate.

32 Robert Henry Graham, judge of the divorce court, 1925–48.

33 *Jones v. Jones*, [1947] 3 D.L.R. 878.

34 Shire town of Kings County, Nova Scotia.

35 Then a Canadian National Railway hotel.

36 *Pew v. Zinck and Lobster Point Realty Corp. et al.*, (1953) 2 D.L.R. 337; the leading case on Nova Scotia's bizarre mortgage law. See T.H. Coffin, "Case and Comment," (1954) 32 Can. Bar Rev. 217. The respondent's petition for special leave to appeal to the Privy Council was granted on 24 November 1953.

37 Turning on whether the mortgagor had the right to redeem mortgaged lands after foreclosure and sheriff's sale by order of the court.

38 [1951] 1 D.L.R. 623, [1951] 2 D.L.R. 667, [1951] 3 D.L.R. 73, [1952] 2 D.L.R. 359.

39 The Pews and the Goulds, who had maintained a summer home on Lobster Point – then as now prime oceanfront property – since 1929.

40 Joseph N. Pew Jr (1886–1963), younger son of the founder of Sun Oil (Sunoco).

41 The Supreme Court Amendment Act (S.C., 1949, c. 37), abolishing the Privy Council appeal, came into force on 23 December 1949 but did not apply to any proceeding commenced before that date. *Pew v. Zinck et al.* commenced 26 February 1948.

42 Lead counsel for the appellants was Donald McInnes QC, of the firm now known as McInnes Cooper; the appeal was withdrawn by letter, 26 January 1955. On McInnes's envy and dislike of Covert see Bruce, *Corporate Navigator*, 228.

43 Porter (1894–1967) was also the first woman member of the Nova Scotia Legislature.

44 "Civic Election Petition Is Dismissed by Judge," Kentville *Advertiser*: 22 April 1954; *Kirkpatrick v. Porter* was a petition under the Municipal and Town Controverted Elections Act.

45 The International Union of Operating Engineers, Local 721, the dismissal of whose application for certification was reconsidered and granted by the Labour Relations Board. The respondent was Robb Engineering Works Limited (Amherst, Nova Scotia).

46 "A Good Board," Halifax *Chronicle-Herald*: 14 February 1956.

47 See generally Bruce, *R.A. Jodrey*, 215–8.

48 With Mrs Stewart and Montreal Trust.

49 Covert confuses the time of the announcement of Stewart's death with the time of his death, which occurred several hours earlier.

50 On Covert's twenty-two years as a highly influential governor of Dalhousie University see P.B. Waite, *The Lives of Dalhousie University, Volume Two, 1925–1980: The Old College Transformed* (Montreal & Kingston: McGill-Queen's University Press, 1998), 477, s.v. "Covert, Frank." Waite, who began his long Dalhousie career when Covert's mentor Stewart was a member of the university's board, describes Covert as "authoritarian" (299).

51 Of which Stewart had been a director since 1941.

52 Among them were Harbour Motors, Super Tire Treaders, Acadian Lines, Avonian Motors, Maritime Accessories, Industrial Machinery, and Consolidated Supply.

53 Less than a year after Covert concluded his memoirs, Canadian Petrofina was acquired by Petro-Canada. At $1,460,000,000 it was the biggest takeover in Canadian history to that time: Peter C. Newman, *The Acquisitors: The Canadian Establishment*, Volume Two (Toronto: McClelland & Stewart, 1981), 472.

54 In 1955 United Service Corporation Limited controlled some 400 retail outlets in the Maritimes. The vacuum created by its disappearance was filled by K.C. Irving.

55 Towards the end of Killam's life, Sir Eric Bowater had been attempting unsuccessfully to persuade him to sell Mersey Paper to Bowater's.

56 Now Merrick Holm.

57 In 1962 Covert became a director of new Mersey (Bowater Mersey) and remained one until his death in 1987.

58 Archibald Robertson Graustein (1885–1969) had been president of International Paper from 1924 to 1936.

59 On Blake Cassels & Graydon, see T.D. Regehr, "Elite Relationships, Partnership Arrangements and Nepotism at Blakes, a Toronto Law Firm, 1858–1942" in Carol Wilton, ed., *Inside the Law: Canadian Law Firms in Historical Perspective* (Toronto: The Osgoode Society for Canadian Legal History, 1996), 207–47.

60 A long ton was 2,240 lb; a ton (short ton) 2,000 lb.

61 Now Bowater Mersey Paper Company Limited.

62 Stewart McKelvey Stirling Scales remains so to this day.

63 Vice-president of Mersey Paper.

64 President of National Sea Products.

65 President of Oland Breweries Limited.

66 Afterwards Hawker-Siddeley Canada Limited. On the Dosco takeover see John Porter, *The Vertical Mosaic: An Analysis of Social*

Class and Power in Canada (Toronto: University of Toronto Press, 1965), 259–63.

67 A superb narrative of Jodrey's fight for Dosco is in Bruce, *R.A. Jodrey*, 221ff.

68 Vice-president of Mersey Paper Company ("new Mersey").

69 On Sobey's involvement in Dosco, see Harry Bruce, *The Man and the Empire: Frank Sobey* (Toronto: Macmillan, 1985), 195ff.

70 Ironically, Fred Smye, Covert's close friend from Munitions and Supply, was Gordon's "closest friend at A.V. Roe;" Smye was managing director of the A.V. Roe subsidiary, Avro Aircraft, which designed and built the fabled Arrow. See generally Greig Stewart, *An Arrow through the Heart: The Life and Times of Crawford Gordon and the Avro Arrow* (Toronto: McGraw-Hill Ryerson, 1998). After A.V. Roe took over Dosco, Gordon became its president as well.

71 In 1969 all the outstanding ordinary shares of Dosco were acquired by Sidbec (now Ispat Sidbec Inc.).

72 Twenty years and many millions of taxpayers' dollars after Covert wrote these words, Sydney Steel Corporation (Sysco), which could not be sold as a going concern, was sold off piecemeal. It continues to exist on paper as a provincial crown corporation.

73 Industrial Estates Limited – now merged in Nova Scotia Business Inc. – was incorporated in September 1957. See generally Roy E. George, *The Life and Times of Industrial Estates Limited* (Halifax: Dalhousie University Institute of Public Affairs, 1974).

74 They were Horace Enman (chairman), Frank Sobey (president), Harold Egan (secretary-treasurer), D.F. Archibald, T.H. Coffin (Covert's brother-in-law), S.W. Kenney, C. LeCouteur, J.C. MacKeen, C.G. MacLennan, and E.A. Manson (minister of trade and industry). Enman was chairman of the Bank of Nova Scotia.

75 See Bruce, *Frank Sobey*, chapter 9.

76 By 1965 the IEL board included the premier and two of his ministers.

77 Covert refers to the Clairtone Sound Corporation plant at Stellarton (Sobey's hometown) and the Deuterium of Canada heavy water plant at Glace Bay – both launched in 1964, during the Stanfield premiership. IEL, which eventually took over the operations of Clairtone, had owned a controlling interest in Deuterium from the beginning.

78 McCurdy left $6,471,000. The province's leading financier, McCurdy had been president of Eastern Trust Company for many years.

He was also a vice-president of the Bank of Nova Scotia and a long-time member and the treasurer of the board of governors of Dalhousie University.

79 Dalhousie was entitled to ninety per cent of the residue.

80 The previous year Covert had been appointed to a select committee of the board "to take whatever action they consider best in connection with the settlement of the McCurdy estate": Dalhousie University, Board of Governors' minutes, 28 May 1957: UA 1–1-A14, p. 79, Dalhousie University Archives.

81 Between probate in 1952 and closing in 1958 the value of the estate declined by nearly $2 million.

82 A. Gordon Cooper, afterwards Mr Justice Cooper of the Supreme Court of Nova Scotia, Appeal Division.

83 Covert is probably referring to a meeting of the McCurdy estate settlement committee, which included among its members three members of the Eastern Trust board: Albert S. Fraser (chairman of ETC), Donald McInnes QC (president), and W.N. Wickwire QC (vice-president). While the McCurdy estate was being closed, McInnes, university secretary and legal counsel, became chair of the Dalhousie board. Until May 1958 the manager of Eastern Trust, Clinton B. Havey, had also been a member of the Dalhousie board.

84 V.J. Pottier, judge of the County Court for District No 1 (Halifax).

85 Jodrey was a director of Eastern Trust.

86 Conspicuous by its omission from Covert's memoirs is the failure of the disastrous litigation involving the attempt by the Jodrey Estate to avoid paying succession duties on bequests: *Frank M. Covert QC, John S. Jodrey and The Canada Permanent Trust Company, Executors under the Will of the late Roy A. Jodrey v. The Minister of Finance of the Province of Nova Scotia*, [1980] 2 S.C.R. 774.

87 Liverpool Regional High School (now South Queens Junior High).

88 John Welsford MacDonald.

89 *Mersey Paper Company Limited* v. *County of Queens*, [1959] 18 D.L.R. (2nd) 19. The case was remitted for further inquiry.

90 J.McG. Stewart had negotiated old Mersey's eighth and final power contract with the Nova Scotia Power Commission in 1950; see F.M. Covert, comp., *Some Mersey Memories, 1928–1986* (Liverpool, Nova Scotia: Bowater Mersey Paper Company Limited, 1986), 32–5.

91 Henry Burton Rhude (1923–1985), by common consent the most brilliant business lawyer of his generation in Nova Scotia.

92 Founded in 1931; J.McG. Stewart succeeded Cyril Stairs as president of Maritime Paper Products on the latter's death in 1953.

93 Afterwards Consolidated-Bathurst.

94 In the Burnside Industrial Park in the·former City of Dartmouth (now Halifax Regional Municipality).

95 Born 1913.

96 See generally Janet Guildford, *Maritime Paper Products: A History* (unpubl. commissioned report, 1993).

97 International Union of United Brewery, Flour, Cereal, Soft Drink and Distillery Workers of America, No. 361, AFL-CIO/CLC. The strike, over wages and the union shop, began on 21 August 1958; it involved about 162 workers.

98 Name changed in 1969 to Venpower Limited.

99 Responsible for the Dominion Companies Act, under which Venezuelan Power was incorporated.

100 Dwyer was president and general manager of John Tobin and Company Limited.

101 The seven Dunn scholarships, tenable at Dalhousie Law School, were unique in Canada when they began in 1959.

102 An Act Respecting the Last Will and Testament of the Late Frederick Carl Manning: S.N.S., 1961, c. 103.

103 Pearson was in Halifax to address the annual meeting of the Nova Scotia Liberal Association.

104 Covert's brother-in-law, Halifax lawyer T.H. Coffin, became national treasurer of the Progressive Conservative party in 1959; his reward was appointment to the Supreme Court of Nova Scotia in 1961.

CHAPTER EIGHT

1 Bill No. 116, An Act to Amend Chapter 295 of the Revised Statutes, 1954, the Trade Union Act, was given the six months' hoist in April 1960. At that time no province in Canada had legislated the compulsory union shop. Nova Scotia did not do so for four years: S.N.S., 1964, c. 48.

2 Judge of the County Court of District No. 6; formerly Liberal minister of labour and afterwards chief justice of Nova Scotia. The McKinnon Report has been called "perhaps the most outspoken critique of the legal system of industrial relations in Canada": C.H.J. Gilson, *Strikes: Industrial Relations in Nova Scotia, 1957–1987* (Hantsport, Nova Scotia: Lancelot, 1987), 198.

3 Now Henson College of Public Affairs and Continuing Education, the then director of which, Guy Henson, was inaugural chair of the Joint Study Committee. See generally Gilson, *Strikes*, 47–55 and sources cited in the endnotes (p. 55) and on pp. 198–9. Covert, interestingly enough, is referred to in his company president not his corporate lawyer persona.

4 See generally Kell Antoft, "Harnessing Confrontation: A Review of the Nova Scotia Joint Labour-Management Study Committee, 1962–1979" in Robert E. Chanteloup, ed., *Labour in Atlantic Canada* (Saint John: University of New Brunswick, 1981). See also C.H.J. Gilson and A.M. Wadden, "The Windsor Gypsum Strike and the Formation of the Joint Labour/Management Study Committee: Conflict and Accommodation in the Nova Scotia Labour Movement, 1957–1979," in Michael Earle, ed., *Workers and the State in Twentieth Century Nova Scotia* (Fredericton: Acadiensis Press, 1989), 190–216; and C. Roy Brookbank, "The Nova Scotia Experiment in Labour-Management Relations" [unidentified offprint, ca. 1965], 1–5. The secrecy surrounding the inauguration and early deliberations of the JLMSC led to accusations that it was "a Halifax family compact." According to Gilson and Wadden (209 n. 56), Frank Covert was "widely believed to be one of the most influential businessmen of the day." Covert, of course, was appointed to the JLMSC not because he was an influential businessman (though he was certainly that), but because he was the only important corporate lawyer who took industrial relations law seriously enough to practise it. In that respect if in no other, Covert was *sui generis*.

5 The notorious 'Michelin Bill', which violated the sacrosanct union shop principle; see generally Brian Langille, "The Michelin Amendment in Context," (1981) 6:3 Dalhousie L.J. 523. Michelin plants in Nova Scotia remain ununionized.

6 Covert attended his last meeing of the JLMSC on 14 February 1979; the Michelin bill, introduced and withdrawn in April, was reintroduced and passed in December: S.N.S., 1979, c. 78.

7 Then president of the Nova Scotia Federation of Labour. On Yetman's implacable opposition to the Michelin Bill, see Beck, *Politics of Nova Scotia...* Volume Two, 350–1.

8 Nova Scotia Pulp Limited was a wholly-owned subsidiary of Sweden's venerable Stora Kopparbergs. An agreement had been reached with the government in July 1957 to build a pulp mill at Port Hawkesbury.

9 Now Shearman & Sterling, New York's oldest and most prestigious law firm.

10 Kenneth Middleton Sedgewick (1911–1970), a Nova Scotian expatriate and grandson of a justice of the Supreme Court of Canada, was at the time a director and vice-chairman of the bank.

11 Executive vice-president.

12 It is not clear what Covert means by Sedgewick's having blown it, though he may be alluding to the folly of Sedgewick's absenting himself from the critical board meeting on 19 December 1960, at which the succession to Walter was decided. On this subject see Duncan McDowall, *Quick to the Frontier: Canada's Royal Bank, A History* (Toronto: McClelland & Stewart, 1993), 358–63. Having failed twice in one year to be elected president, Sedgewick immediately resigned from the employ of the bank and as a director.

13 In 2004 the newspaper remains owned by the Dennis family.

14 A.E. Johnson, whose acquisition of control of Farmers Limited Covert had negotiated for Maple Leaf.

15 Company now called Farmers Cooperative Dairy Limited.

16 Charles Benjamin Moir Jr (1900–1973) became a director of Ben's Limited in 1920 and president in 1934.

17 John J. Jodrey (born 1913).

18 In October 1962, while visiting Toronto, Covert mislaid his diary; as a result, "I am too lazy to dig into office records to see what I did in 1962."

19 Now Nova Scotia Power Inc.

20 In 1955, on the death of J.McG. Stewart, who had been a director since 1926 and vice-president since 1931. NSL&P was one of the very few directorships held by Stewart at the time of his death which Covert did *not* inherit.

21 Covert was one; the other was the company's solicitor and Covert's law partner, Gordon Cowan; information from A. Russell Harrington. The board compromised in the choice of A.S. Fraser, president of Eastern Trust Company. It seems probable that Covert's extreme antipathy to Eastern Trust dates from Fraser's appointment, in May 1955, to the NSL&P board.

22 Liberal senator.

23 In August 1962, thanks to the sudden death of the company's president, W.N. Wickwire.

24 August 1962 to April 1963.

25 An Act to amend the Income Tax Act (S.C., 1963, c. 12) was passed on 5 December 1963.

26 Not only was MacKeen the second senior member of the firm to serve in that office (the first was Malachy Bowes Daly); his father, Senator David MacKeen, had been appointed lieutenant-governor in 1915.

27 The Study Committee on Financial Institutions, appointed in December 1965, was chaired by economist Jacques Parizeau, an influential economic adviser to successive provincial governments. In 1968 Parizeau joined the Parti québécois, eventually becoming leader and, in 1994, premier. He was serving as minister of finance in the Lévèsque government in 1978, when Sun Life finally did move its head office out of Quebec. Ironically Parizeau's father, Gérard, was an insurance executive.

28 In 1968 Hurlburt, then general counsel, became vice-president of Sun Life.

29 John Laylin of Covington & Burling.

30 The definitive account of Covert's role in Sun Life's head office move from Montreal to Toronto is Laurence B. Mussio, *Sun Ascendant: A History of Sun Life of Canada* (Montreal and Kingston: McGill-Queen's University Press, 2004), chapters 17 and 18.

31 Arnold Hart (chair and chief executive officer of the Bank of Montreal), Louis Hébert (chair and president, Banque canadienne nationale), Hartland Molson (chair, Molson Industries), and Ian Sinclair (president and chief executive officer, Canadian Pacific).

32 See the following chapter.

33 Members of Local 446, Bakery and Confectionary Workers' International Union of America.

34 John Simonds.

35 Earl Bennett, president and business agent of Local 446.

36 The strike against the breweries in the autumn of 1958.

37 Now TrizecHahn Corporation; in 2000 it ceased to be a real estate company.

38 Trevor Eyton (now senator).

39 An ironic anticipation of the title of the second volume (1981) of Peter Newman's *Canadian Establishment*: "The Acquisitors."

40 On this subject generally see Peter Newman, *Bronfman Dynasty: The Rothschilds of the New World* (Toronto: McClelland & Stewart, 1978), chapter 17.

41 Fred Manning's son-in-law.

42 In 1971 Covert was elected a director of Standard Brands Canada Limited.

43 A tract of forested land where a company has the right to cut and remove timber.

44 Then president of Bowater Mersey Paper Company Limited.

45 Moirs chocolate factory, at 375 Pleasant Street in the former City of Dartmouth, remains in operation.

46 A shopping centre constructed by Halifax Developments Limited, in which supermarket magnate Frank Sobey was a principal.

47 A state-of-the-art plant when rebuilt in 1891.

48 A former minister in the St-Laurent cabinet, R.H. Winters re-entered politics at the urging of Lester Pearson, was elected for York West in 1965 and named minister of trade and commerce. In 1968 he was only narrowly defeated by Pierre Trudeau for the leadership of the Liberal Party.

49 An Act to amend the Criminal Code, S.C., 1967, c. 15. In April 1967 Trudeau, who was serving as parliamentary secretary to the prime minister, became minister of justice.

50 Pearson announced his retirement in December 1967; Trudeau's letter to Covert is not extant.

51 After Covert became head of the firm in 1963 Cowan's departure was only a matter of time. The Judicature Act Amendment of 1962, creating Trial and Appeal Divisions in the Supreme Court and assigning the judges to one or the other of them, did not come into force until 1966, and the timing of its proclamation may well have been dictated by Cowan's desire for a judicial appointment. The promotion of a senior puisne to be chief justice of the trial division opened a vacancy which Cowan filled. Within seven months, though the most junior judge, he was appointed chief justice of the trial division. Cowan remained chief justice until his retirement fourteen years later, in 1981.

52 It was thanks largely to Cowan's efforts that a new Judicature Act was enacted in 1972.

53 James S. Cowan QC, who articled with Covert, is a senior member of Stewart McKelvey Stirling Scales.

54 Three shares in Bell for every five in MT&T.

55 The legislature was called back into session and the bill introduced by Premier Stanfield, whose older brother, Charles, was a director

and member of the executive committee of MT&T. The Liberals supported the government; see Beck, *Politics of Nova Scotia...* Volume Two, 291.

56 Legal only because MT&T, though a public limited company, had a legislative charter: S.N.S., 1910, c. 156. It is now merged in Aliant.

57 An Act to Amend Chapter 156 of the Acts of 1910, An Act to Incorporate the Maritime Telegraph and Telephone Company Limited (S.N.S., 1966, c. 5), passed on 10 September 1966. It limited the number of voting shares held by one shareholder to 1000.

58 Vincent William Thomas Scully was deputy minister of reconstruction and supply, 1945–48; of national revenue, 1948–51.

59 In 1951.

60 Striking against Canadian Keyes Fibre Company Limited (Hantsport, Nova Scotia) was the International Brotherhood of Pulp, Sulphite and Paper Mill Workers, Local 576.

61 The writ was dropped on 20 April; the strike began on 3 May 1967.

62 I.e., of Minas Basin Pulp and Power Company Limited.

63 At the time of his premature death in 1983 Gravefell was Atlantic regional vice-president of the Canadian Paperworkers Union.

64 Dr T.J. MacKeough, "a Tory of the left" in the words of J. Murray Beck.

65 A reference to the Boston police strike of September 1919, when Coolidge, then governor of Massachusetts, made the pronouncement, "There is no right to strike against the public safety by anybody, anywhere, any time."

66 An Act to Amend Chapter 311 of the Revised Statutes, 1967, the Trade Union Act, S.N.S., 1969, c. 79.

67 Canada's first legal police strike took place in Sydney NS 19–20 August 1971.

CHAPTER NINE

1 On this subject generally see Laurence K. Shook, *Catholic post-secondary education in English-speaking Canada: A history* (Toronto: University of Toronto Press, 1971), 73–4.

2 In the south end of the former city of Halifax.

3 A mortgage in which the interest payable on it is applied to reducing the principal.

4 An Act to Amend and Consolidate the Acts Relating to Saint Mary's University, S.N.S., 1970, c. 147 (24 April 1970).

5 Colin Campbell, then vicar general of the archdiocese of Halifax and afterwards bishop of Antigonish. The unnamed assistant was Fr Thomas White, chancellor of the archdiocese; information from the Most Reverend Colin Campbell.

6 On Covert's role, see Bruce, *Frank Sobey*, 305–6. The reference is to the "principal agreement" (18 August 1966) for the sale to the government of Nova Scotia of Deuterium Corporation's 49-per cent holding in Deuterium of Canada Limited; the "licence agreement" (26 August 1966); and the "patent agreement" (8 February 1964).

7 "A form of water consisting of deuterium oxide, used as a moderator in nuclear reactors" (*Canadian Oxford Dictionary*).

8 By 1970 the province had spent $130 million on Deuterium; the total was perhaps as high as $250 million. Under the Deuterium of Canada Act, passed in 1966, the province was not to lend Deuterium more than $15 million. See Roy E. George, *The Life and Times of Industrial Estates Limited* (Halifax, 1974), 77–90; Bruce, *Frank Sobey*, 277–9, 300–7; Beck, *Politics of Nova Scotia...* Volume Two, 281–319 passim. The best and most detailed published account of DCL is the consecutive five-part "special report" by investigative journalist Linden MacIntyre in the Halifax *Chronicle-Herald*, 13–17 April 1971.

9 A personal services contract covering consultancy, patent use etc.

10 In the Legislature Premier Smith referred to Covert as "counsel for Deuterium of Canada Limited": *Debates and Proceedings of the House of Assembly ... of Nova Scotia*, 24 March 1970 (p. 1539). Covert's law partner, J.W.E. Mingo QC, solicitor to Industrial Estates Limited, was an ex officio member of the executive committee of DCL.

11 By Atomic Energy of Canada Limited.

12 Now Mr Justice Chipman of the Nova Scotia Court of Appeal.

13 Release agreement from Deuterium Corporation and Jerome S. Spevack to HM The Queen in Right of the Province of Nova Scotia, Deuterium of Canada Limited, Industrial Estates Limited and Cape Breton Heavy Water Limited; Order in Council, 70–269A (20 March 1970).

14 Of the Montreal law firm now known as Ogilvy Renault.

15 17 March 1970.

16 Ruth Spevack was secretary-treasurer and a director of Deuterium Corporation, the US parent company, of which her husband Jerome was president and chairman.

17 "Spevack signs claim release," Halifax *Chronicle-Herald*, 25 March 1970. "The task was a very difficult one of great importance," Premier Smith wrote. "The satisfactory outcome clears the way for further necessary action which could not be effectively carried out until the Spevak [*sic*] problem was solved": Smith to Covert, 25 March 1970, Frank Covert papers. The further action, of course, was an infusion of federal government money to secure Deuterium's contract to supply heavy water to Atomic Energy of Canada Limited.

18 "In October 1971, AECL took over management of the project and undertook to reconstruct the plant for $30 million, in exchange for the heavy water production. However, AECL underestimated the repair costs by $158.5. million. In 1978, AECL bought out the plant for annual instalments of $3.3 million per year over 20 years. It was not until 1979 that the Glace Bay HWP reached full production. When CANDU [nuclear reactor] sales failed to materialize in the late seventies and early eighties, huge quantities of heavy water had to be stockpiled, and finally, in March 1985 AECL shut down the Glace Bay HWP": David H. Martin and David Argue, *Nuclear Sunset: The Economic Costs of the Canadian Nuclear Industry* (Ottawa: Campaign for Nuclear Phaseout, 1996), 43–4.

19 Covert was in Montreal on Sun Life and Royal Bank business.

20 Under the Nova Scotia Companies Act.

21 Sydney R. Kennedy was CBC regional director for the Maritimes.

22 Mingo and Rhude both became members of the firm (partners) on 1 January 1958. "Placing Rhude on one side of my office and Mingo on the other certainly made my workload easier": Frank Covert, quoted in Eleanor O'Donnell MacLean, *Leading the Way: An Unauthorized Guide to the Sobey Empire* (Halifax: GATT-Fly Atlantic, 1985), 12.

23 The head of the firm was the senior member with the most seniority, the senior members those partners whose names appeared on the shingle.

24 Between 1963 and 1970 the firm grew by 300 per cent.

25 Out of deference to Covert, the executive committee did not have a chair until 1978, when Covert retired and J. William E. Mingo became head of the firm in form and in fact. He remained chair of

the executive committee until 1992. In 2004, after more than half a century with the firm, Mingo is still practising.

26 An ironic foreshadowing of the four-firm interprovincial merger which would lead in 1990 to the creation of Stewart McKelvey Stirling Scales.

27 The result was the creation of Nova Scotia Power, a provincial crown corporation. It was reprivatized by a Conservative government in 1992. An excellent short account is to be found in Stephen Kimber, "*Not Guilty*": *The Trial of Gerald Regan* (Toronto: Stoddart, 1999), 135–7.

28 A. Russell Harrington (born 1914), nephew of a former Conservative premier of Nova Scotia.

29 S.N.S., 1973, c. 47.

30 *Imperial Oil Limited* v. *Nova Scotia Light and Power Company Limited*, [1977] 2 S.C.R. 817. Lead counsel for the appellant was John J. Robinette.

31 Canadian subsidiary of AT&T.

32 "Ex-Executive Admits $500,000 Fraud," New York *Times*: 6 June 1973.

33 Before pleading guilty to 27 counts of grand larceny and conspiracy, he asked Covert to defend him; Covert declined (private information). The scam involved imaginary or exaggerated charges for ships to warn away fishing vessels from undersea cables.

34 Son and namesake of Angus L. Macdonald, Macdonald *fils* entered the firm while his father was premier.

35 In March 1973 the appeal division of the Supreme Court of Nova Scotia was, for no apparent reason, increased from three judges to four. The amendment to the Judicature Act came into force on 21 December 1973; Macdonald's appointment was announced a week later. Between March and December, the chief justice of the province, who presided in the appeal division, died and was replaced by a member of the practising bar – an almost unheard-of elevation. Had a fourth judgeship not been so fortuitously created, there would not have been a vacancy in the appeal division for Macdonald to fill.

36 On this subject generally see Theresa Corcoran SC, *Mount Saint Vincent University: A Vision Unfolding, 1873–1988* (Lanham, Maryland: University Press of America, 1999), 331–5. Covert, who was the Congregation's lawyer and a member of its financial

advisory board, represented it on the joint congregation/university negotiating committee on the transfer of ownership. So sensitive are the minutes of this joint committee that they will not be open for historical research purposes until 2049.

37 The university was not secularized until 1988, after Covert's death.

38 The petition was tabled in the Senate in October 1975 by Harold Connolly, the former Liberal premier of Nova Scotia.

39 The road through Parliament was rocky; see Reuben Cohen, *A Time to Tell; The Public Life of a Private Man* (Toronto, 1998), p. 117. Originally introduced in the Senate, the chartered bank conversion bill failed to pass and had to be reintroduced in the Commons. The Act to incorporate the Continental Bank of Canada (S.C., 1977, c. 58) received royal assent on 14 July 1977. Continental Bank commenced operations in 1979 and in 1981 merged with IAC Limited. Continental did not flourish; by 1986 it was no longer viable and in 1987 it was wound up.

40 Covert was both – Royal Bank and Montreal Trust.

41 Keith H. MacDonald.

42 Struan Robertson, president and chief executive officer of MT&T.

43 Now merged in Dalhousie University.

44 At the time, Covert was still a member of Dalhousie's board, and its honorary treasurer. After becoming chair of NSTC, he resigned from the Dalhousie board, to avoid any appearance of conflict of interest. When Covert's unexpired fourth term ended in May 1978, Dalhousie's president offered him a further three-year appointment, which he could not accept because he was still on the NSTC board.

45 Order in Council 76–1387 (30 November 1976).

46 George W. Holbrooke was president of NSTC from 1964 to 1970.

47 A.E. Steeves, dean of students.

48 On the 1972–75 merger initiative see generally Waite, *Old College Transformed*, 347–8. Bill 110 ("An Act to Amend Chapter 214 of the Revised Statutes 1967, The Nova Scotia Technical College Act") was given the six-month hoist in November 1974. See also *Report to the House of Assembly of the Select Committee on the Nova Scotia Technical College Act* (March 1975), which recommended that the proposed merger of NSTC and Dalhousie proceed.

49 Thus was the marriage deferred for twenty years; The Dalhousie-Technical University Amalgamation Act (S.N.S., 1996, c. 24) became law on 20 December 1996.

50 Formerly dean of engineering at Concordia.

51 S.N.S., 1977, c. 41 (19 May 1977); Covert himself drafted the bill.

52 Under the amended NSTC Act, the Association of Professional Engineers of Nova Scotia had ex officio representation on the board of governors.

53 An Act to Change the Name of the Nova Scotia Technical College to the Technical University of Nova Scotia ...: S.N.S., 1980, c. 42 (26 May 1980).

54 Covert's successor on the NSTC board was another member of his own firm, Donald H. Oliver (now Senator).

55 Lawyer George W. MacDonald, an electrical engineering graduate of NSTC, remained chair until 1987.

56 *In the Matter of Section 253 of the Railway Act; and In the Matter of the Application of Canadian National Railways to abandon their operations over the Caledonia Subdivision from Caledonia Junction (mileage 0.00) to Caledonia (mileage 21.92) in the Province of Nova Scotia, a distance of 21.92 miles*: Canadian Transport Commission (Railway Transport Committee) case no. R-22/76.

57 Willis G. Forrest Company; Bowater Mersey bought 17 per cent of its woodschips from lumber mills in Caledonia; "Residents against abandoning rail line," Bridgewater *Bulletin*: 22 September 1976.

58 Queens County, Nova Scotia; the first train went through in June 1905.

59 Mr D. Arthur, regional superintendent of transport.

60 Counsel for CN was David Bekhor.

61 An Act to Amend Chapter 258 of the Revised Statutes, 1967, the Public Utilities Act (S.N.S., 1976, c. 32), declared Nova Scotia Power Corporation a public utility.

62 *Nova Scotia (Public Utilities Board) v. Nova Scotia Power Corporation et al.* (1977) 75 D.L.R. (3d) 72.

63 The hydroelectric power plant was built under the terms of a 1928 agreement between I.W. Killam's Royal Securities Corporation (the promoter) and the Nova Scotia Power Commission.

64 The banner headline in the Halifax *Chronicle-Herald* (11 March 1977) read, "Special Power Deals to End."

65 The charter of the French language made French the sole official language of Quebec.

66 Presumably Dr Claude Bertrand, the Montreal neurosurgeon who was one of only two francophones on the Sun Life board; the other was Louis Hébert, chair and chief executive officer of Banque canadienne nationale.

67 A reference to Parizeau's caricature of Sun Life as a $400-million exploiter. His statement on the proposed head office move may be found in Montreal *Star*: 7 January 1978, A8.

68 In 2000 Sun Life was demutualized.

69 The prime minister's father-in-law, James Sinclair, was a director of Sun Life.

70 Campbell and Galt were called to 24 Sussex Drive on 12 January 1978 to hear the prime minister's objections to the proposed move.

71 Campbell, who was then in his seventy-third year, had been president 1962–70.

72 On Rhude's career as a trust company executive, see Patricia Best and Ann Shortell, *A Matter of Trust: Greed, Government and Canada's $60 Billion Trust Industry* (Markham: Penguin Books Canada, 1986), 118–32, passim. Rhude had been president of Central Trust since 1973. Such was his pre-eminence that, by 1975, an article on Halifax's "powerful dozen" characterized him as Covert's "only serious challenger," who was "fast overtaking him" in the fields of corporate finance and law: Brian Currie, "Power for progressive change sadly lacking in Halifax," *4th Estate:* 5 November 1975. Rhude was to predecease Covert, dying prematurely, aged sixty-two, in 1985.

73 In Bomber Command, aircrew sent ahead of the main bomber force to locate and mark the target for bombing purposes. The Pathfinders were No. 405 Squadron RCAF.

74 In 1977 the Sobeys and H.B. Nickerson & Sons Limited of North Sydney acquired joint control of National Sea Products. Before the year was out, the Nickersons were in sole control.

75 In 1980 Rhude was suceeded as chair of National Sea Products by J. William E. Mingo QC.

EPILOGUE

1 "Of Bench and Bar," *Chronicle-Herald* ('Mayflower' supplement): 6 May 1977–10 March 1978.

2 J.L. Dubinsky, *In and Out of Court* (Hantsport NS: Lancelot, 1981), 281–8. The first Jewish barrister appointed to the Supreme Court of Nova Scotia (in 1967), Dubinsky replaced Covert's associate, Gordon Cowan, promoted to chief justice of the Trial Division. Dubinsky's otherwise distinguished career 'in and out of court' has been overshadowed by the 1971 prosecution of Donald Marshall Jr.,

where he served as trial judge. Ironically, Covert's manuscript mentions only in passing the one time he and Dubinsky crossed paths professionally: the coal conciliation board of March-June 1953. Covert represented Dosco and Dubinsky the United Mine Workers. Though chaired by eminent United Churchman, the Reverend Dr Clarence MacKinnon Nicholson, principal of Pine Hill Divinity Hall, the board could not agree among themselves and Dubinsky submitted a minority report: *In and Out of Court*, 283–4. "I had quite a list of labour work," Covert writes, "including ... three big conciliation cases, one for Dominion Coal Company, one for Eastern Car Works and one for Trenton Industries Ltd. These took many meetings in Sydney, New Glasgow and Trenton, but we secured unanimous reports in all but one." That want of unanimity clearly rankled, for it was the first occasion on which Covert had served as Dosco's nominee on a conciliation board and he wrote the decision. See generally *Annual Report of the [Nova Scotia] Department of Labour* (Halifax: Queen's Printer, 1954), 34–6; Paul MacEwan, *Miners and Steelworkers: Labour in Cape Breton* (Toronto: A.M. Hakkert, 1976), 287–8.

3 Peter C. Newman, *Debrett's Illustrated Guide to the Canadian Establishment* (Agincourt, Ont.: Methuen, 1983), 156.

4 See generally Rick Williams, "The Restructuring That Wasn't: The Scandal at National Sea," in Gary Burrill and Ian McKay, eds., *People, Resources and Power: Critical Perspectives on Underdevelopment and Primary Industries in the Atlantic Region* (Fredericton: Acadiensis, 1987), 74–83. See also "A Corporate Captain Mixes with 'Big Fish' to Land New Business," *Business Focus* (Halifax): May 1983.

5 *Some Mersey Memories, 1928–1986 = Some Important Events in the History of Bowater Mersey Paper Company Limited and Its Predecessor Mersey Paper Company Limited* (Liverpool NS: Bowater Mersey Paper Company Limited, 1986).

6 NSBS Council minutes, 20 November 1987; courtesy Nova Scotia Barristers' Library.

Index